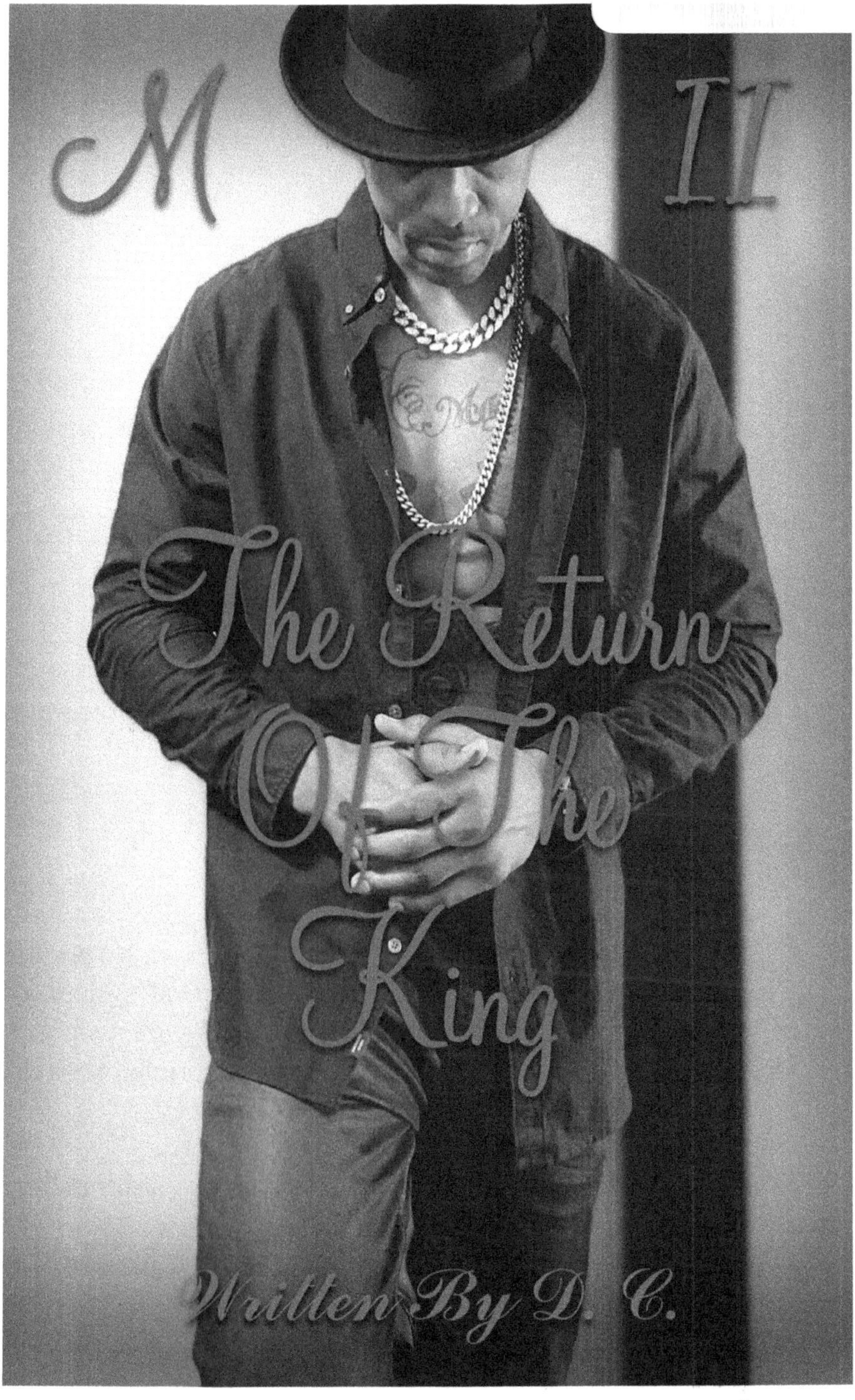
M II
The Return
Of The
King
Written By D. C.

CLF Publishing, LLC.
www.clfpublishing.org
909.315.3161

Copyright © 2020 by Dontae Cottrell. All rights reserved. No portion of this book may be reproduced, stored in a retrieval system, or transmitted by any form or any means electronically, photocopied, recorded, or any other except for brief quotations in printed reviews, without the prior permission of the publisher.

Cover design by Senir Design. Contact information: info@senirdesign.com.

ISBN # 978-1-945102-53-0

Printed in the United States of America.

DEDICATIONS

I dedicate this book to my grandfather, Otis Manning, who has inspired and helped shaped the man who stands before you. Losing you, Grandpa, I lost my way. It wasn't until you came to me in a dream and asked me what I am waiting for. "The world is yours," you said. It was then, and only then, I began writing again, expressing myself with the pen. Even gone, you are still inspiring me to be me. I thank you, miss you, and love you, Grandpa.

ACKNOWLEDGEMENTS

First, I would like to thank my Heavenly Father for guiding my footsteps, strengthening my faith each and every day that I wake.

I definitely have to send a big thank you to my wife Christina, for not only staying up with me listening to early drafts in the late hours, but from also giving me ideas about my cover, to actually becoming a part of the cover itself.

Thank you, my love.

To my mother Tammy, thank you for keeping me in good spirits through the rough patches. I love you, Mom.

To my publisher Dr. C. whom I owe a great deal to. Thank you for everything; you are the greatest.

To the ones who have inspired me in this time of writing my Masterpiece, you know who you are.

To my photographers Karen and Jesse.

To everyone who worked on my book, I thank you.

And to my die-hard poetry fans, I thank you from the bottom of my heart. Thank you for giving me a reason to continue to do what I love. I can't say it enough.

Thank you.

R. L.

TABLE OF CONTENTS

The Return of the King (Intro)	11
My Love Knows No Limit	13
Showing You a Love Like Never Before	14
Just Right	16
Lose Control	18
Blessing You	20
I Won't Settle for Less	23
Flash Backs	24
Invitation Only	27
I'll Be There	29
All I Think of Is You	31
My Promise	33
Class Is In Session	35
Let Me Put A Smile on Your Face	37
Room 143	38
Supreme	40
My Sweet Melody	42
Keep Your Heels On	44
The Key to My Heart	46
A Different Woman Every Night	48
Soul Mate	50
Take You There	51
Can't Live with You, Can't Live Without You	52
Soul Searching	53
Your Erotic Zones	55
Games, Lies and Deceit	56
Taking You for Granted	58
Fill This Hole in My Heart	59

Love and War	60
Our Chemistry	62
Blue Dream	64
I Got a Woman at Home	65
Falling in Love	67
Tonight Is the Night	68
Sitting Here Thinking About You	70
Another Man's Girl II	71
Rock You Slow	73
Taking My Time II	75
Your Curves	77
Drunken Night II	78
Greenlight Special	80
A Feeling You Never Felt Before II	82
Lazy Love	83
Baby Making	85
My Program	87
Ready, Set, Go	89
Let Me Be Your King	91
Royal Challenge	93
Kissing You	95
Love Triangle	97
Come Back Home	99
Down Low	100
Mr. King (Back at The Party)	102
Take Care of Home	104
My Heart Is Yours	106
Any Place, Any Time	108
My Comfort Zone	110
Relapse	112

I Can't Let You Go	*113*
My Heart Forever Yours	*115*
Run Away with Your Love	*117*
Love at the End of the Tunnel	*119*
The Last Time	*121*
Fill My Empty Space	*123*
Can I Hold You Close?	*125*
Anything Your Soul Desires	*127*
The Places I Want to Kiss	*129*
You Give Me What I Need	*131*
My Royal Bed	*133*
Our Heartbeats	*135*
I'm Wide Open	*136*
Easy	*138*
The Perfect Match	*140*
One More Time	*142*
I Will Do the Things Your Man Won't Do	*145*
Secret Lover	*147*
Forever I Will Adore	*149*
Thanking My Past	*151*
Pushing Inside of You	*153*
On Repeat	*155*
My Beautiful Find II	*156*
A Crazy Night	*158*
I Wanna Be	*160*
Good Girl Turned Bad	*162*
Our Conversation II	*164*
Second to None	*166*
Royal Lover	*167*
Slow Strokes	*169*

I'm What You Need	171
My Paradise	173
Untitled Love	175
You Are In Control	177
Holding You Close	179
Once Upon A Time	181
Follow My Lead	183
Others After You	186
I Can't Stop Loving You	187
Emotional	189
Window Pane	190
Take Away Your Pain	191
Blinded by Your Love	193
Lights, Camera, Action	194
Missing You	196
Ups & Downs	197
Before You Came into My Life	199
No One Above You	200
Giving You All That I Have	201
I've Prayed for A Love Like Yours	202
Ignite My Fire	203
Your Worth	204
Your Every Wish Is My Command	205
I Won't Settle for Less	208
My Sweet Lady	209
Royal Therapy	211
Exploring Your Fantasies	214
Sorry, I Let You Down	216
I Can't Take This Pain	217
To Feel Your Touch Again	219

You're Incredible	*220*
Lift Off, Take Off, Blast Off	*221*
Crushing on You	*223*
A Really Good Feeling	*224*
Team Us	*226*
Chocolate Strawberries	*228*
Making You Mine	*230*
Enough Is Enough	*233*
Eye Candy	*235*
You Are My Destiny	*236*
When My Love Calls II	*238*
I Can't Get You Out My System	*240*
My Spanish Rose II	*241*
Turn Up the Heat	*242*
Break You Down II	*244*
Wonderland II	*246*
Palace of Pleasure	*248*
One Special Night II	*250*
I Didn't Mean It	*252*
Kryptonite	*253*
Float	*254*
Unpredictable	*255*
Sounds of Love Making	*256*
The Pursuit	*258*
Feel Me	*260*
0-100 (Real Quick)	*262*
#923	*264*
Happiness	*267*
A Desired Feeling	*269*
Sneaky & Freaky	*271*

POISONOUS LOVE	*273*
Let Me Love You	*275*
For You I Will	*276*
Since I Met You	*278*
Inhale Me	*280*
My Ego	*283*
Naked	*285*
So In Love	*287*
King	*289*
Private Party (Outro)	*292*

THE RETURN OF THE KING (INTRO)

Let the trumpets sound, Let the drummers beat their drums, King is arriving back in town, yes the royal one, the time has come for me to return, this is the year of the lover, the inventor of love making, the chosen one under the sun has come here again to show you why I am number one, riding in on my horse are you ready to take the next course, a party is about to get started, welcome to my palace where anything can happen, imagine all your fantasies playing out like you want them to be, your inner desires I seek come and join me on this adventure, with one touch your body will quiver, the King is here to deliver, never cold like the month of December, speeding, keeping you warm like the month of September, memories of this night you will forever remember, the King is back to stay taking my rightful place here on the throne, I'm home let's get it on until the break of dawn, a real lover is what this world has stumbled upon, ladies come in and enjoy this ride for tonight will be a joyous night, your hearts will take flight, I will leave a loving impression on your life, I got that Just Right, what you see and fiend from my Royal Room, the way I put it down when I told you I can Pleasure you with my tongue Until You Climax, yes that was the one that had your palace soaked and wet, hot like the sun, so many feelings are showing, putting you in a different groove inside my Kitchen of Love, showing you how I was a different type of dude, taking you high and above, My Back Bone I couldn't get enough, I Can't Resist the touch of your soft skin, it was All About You, I was all in The First Time, the temptation of the fire that I possess has arrived, Our Conversation your thoughts I caress, never leaving you deprived, again In Due Time your head will be laying on my chest, an Unbelievable Night, yes you can bet, that's why they call me the best, the greatest of all time at this love making, turning you into My Love Slave once I start back breaking, going deep into your soul, Tic Toc Tic Toc never watching the clock, time is under my control, giving you A Feeling You Never Felt Before, your body I explore with My Twelve Royal Ways digging into your love cave, your

D. C.

body I know it craves when My Love Planet came to your town loving my Showdown the way I put it down when following your road signs through your tunnel of love, adorning My Beautiful Find, my gorgeous dove you are, taking you far when I allowed you play the part of my Co-star, showing me You're a Love Freak, the way you had me in the palm of your hands, weak, making me reach my peak, I couldn't speak after that release, Just You and Me, King and Queen, real love between us two becoming one, you didn't know what to do when I had your hands up, no lust, My Roller Coaster Ride made you erupt, from the look in your eyes you love every stroke when I push and touch inside, the heart never lies when in my Promise Land, you couldn't understand how I grabbed ahold of your heart, I had that Master Plan, I couldn't stand being far away from you, even when the Rain Drops I couldn't stay away rushing over to your place just to give you a taste, Filling Her Empty Space, when In The Middle Of Your Love, on that Drunken Night, inside A Love Groove Called You, can you Imagine what I'm going to do next, my Dream Catcher, Everlasting when Body to Body, soaking my sheets, getting wetter and wetter, Thoughts of You will go on forever, Perfect in My Eyes after that One Night, the way I hit you with that boom and thunder, showing my might Loving You to the Tenth Power, my love is outta sight, your passion I devour, when sending you that Formal Invite, My Computer Love, you couldn't put up any fight, Blow Your Mind again I just might, Take My Time, my Never Duplicated, baby you're so fine after one night you will want to spend A Lifetime with King being Deep Inside giving you that Unforgettable Night on Borrowed Time, Who Am I when Our Love becomes intertwined, all in your spine showing you why I'm One of a Kind, I Surrender to you Remember That Time, going around and around all night until the sunlight, no one does it better, yes I've returned to show you what I've learned, you yearn when inside My Wonderland can I take your hand, can I have this dance once more For Eternity you will score, trust there's more in store, this time I won't leave you wanting more, the total package is what you're about to explore, so I welcome you to my Memoirs II, I hope you're ready for the things I'm about to do.....The Return of the King is here.

MII: The Return of the King

MY LOVE KNOWS NO LIMIT

It seems like you're Ready, Set, Go; I want you to know My Love Knows No Limit; once I start, I won't finish until you're finished and even then that will be the beginning; you have opened my eyes to the other side of the love that you hold inside; kissing you slowly, soft and gentle is a must; there's no rush when our lips touch, when our tongues twist your love I Can't Resist; as I flip the script and take complete control of this situation, anticipating you are, please don't take me for being crazy, but I'm ready for my love to come down; I wear a King's crown for a reason; this is the season that a Queen bares my child, the heir to my throne; baby, show me you belong; My Love Knows No Limit; I want you until my life ends; let's start a new beginning; you answer with a yes I want to go on this forever quest with you, forever by your side, two can be one, let's make love until the sun comes up and you fill me up with a bundle of joy I am all yours to keep warm, to hold close at night, baby call me your Queen, your Mrs. Right; I reply, your worth is more precious than gold, my love for you will never grow cold, forever you're close to my heart, never will we part as you said two can be one, your second to none, you are the one I've been searching for all my life, there's nothing I won't do for you, I stay ready, opening my heart and giving you the key, giving you my all, real love sleeps inside of me, spending my life with you my love there's nothing more I want, this is true my groove beats to the rhythm of you, we belong together, our love can never be measured by a stick, my love will never cease, never will it quit for you have equipped me with the sense of stability, just you and me forever we will be until the death of me, your love will flow through my veins, my body, after the first time I looked into your eyes I knew then I was hooked, shook like a crook caught by the laws I was stuck in between your walls of love, your rain came down over me, finally a real Queen I can give everything to, My Love Knows No Limit, I'm so caught into you, this is only the beginning, you're in store for a grand finish.

D. C.

SHOWING YOU A LOVE LIKE NEVER BEFORE

We have been here many times before, we have dealt with each other for years; throughout this time, there have been more tears than cheers; as time winds down, I fear I'm losing the one I love most; bags are packed, I see you about to become a ghost; I get up and run to the door, standing in front of you blocking your way, closing your path; before you go, can you please hear what I have to say, pause you do, then you answer with a yes I could I shouldn't, but I want to hear what you have to say, reaching for your bags as I say okay first, allow me to state that at the end of my plea I hope you can see that I know your worth, I'm willing to do whatever it takes to make us work, know that I am not perfect, but I can love you like no other, lost in my work not showing you no attention let me say I am sorry my love as I mentioned I want to release your stress and tension, this love we have will never be finished, when we started in the beginning, I told you that there will be no ending, again I am sorry for hurting your feelings and putting everything else before you, there's nothing I won't do for you, ready I am to show and prove that I can love you better, respect your mind, body and soul, value your opinion. I don't want you to let go, there's no "I" in team I now understand what that means, never have we had a problem when I go in between, but now when I enter your palace love is what you will scream, baby change has overcome, me losing you I won't be the same, I wouldn't be able to breathe baby I'm down on my knees, I need you next to me for the rest of my days, I will be Showing You A Love Like Never Before, in many ways, in so many different forms. There are so many different acts of love I want to perform and explore with you, believe my love is true; from now on I won't put nothing or no one before you, it shouldn't have to take you packing your bags ready to walk out mad on my ass to realize what I have standing right before my eyes; my ride or die, I need you at my side, I'm letting go of my ego setting my pride aside with everything else, you know you love it when I go below your belt, your smile makes me melt true feelings are felt when it's real and this is real; give me a

MII: The Return of the King

chance to show you that my love for you would forever be held close with mine, In Due Time you will be my wife, willing I am to sacrifice all to stay inside your walls of love; I never want us to fall or fail that will be hell on earth; baby, now I know your worth. Yes, I will attend church with you every Sunday standing in place right by your side. I hate to see you cry no more tears, no more reasons to fear that my heart and soul is not here with you, ready I am to do this thing right, no more fussing; I don't want to fight talking loud screaming with all our might, I understand your feelings now wiping away your frowns forever I will be down for you, I don't need a crew when I have you my Bonnie, I'm your Clyde, let's set aside and start a new life, like Bill and Claire, baby you are my air, stay beside me at the throne your heart is home, I your King is who you belong with, never will our love quit; we have a forever bond; for the rest of my time, I will keep you as mine, Showing You A Love Like Never Before,
always I will be yours.

D. C.

JUST RIGHT

Where did I, how did I come to find my Just Right, all through the days and nights, I think about my Just Right, the love we share, the way you take me there each and every time we become joined at the hip, giving me that lazy love, taking my mind on a trip you flip the script, you have me on tilt, drunk off your love, my Just Right; when I look upon you through your eyes, there's a feeling that comes over me on the inside, it's like a party has jumped off, staying hard never going soft when inside deep lost in your palace, I can't even imagine life without you; you have me doing things I normally won't do, falling victim to your love. You got that "I don't want to go nowhere" type of love, my Just Right sent from above, you're feeling so right my Just Right. I promise what I'm going to do tonight will ease your soul as I push through your spine; these feelings are so hard to fight going high taking flight, I'm reaching from deep down inside, my love is steadying at a climb, raising high, forever I want you to be mine, relaxing your mind as I unwind your body; at the end of this escapade, you will come to find why you can't find another Just Right, feelings are coming unraveled, breaking loose as I go through and through with my tongue pleasuring you, pleasing you my Just Right; tonight it's your night, from your Oh's and Ah's, I know you're feeling good inside, my body giving off that Just Right as I proceed to give you what you fiend, picking up my speed with my tongue feeding you your drug, as I dug I mean dig, calling out switch my Just Right grabs my royal stick to show me what she working with, showing me why she is my Just Right, giving it to me the way I like, kissing and licking down the side looking softly into your eyes as my toes begin to curl; it's about to get live, I want you girl, climb on top and drop me into your juice box, sliding in slow as you proceed to rock the boat now we on cruise control, yes a slow coast until you feel that undying flow, fast and faster you start to go, hitting your spot ready for that splash I grab your ass tightly as you release your passion, tonight will be an everlasting memory; you just watch and see I have a few tricks up my sleeve, yelling out switch so I can continue to make you weak in the knees as I proceed I drop back

MII: The Return of the King

to my knees pulling you towards the edge of the bed; no, no, no I don't need any guidance; get your hands off my head (smiles) I got this watch this as I suck and lick, lick and suck, kiss with a soft touch of my tongue with a twist I flip you over to pick you up now I'm licking you deep while I stand up my Just Right I told you this will be passion and love all night, you feel my strength and my might as you play with my royal mic, putting you down so I can give you what you like, what you will love once I am done, I'm the one, the only, the King of your palace no one can match this as I flip and twist your body in positions you never been in before my love you I want to explore, adore this passion we dishing no more hoping and wishing my Just Right, I want to show you this type of love for life, show you how it really feels to be loved by someone who's real, my heart I spill for you my special girl you are my world as I give your body a twirl pulling out to play with your pearl, in you I found a winner; are you ready to run your victory lap flipping you over so I can go deep, from the back slow with my attack you throwing it back, arch deep down the middle, picking up the pace just a little, you're giving me what I need, feeding of your vibe, no way my feelings can hide, this love making will go all night until the morning sun, weak I have become in my knees staying deep in between, you're ready to cum you scream, so am I my Just Right as we drift off into an Unforgettable Night.

D. C.

LOSE CONTROL

Ready I am to Lose Control and just let go; I want to show you how love is supposed to go, show you how love is really supposed to be given, with me in your life there will never be no ending; I can't wait any longer; you need to be finished, done with his mess; I believe in us this you can bet that I will never take your love for granted; I can't stand it the way he does you, bruising my heart, doesn't he know real love don't cost; baby, you're more than beautiful; you wouldn't have to worry about me because with you is where I want to be forever you and me, ready I am to start making plans for our future; see I want nothing more than to do you right, baby; allow me to come inside where those feelings of yours hide, allow me to break you out of those shackles; with me you will be free, able to spread your wings and fly, taking you high I will this is a lifetime ride, ready to settle down with you I am; I've traveled all around the world and seen and met so many different type of women, but in you, I see my world, the man you're with right now can't treat you like I can, you said it yourself, he only cares about his wealth; materials things holds no bearing over my life, with you by my side, I will be rich in my heart, my love will be complete my Mrs. Right, I can't take another night without you in my arms, about to Lose Control I am, I feel it riding around the city looking for you my one true Queen; you told me you were going home to pack all your things; I've been waiting patiently, driving slowly searching high and low to your home I must go. As I pull up, cop cars are the show, ambulances and a crowd is the scene, giving off a bad feeling as I get closer and closer, slowly realizing that it is you lying in the front door with bags tossed in the front lawn; my attention is drawn towards a cop walking a man to the back of his cop car, tears roll down my jaws in awe; I am not knowing what to do; I bust through the yellow tape to steal one more hug from you; Losing Control I am feeling blue, what have I've done, feeling like it's my fault consumed by my lasting thoughts, forever now I'm lost, sorry I am you paid the cost with your life, throughout the rest of mine I will

MII: The Return of the King

*cherish our time and love that we once had, bitter sweet, but glad at
the same time knowing that you are in a better place,
your love I will never erase.*

D. C.

BLESSING YOU

As I glance over this bar that I am at, my eyes stumble upon a beauty like no other; every man in the room was trying to rush her, but she paid them no mind, her attention was on me, I guess she can see the King that lives inside; as she starts to creep towards me, I sip my drink; she sits down and speaks, I don't know what it is about you that has me weak, but all I keep telling myself from the very moment I saw you is I want to feel you deep, I want you to bless me with that power you hold in between your thighs, let's make tonight a memorable night; as I reply with your beauty is outta sight, it will be my pleasure to hold you close with all my might, all through tonight I will be doing you Just Right, Blessing You throughout the night until the sunlight intrudes, you are about to love my groove; as we both get up to move towards the exit leaving this bar giving your back a gentle rub with a kiss to your cheek saying since we both drove you follow me, I'm about to lead you to my land of ecstasy; as we proceed, in my car alone I'm thinking about how I'm about to show out and perform, show her I'm what she's been looking for, if only for one night, her body I am about to bless and explore show her what it feels like to be adored, with the pedal to the floor coasting through these streets let's see what's on her mind, what she's thinking as she follows behind, listening to trading places, love faces is on her mind, searching and searching trying to find a guy of his kind, King is too fine, I can't wait to kiss his lips and look him in those eyes, they're so seductive, you make me what to scream it to the public, preaching about what I have found. Snapping back into reality, as we pull up to my castle, I walk over and open your car door for tonight love is not about to be ignored, like a lion you will hear me roar; as we walk through my doors, I take your purse and jacket, tell you to have a seat as I grab two glasses to pour us a drink of that exclusive Ace of Spades; tonight, there will be no games played, your feelings is what led you to my kingdom of love sent from above, so let me begin Blessing You my beautiful dove, taking my time with you I will, my skills are real; no this isn't a dream; once I start to stroke and coast, you will scream passionate sounds, taking you by the hand pulling you into my arms as my lips start to perform, kissing our tongues move, twist putting you in my groove, under my spell, slow while giving you just enough, another twist love is what you have missed in your life; tonight; I will show you what it's like to be Blessed in the act of love; as my hands feel your body up and down, all you can think is who is this I have found, I see why he wears a crown, and I haven't even put it down yet, undressing you slowly by pulling off your top dropping it to the floor, your neck and breasts I start to explore; with each touch from me, I'm making you want more and more, as I pull your pants and thong to the floor, sweeping you off your feet to lay you on top of my sheets so that I can adore your body my beautiful flower, we will be going for hours; I won't stop until I give you meteor showers, your palace I'm about to devour, as I dive in head first making a big splash with my tongue landing in your pleasure zone you're about to find out why I am the one baby, say you're ready, are you ready for what I'm about to do, licking you slowly down below in between your thighs where no sun shines, tears of joy begin to fill your eyes, as I take you high in the sky, call me the captain this pilot has you on a rise, going through your palace, my tongue has you at a loss for words with my hands playing through your curves, no need for air I can dive for days, Blessing You I am, your love slave has awakened your cold heart that was in that trap cave, I am here to slay and conquer your walls, past overdue, it's time your love falls in the right hands, I can see you in my life's plan as I stand to come up out of my clothes, fully exposed I climb on top to hold you close so you can't run once I enter your love, taking that friction from your lips as I dip in between your hips, hitting spots that your last missed, tapping and quitting is not an option, I won't stop until you're finished; from the beginning until the ending, I will keep you spinning in love, me Blessing You is becoming your drug, as I dig, you dig your nails deep into my back, my attack is real; with each thrust, you can feel the passion in my actions, giving nothing else but love, you never dealt with a realist, I feel it just like you feel it, I'm the one you should be with as I hit your spot back and forth, north than south, candles been blew out, even in darkness you shine, forever be mine is on your mind, hoping and wishing this won't be the first and

D. C.

last time of me Blessing You, Blessing your soul going strong and deep, pulling on the sheets as my knees and legs get weak, I continue to creep, kissing you on your cheeks, as I give you all of me, wrapping you tightly in my arms, showing you that I will protect you from any hurt or harm; no matter the storm, my love will always outperform when Blessing You.

MII: The Return of the King

I WON'T SETTLE FOR LESS

Putting my foot down I am, I Won't Settle For Less, I want nothing but the best, no ordinary love, I Won't Settle For Less, an exceptional love is what I'm looking for, someone who can fill my soul with joy, exploring my mind, my every thought; true love can never be bought; all it costs is your heart, two becoming one, not allowing nothing or no one to come in between, inseparable is what I mean, my one true Queen, no I Won't Settle For Less; my love is ready to explode through my chest; where are you my real love; I will play the part of a fool just for you; I will show and prove with me you will not lose; I choose not to settle for plain happiness; I want that "I can't live without your happiness" type of love; read my lips, I need a lifetime partner for this forever trip, a love that will never quit, enriching the love you already have deep inside your soul, making it evolve so that it will last, never will my love grow old, so many from my past who had the chance, who had their taste of what love should be, they couldn't handle this King; I will worship your feet, the very ground that you walk on, grown man status, no boy in me, no time for games, beauty is not the only attraction that will hold me my dame; follow me as I explain; it's your mind, your personality, being a professional woman turns me on you see, becoming that freak when it's time to be, excites me, a woman with motherly instincts, holding common sense, down to be my backbone for life, I'm looking for that one I can call my wife, that one who is going to add to my pot not just take, that love that makes you ache when you are apart, away from each other, I Won't Settle For Less, love me from deep down under, show me that caring compassion, a love that's satisfaction guaranteed, become my drug and turn me into your fiend, be my friend, my confidante and give me what I desire, what I need, I Won't Settle For Less, make sure your love making is at its best, I need that someone who brings no stress, a love that will never rest, I Won't Settle For Less.

D. C.

FLASH BACKS

No matter what's going on, you always seem to enter my mind; thinking about those times that we performed Love Acts, I think back to the first time I told you I was going to blow your mind, popping that Remy bottle before I explored you low, you gave me a sexy dance, giving me a show, you winded so slow, to the shower we go, undressing entering that steamy wetness, pressing close, washing your back with that rose petal soap, taking my time rubbing down your spine and curves, you turn around telling me you yearn for my royal, grabbing me low with a slow stroke I kiss you, here we go, soft and sensual as we flow, turning the water off to the bed we head without drying instead we allow our wetness to consume each other bodies, lips lock, I'm going to stretch you out like Pilates; you found yourself in a place tonight where there will be no escaping, nothing but love making; I'm about to put you to sleep, my finger takes its place starting this marathon race, massaging your pearl; after tonight, you're going to want to be my girl, my woman, my Queen, climbing on top I am, damn my phone rings, snapping me back into reality; at night, I can't sleep when I close my eyes you are all I see, Flash Back to where I was at that second time we didn't waste no time, walking in your room to find you in your birthday suit, different flashes always seem to appear of you this is true, I undress before getting closer to you, pulling you to the edge of the bed spreading your legs so my tongue can go deep in, giving you a piece of heaven, it's a quarter past seven, your body is blazing, you rise up to show me what you got, deep throat, hitting that spot, my spot, curling my toes inside my socks opening my eyes wishing you were here on top; these are Flash Backs, they never stop, getting out the bed to take a shot while watching television looking at these guys run from the cops, trying to do anything to make these Flash Backs stop, but as I watch I go off into this trance, remembering that time I pressed you up against that wall, what did I say once before I started to explore, if the neighbors not complaining than I'm not doing you right or doing my job, kissing and licking while I fill you up, with each thrust your passion erupts with a river flowing downstream, you let out several screams, deep into your spleen, showing you my strength with a twist, holding you at the wrists, turning away from the wall, I got you baby you won't fall, there go those neighbors banging on my ceiling walls from downstairs, you weren't prepared for my Everlasting that night, I gave it to you Just Right, waking up to the morning sunlight that's coming through my blinds, up I am getting ready for work as I come to find you entering my mind once again, that one night when you took my emotions for a spin, from the bed to the floor, that night I was all yours, rolling around going in circles, cater to you is playing on Pandora as I enter your pleasure box, Tic Toc, Tic Toc, it's only a matter of time until your juice box pops, your legs wrap and lock around my waist, deep into your space from the look upon your face I can tell this passion is real with each passing stroke I feel love back and forth into your world, tight as a glove you were, taking you high and above, I can't get enough, switching it up, damn I'm driving, I was stuck, this bus honking loud snapping me back into reality, moving on with a smile, these Flash Backs are wild, what have I gotten myself into, what is this I found in you, a Queen, baby tell me this is no dream, at the office behind my desk staring off into this computer screen, Flash Backs enter my space, remembering that one day, yea that day takes the cake, a freak in me is what you brought out, let me explain so that you can see what I'm talking about, kissing with tongue lashing from my mouth, stripping you down to your thong, tonight it's about to be on, that Malibu Red is about to be fed with passion strokes, the heavens have invoked me with powers, your body will bloom within the hour, down low for fifteen, passionate moans and screams enters this scene, the next fifteen I'm giving you that Greenlight Special, flipping you over to see them lips smile, it's about to get freaky, your love so wild, under hooking your legs with my arms lifting you up to please you greater than the normal you have received, your legs are wrapped around my neck, deep into your pleasure chest I go, wet and sticky face as I flow through your waterfall, gripping you tight at the waist until this day you never had it this way, love is read off your face, my manager bangs on my desk making me get back to work putting my

D. C.

Flash Backs to rest until the end of my day, love what are you doing to me, in you love is all that I see, these Flash Backs are getting the best of me.

INVITATION ONLY

Blessed you will forever be, if you ever get to witness greatness at its finest, come close so I can give you a sneak peek, a look into the mind of the Royal Lover; when I'm done with you, you will want to rewind me, rewind the things I've done to you in between my sheets; you walk up, the sign says Invitation Only; do you have your slip Ms. Fine, the type of fine that constantly stay running through your mind; are you ready for one perfect night, opening the door wide saying please come inside, with candles and roses to your right and to your left chocolate covered strawberries with the best wine money can buy, just for you, Ms. Fine; I have all night; we can take our time; once I start, forever you will be mine; never will you come to find another of my kind; the way I wind through your body with my body, our Body To Body blowing up your past feelings when I reach inside, you came to me for a reason, summer is the season; I am the love King; it's a Virgo thing; love making is what I'm going to bring; I know the meaning it's what you need, what you fiend, what you crave, tonight you will become My Love Slave times three; I'm about to give you all of me; are you ready baby, follow me, grab your drink, let's make a toast to you and I, to real love being restored; forever, you will be adored as I explore your canvas, I'm going to make you forget about the madness you've been through with the things I'm about to do, first allow me to kiss those soft and sexy lips, sending you on a love voyage trip, soft is the touch, giving you a rush through your body with a single lick from my tongue to your bottom lip, showing you we about to get naughty, it's my nature, to the sky beyond the clouds are where I'm about to take you; in love I'm going to make you fall deep after I take my place into your palace walls, I pause to set my drink down, putting my focus back on you; it's time we get down to making your dreams come true, a kiss from me to you while kicking off my shoes; I have one rule- you keep your heels on; I love the way those legs, hips and thighs look when I pull up from behind or when I spread you wide to go deep inside, smooth is your skin to my touch, ready I am to dive in until you can't get enough, climax after climax as I begin to licking you low gripping your thighs, oh how warm you feel inside, tonight's your night, it's all about you and the things you need me to do, continuing to move, dash in and out with my tongue as my finger moves like I'm pulling a trigger to a gun, but it's you my love clinching tight, legs wrapping around my body like a snake busting uncontrollably calling me the one, they call me the great, I can make it rain, and I'm not talking about money like the rest of these clowns, I'm not talking tears streaming down your face, so have no fear, I'm talking what's below your waist in between those thighs as I rise to no surprise the look from your eyes once you caught a glimpse of my perfect size ready you are for me to enter, flow deep inside, those feelings you hold inside about to pour out tonight, playing with your pearl before I show you my might, I'm here to give your body things those others couldn't, Out Of Sight, when I slow stroke you moan soft and low, wetter you become, I groan, you moan a little louder as I swim in your pool of passion, cannonball splashing, feeling good better than satisfaction, showing you different love actions with your legs to my shoulders so I can go deeper, King you call out you're a keeper, I'm no rookie baby, I'm a vet call me Mr. MVP, Invitation Only you can't just walk up on me, if this was tennis the match would be set, the greatest love stroking high from above, in my pushup position taking your love on a royal mission, I can change whatever condition your heart is in, make you believe in love once again, screams coming from within your soul, into your world I go, flowing to a steady rhythm, giving you your much needed sexual healing, bringing back those lost feelings, you hoping and wishing you can get a forever pass to my Invitation Only class, kissing when I go deep into your abs, with your nails in my back, attacking your palace showing you what it means to be loved by a King all night you have been singing I want to be your Queen and hold down everything that word means, now that I gave you a sneak peek you see why I reign Supreme, the one and only baby your King.

MII: The Return of the King

I'LL BE THERE

All you have to do is hit my line, call me up on the phone and I'll Be There to satisfy your every need; whatever it may be, I will do whatever, so that you can see there are no Lies, Games and Deceit living inside of me, forever by my side right next to me, no one else can creep in between these feelings we have for one another I am here for you and only you, my love you're the fire that burns deep within my soul, completion is what you give me; never will I let go of that love you possess; you have me under your spell; without you, I would be a mess, stress, not knowing what to do; I love it when you lay on my chest as I caress your body, stroking my fingers through your hair baby I can't compare any feeling I ever had before you; the things you make me do are out the norm; this love is true; I can't let go; no matter the time or place, I will race over to you with action I will show and prove that I'll Be There whenever you call, not even the laws can keep me from your love, from your passion which is my drug you beautiful dove; you give off a feeling that is so right sent from heaven above; tonight, we're going to have some fun with your hips, your thighs, damn those sexy ass eyes, with your fragrance of love as I arrive on time falling in my arms with a smile, you are by far the one I want to bare my child; my heart was lost in the wild before you came around, stumbled upon, look at what I've found, love flowing through my veins as I play my part, priceless like the art on my walls in my arms catching you if you should ever fall, never will my love for you pause or dissolve, with you I have evolved, spreading my wings an all, floating high against the laws of gravity just you and me is all I see perfectly blind when in your presence, my heaven sent, this love I know was meant to exist, loving this love trip, you have equipped my heart with passion again with you I can't do nothing, but win, turning me into a great man, for us I have set a master plan to always provide and be the man you need until never ends, even then I'll be here when life starts all over again, no one need will go unpleased, unfulfilled, I have mastered the skills of love making, headboard breaking, legs shaking when I enter your soul, never will this love run cold, I'll Be

D. C.

There never letting go, my love is a for sure thing, I will now and forever always be your King.

MII: The Return of the King

ALL I THINK OF IS YOU

I start my day with a "Thank you, Lord for yet another day" with a smile across my face, as I wash the night away. On my mind you stay; I am blessed to have someone like you next to me at my side; I don't even have to tell you, you know you're the love of my life, my happily ever after, I want to be with you for the remanding chapters of my life, when out of my sight I close my eyes to see you from within; deep down, you live within my core, my soul; my heart is overflowing; I'm Losing Control; my love is ready to explode; you have a hold, a grip so cold; I never want to let go of these feelings, emotions running high when I go low to give you a show, oh how my mind floats when I think about the times I held you close while I stroke you slow, kissing you even slower all night when my special delivery enters your warm delight, remembering that one night when we were fussing and fighting, that make up love was Just Right; I reminded you who is your King that night I came into the room after the fight feeling good off the Remy and Sprite, with one kiss it was on for the rest of the night, making up is alright when in love, I place no one above you my love, I know from high above heaven is missing an angel, loving you from different angles, caring about the things that you care about, my love is a hundred percent, grade A, I value your goals and the way you stay so humble and grounded, lost in you, happy I am I found my rose, it is said nothing is as precious as a rose, I beg to differ because with my love we will grow, even if you water that rose sooner than later it will die and go, my love is a lifetime show, so happy I am that I have found the other half of my heart, completion, making me whole; All I Think Of Is You when I'm in my zone, to you my love will always be strong; like rights to a song; I will always belong can't nobody own or duplicate, this love we have is fate, no matter what this can't be erased, there's no escaping this place; you're a full-course meal, my dinner plate, love it when my hands rub up and down your cakes and are lips takes their place, you have brightened up all my days, even shining at night, your love I will always crave; there's not a minute that goes by that I don't feel you deep inside; baby, I can close my

D. C.

eyes and see your smile that drives me wild, your style is so perfect to me, you're all I will ever need, exceeding my expectations, putting them all to rest, my doubts when you lay across my chest; my love, you are the best the greatest I ever had, out doing my past, I am glad they couldn't last, they gave me the opportunity to be loved by someone real; I love how this feels; when thinking of you my groove changes; I will never be the same, my heart I have no complaints, breaking away from my shackles and restraints the day you came and took my heart away, with each passing day, my love is growing stronger, no longer alone; All I Think Of Is You, my love will always be in your hands where it belongs, your heart is my home, satisfied I am sitting next to you on my throne.

MII: The Return of the King

MY PROMISE

With every day that passes, with every night that falls, your heart will be protected behind my love walls, proving nothing will tear us down, a real love only comes around every so often, if love could be bought then I would have spent my last on yours, oh how I love to adore you, bringing comfort to my soul, my love, My Promise is forever yours, never will we end, Marry you I will so we are not living in sin, you give me peace of mind when I'm rubbing on your skin, you will never find the type of love I hold within from another, I want you to be the mother of my kids, raising a happy family, oh what a gift you are, I am by far the luckiest King here on this planet, without your love I couldn't even manage, My Promise, I Promise to remain honest, respecting your thoughts and opinions, this is the start of a never ending, My Promise, I Promise to never hurt you, I want nothing more than to love and care for you, show and prove that love is real, that love exists, it is not a myth, by the way I love your palace and those hips when I dive deep to take a dip your warmth makes my heart do flips, you take my soul on a trip, this is too good to be true, it feels like a movie script, My Promise, I Promise to forever and only kiss your lips, both pair, I breathe you baby your my air My Promise, I Promise to never go back on My Promise from this day you and I will forever stay in love, I Promise, My Promise, my heart is yours to keep to hold, My Promise is to never leave you in the cold, to keep your heart intact, warm, whole, never shattering your feelings like broken glasses I will outlast your last, rearview mirror to your past, even though objects may seem closer when you glance, but they don't stand a chance, my seed I plant, doing this love dance, around and around we go, setting sail on my boat as we coast just float away, hand and hand, this is God's plan, it was written before you knew life, at this altar ready to make you my wife, My Promise, I Promise to always do what's right, no outside light will ever be able to shine in, I'm all in my Queen, you love it when I slip in between, those love faces you make do something to me, your moans, screams and shouts leaves me without a doubt that pleasure is being restored, my love, My Promise, I Promise to always

D. C.

be yours, you're so sweet, so beautiful to me my find, I will always adore, your love I am going to conquer and explore, waving my white flag this game is over, My Player Bone is gone, I am all yours, My Promise, I Promise.

MII: The Return of the King

CLASS IS IN SESSION

Walking into a class of women with my briefcase in hand laying it down on my desk, taking off my jacket and hat as I quote, good morning class, I hope all had a good night's rest, turn in your homework please, as I get ready to go over today's lesson plans, settle down everyone, Class Is In Session, all eyes are on me, oh my look at all these beautiful ladies, stunned for a second, popping my briefcase open I'm just going to dive right in, today I will give you all the tools on how a man should please his woman when laying in between the covers, you might want to take notes because if he's not doing it like this, then he is not exploring your world properly, to the chalkboard I go, you will be tested Friday also I say with a smile, moving right along, now when you come home from a long day, your man should have a hot steamy bath with candles lit, also with a glass of wine waiting on you so that you can unwind after a long day of being on your feet or behind a desk dealing with stress, this will ease your tension, I almost forgot to mention that shot of patron to welcome you home, dinner should be made, when you two are done, to the room you will go so that you can lay in each other's arms, Love Acts is what is what should be performed, allow him to take full control, being submissive is your only mission in this quest, kissing from your head to your chest, from your chest to those thighs, your toes should be curling by now, feelings should be on the rise, this love should be given to you all night, removing your thong he should, so he can put his tongue where it belongs, now you start to moan, your pilot light is lit, there's no stopping, his tongue should never quit, lick, lick, until he feels you shift, tightening up your grip, grabbing a pillow to squeeze as you release, that's just the beginning of a real King pleasure treat, undressed he becomes so he can go deep in between them sheets, penetrating so deep with his creep, creep, creep a tears falls down your cheek, making you weak with every stroke, wrapping your legs around his waist so deeper he can go into that place, into your palace by now your nails should be with passion back scratching while kissing on his neck, you know he's working if he drips a little sweat, with his back and forth pushing your legs farther towards your head to go deeper north, picking up speed like a Porsche, neighbors should be complaining about the noise, but you can't help it, the way he's getting it, rocking and dipping, hooking your legs with his arms with your back slightly bended, as he presses deep, you're in his submission, splitting that thang wide open, coasting slow no need to rush as he rocks your boat, you float busting down low for the second time, changing positions giving you a royal show, taking you up with no parachute, you should have strapped on your seatbelt for this ride flying high, grabbing your thighs to lift you up, deeper into you is a must, multiples you should have bust, sending a rush through your body, showing you strength, as he goes through your love, taking you higher and above, not holding nothing back, attacking you with love not lust, putting you down, turning you around grabbing on your butt, kissing up and down your back before he continues with his attack, sliding your hair to the side to look into your beautiful eyes, as his finger slides back inside, kissing you on the side of your cheek, to your lips, y'all tongues starts to do flips, you feel a thrust back in your hips once again he begins to dip, dive, drive back and forth, in and out, you scream, he shouts, the candles should have burned to the wick, moving fast, moving quick, no doubt this is an all-night script, the plot is this, it's all about you tonight, this was yours to have my boo, he says, with feelings on edge, legs are going dead, an explosion is what ya'll are meant to have, taking you above the clouds, love will be the only thing coming from your mouth, as he explodes down south, this is the type of love making I'm talking about, a student shouts, (class laughs) settle down, settle down I say, next session will be on how the woman should please her man, class is dismissed until we meet again.

MII: The Return of the King

LET ME PUT A SMILE ON YOUR FACE
(INTERLUDE)

Baby, can you get away; I see the sadness written across your face, the way he treats you is a disgrace; I wanna take you out that evil place, hesitating you are, my love will take you far, I can see the scars, the pressure from afar, how he who would rather be your stressor, than your stress reliever, no smiles, but cries in your eyes, hoping you change your mind before you run out of time, he's running you down to a penny from a dime, a one of a kind, happiness is what you will find, if you allow me, if you Let Me Put A Smile On Your Face, give you better days, no more of those cloudy, dark days, I see your heart craves, so young, but with him you've aged, no loyalty should be given to that sucka no way, if he should ever touch you in a harmful way, blacking your eyes because of something you may say, spending time in those hospital walls, making you crawl towards his feet, why should you stay, with me you should be, so I could show you how a Queen should be treated, I need you to get away, don't you want to escape to my Lovers' Land, just take my hands, I wanna see that smile, a lesson in love has come around, you don't have to hide no longer, let me come inside your heart, tearing you apart, breaking loose from his shackles, setting you free, with me showing you things you've never seen, that beautiful smile puts my heart at ease, times I just want to freeze, back to reality, as she walks away from me, back to him she shouldn't be, shouldn't go, I hope and pray she stays safe, my God protect your angel, I just wanted to Put A Smile On Her Face and show her the way to Room 143, where she will never be able to get enough of me.

D. C.

ROOM 143

You are now entering my room of love; prepare yourself to fly high and above; once I open my heart, passion will fill the air; the love I pour out cannot be compared; this love you will not want to share; stepping in my Room 143 I will take you there, showing you a love like never before, through your eyes I can see your love is starting to glow while holding you close and tight, our hearts are beating as one with the might of ten men; after tonight, you will be all in, for being in my Room 143, I will give you what you need and what you want; you don't have to second guess love no more, bringing your walls down I am with a single kiss to your lips; tonight, I will make you forget about your past, those lames couldn't last, glad at that fact that my love is true, I will show you that I am who you belong to; those clowns was jacks and jokers; allow me to bring you into my world to show you how love is supposed to be, how love is supposed to feel, real I am, King of your world; now as I lay you down gently Taking My Time, no rush I have nothing but time to show and prove this love you will never lose as I begin to kiss you ever so softly, from your lips to your neck with my hands moving up your thighs and my tongue going down in between your breasts, making your feelings go crazy inside this is a love making night, showing you that there's more to it than just having casual sex, yes you can bet you haven't seen nothing yet. Ready, Set, Go, flowing down to your palace of love in between your thighs now with my legs parallel to the floor your love I am about to explore, conquer and devour, I've been sent to you by a higher power, we will be going for hours, like a beautiful flower in the spring time your blooming as my tongue consumes the inside of your womb, deep into your walls, your sweet wetness steams down my chin as I give you my all, catch you I will once your walls fall completely, loving you deeply, undressing so you can feel me deep; with one stroke your legs will become weak, holding them up in that V shape, your body gives off that vibe of being at your peak unable to control your natural flow, you let go and this is just the beginning of my 143 show, with your hands wrapped around my back as I attack, you scratch while

MII: The Return of the King

moaning in that sexy tone, taking you places where you never been before, places you only imagine what real love felt like, all through the night, I will be giving you a love that you will forever place above the rest, once your heart was cold and in a mess, I broke the mold when I was created by the heavens, ever since I was eleven I knew I was blessed with a gift that will have all your feelings in a twist, no place on your body will go missed, untouched, wide open you have become as you begin to bust like a gun again and again as I swim through and through back and forth in and out doing circles with our tongues as we twist, I flip your body over to your backside, so I can go deeper inside I know how to please you right, each and every time that you step into my Room 143 you will walk out pleased with a smile on your face, stroke after stroke from the back with my hands on your waist, so that you can't run there's no escape, taking you to a higher level, making you cum again and again and once more your body I'm deep within as I explore, with one more trick up my sleeve, I'm about to give you what you will forever want, forever need, you ask if I can handle you in my arms and lift you high, never before have you enjoyed a ride of that kind, when I'm done you won't be able to find another guy like this King you are dealing with tonight, with a finale stroke from behind I turn you around to give you what you ask for, with my feet planted on the floor I wrap your legs around my waist so that you can finally explore deep within your core, I'm about to go I hope you ready for the grand finale show, sliding in slow as I lift you high with my hands on your hips and thighs, gripping your butt spreading you apart so that you feel me deep into your guts as you bounce and ride, I slide and slide through your palace you never would've thought, never did you imagine the passion you were about to feel once you step into my Room 143; yes, this is no dream; I am real, now your eyes are wide open, walls have fallen to my love you feel a feeling you never felt before as we go off into the night exploring this thing called love as I send you off into heaven's bliss with a smile and a kiss; my love for you will never be able to resist; each and every time I will take your mind, body and soul on a new trip.

D. C.

SUPREME

I sit on the highest throne; I want to make your palace my home; I want to perform some hidden acts, (and a half when I pull out, all facts, can you handle my royal Supreme, not wasting no time, not playing no games, no cameras, no tricks, your lips pressed up against mine, your body unwinds in my arms, alarm, your sirens goes off as I push you gently, softly to the bed where I reign Supreme, you're about to find out what I mean when I deep sea dive into your groove; I move closer just to drop down to one knee; you sit up to kiss me; I take my hand to your chest pressing you back as I move down your crossroads, pulling off your clothes, a sweet, sweet smell hits my nose, rose petal blossoms, cherry red, my tongue is led from your canvas to your thighs, temperatures rise, your eyes starts to close and roll; in I go, spreading you just enough to peek and see, touch and feel, yes I'm real, I possess a set of skills never seen before, All Yours, call my name, King, I reign, taking away your pain for many nights to come, yes you cum, with just one touch you erupt, I play with your pearl tongue, giving her a little twirl, oh baby girl you're becoming more and more moist; I am the right choice, a choice you made that's going to change your way of love making from here on out; I'm number one under these clouds from the heavens; I was sent to show you what love is all about, without a doubt when I pull up to pull in, you will scream softly, shout my name King who reigns Supreme when in between the sheets, just as I feel you getting weak, ready to explode again I stop, to look you deeply in your eyes, spreading your hips and thighs, gently and slowly I rise to go inside of your world, so precious , MY Girl, nice and warm, with your embrace, that smile upon your face takes the cake, says it all, pleasure your walls, evolving you are, we becoming one until I'm done, that number one under the sun, here under this roof I'm living proof of the art of love making, your back I'm breaking, your soul I'm taking, your body is shaking, I'm pushing with a groove that just can't lose. my tool rules these parts, your parts, this [palace, I'm thrashing and smashing through, wearing my crown as I put it down, showing you why I reign Supreme here on this block, on top

MII: The Return of the King

nonstop I go with this Rollercoaster Ride, up and down, side by side, in too deep in your tunnel, I funnel your love in different ways making you misbehave, I'm the ruler of your cave, My Love Slave you will become after, forever we are one when I come around top gun around this town, no frowns I wipe them away, your heart I break free, forever to escape when I take my place in your love potion number 9, you're on cloud 9, as you deliver that perfect quiver and shiver, body, mental on relaxed, I gave you this Relapse on repeat, sleep until next time we meet remember me in your dreams all hail the
King who reigns Supreme.

D. C.

MY SWEET MELODY

Seeing you for the first time blew my mind, right there in that moment, in that time I told myself you will be mine, that I will take your hand and guide you to that light at the end of the tunnel where there is nothing but love that will consume your every feeling every thought, there is a cost, your heart forever to be mine no matter how much time passes us by; no matter how long we're apart, our hearts will always be one to never part, that body, yea your body, a work of art, your eyes looking deep into my soul captivating my feelings trapping my heart exploding with joy when I see that smile of yours I just had to explore your core, bring you into my world to share what you have missed, to share what your body so desperately needs, to give you things those others couldn't give with just one touch, no baby, no rush, we taking it slow like H-Town, a King is what you have found, weeks pass before I get to put it down, patience is a virtue, I can't wait no longer, I want you, but more importantly, I want to show you what it means to be touched by a King, showing you why I am that Royal Lover, under these covers I rule, your body is my kingdom, watch me show and prove I can reign supreme when I hit you with my royal groove you won't lose when in my hands I know exactly what your mind, body and soul needs, believe in me I will deliver, your body will quiver and shake, taking you to another place when I go deeper, you're becoming wet as the ocean seas, weak in your knees when I drop to mine to give you that divine tongue between your hips, your thighs I lift, spreading you wide, pulling apart your lips with my tongue, playing with your pearl, giving you the world in this one feeling, healing all your scars, taking you far, singing loud, you're a rising star, not done by far, freezing time with the powers I hold in my tongue, shout out I am the one, shout out nobody can even come close to making me feel the way you have me feeling King do your thing, as I proceed to give you what you need standing to my feet, in between your thighs, pulling you closer, lining my Royal up with your palace in sight, pulling in slow, deep, deep, loving here I go with my strokes, here you go with your Sweet Melody, you feeling me in your core, hitting you with the powers

MII: The Return of the King

I hold inside of me, my love continues to creep through your walls of passion, your mind starts to wonder and imagine, is this really happening, is this magic, could this be a real King in your presence, blessing me with the heavens from up above, my dove I reply, reading your mind as I flip you over to stroke you from behind, one leg up if you don't mind, lean your torso towards the bed with an arch in your back, you feel the difference when I stroke like that? You feel that fiery sensation in this position? My mission is to give you A Feeling You Never Felt Before, your body, your canvas I want to explore, I want to know more and more, as I give you more than you can handle, switching gears, pause as a tear rolls down your face, I stop to kiss your face then your lips, flipping you back over so that we can be chest to breasts, face to face, lips to lips, in between your hips with my hips, I dip in with no hesitation, your love you're professing in my ear, your deepest fear is not having me near when in need, as I continue to feed your love I whisper my dove whenever you start to sing MY Sweet Melody, I will be right there to take care of all you need me to, each and every time it will always be about you.

D. C.

KEEP YOUR HEELS ON

Walking back to my room after a long night of work, unlocking my door to only see a trail of roses on the floor with a ready Hennessy drink on the table made for me; I pause and sip, think and wonder as I sip again, who could this be in my room; I start to walk towards the flick of candles, the smells of passion fill my room, it takes my mind, thoughts all consumed, opening the door to find you standing in my sight; everything about you is right, from your long black hair to those heels you wear, my eyes are set to stare, as you move over to where I stand; even with the fan, it's hot in here, having no fear, ready I see you are to show your skills, looking so good in your lace teddy you ask me if I'm ready to receive what you have in store for me; yes, I preach, you're taking my glass, placing my hands around your ass, your lips I feel, it's about to get real, pushing me down onto the bed, in control you are, love is about to be fed to my soul, first thing you do is take off my clothes, climb on top to feel me close, whispering in my ear we're about to make the best love you ever had before, forever I will be yours to adore, kissing slowly down my neck to my chest, back to my neck. Tonight, we won't be getting no rest, sheets are about to become a mess, I'm rubbing on your breasts as you creep low to give me a show with your tongue, squatting in those heels, showing me you are the one as I feel the chills through and through, keep doing what you do with that tongue lashing, licking and sucking, back and forth satisfaction, making me clench my sheets, toes curl damn baby I'm weak say forever you will be my girl staying close to me, I need you in my world, keep giving it to me, my mind takes a twirl with those oh's and ah's sounds I'm making, my walls you are breaking down you coming up from being down, reverse cowgirl is how you getting down, turning around to drop it low deep inside I go, you begin to coast, holding me tight at the ankles, your palace starts to flow, splash as you pick up the pace, going fast, splash each time you come up to stroke back down, spreading you wide, moving your hair to the side so I can see that smile, in my kingdom there's never no frowns as we switch position you killing all the competition, with you I'm winning from the beginning my heart was swimming in your pool of love, as we stand so I can pin you against the wall, heels on and all, deep into your walls I go with one leg up making you erupt is a must, splash when I enter deep in with a thrust, dash as I go fast and fast, I mastered my craft, floating as if you were on a raft, gripping your other leg, so I can go deep with my attack, French kissing your lips your heart is doing flips, laying you down before we finish this trip, rocking my hips between your thighs, your heels I rise to the sky I slide and glide all through the night, reaching my peak as I thrust away with all my might, this love making has been outta sight, oh what a night, my one of a kind, reading my mind by Keeping Your Heels On as you perform unlike the norm, loving your warm embrace, can't one take your place.

D. C.

THE KEY TO MY HEART

Trials and tests you will have to go through in order to earn The Key To My Heart, promise to never break a promise, take me far, show me the star you are, once it is given never scar my heart, once its close apart we will be, lost like priceless art, take me on a ride called making love, show me why I will never get enough of your love, I want to know why you are the one and only woman who should wear this crown and sit aside my throne to run this town; I want my feelings to be "Wowed", running together for life and not just for a few miles, look at what I have found, you go crazy wild when my body whispers in between the sheets, the way you give it all to me takes my breath away, you are the woman for me no need for me to seek no longer, with you I will grow stronger, able to cry on your shoulder when the going gets tough, in you I give all my trust, I've been wanting for real love to enter my life, in you I see my wife, sitting back I did think twice and once more just to make sure before I handed you The Key To My Heart; this is right for me, for you, together we can't lose, we have a lifetime to prove that we're supposed to be, us two here I go giving it to you, open your hand so I can place The Key To My Heart in your possession professing my love, never will I put no one else above the love we share, forever we will be intertwined, floating high in the air this I swear, I will always be here to cherish the very ground that you walk on, this love will live on even after I'm gone, my love is just that strong, putting on the armor of your love, you're the key my dove, I thank you for no rush, you hung in there which is a plus, stood by my side until I was ready for you to come inside; you have me on a natural high, I'm in love with you my Queen, you hold down everything that word means to me, glad I am I chose you to represent me, you're all I will ever need, you keep The Key To My Heart close, wear it around your neck so no one can ever come close to intervene in this destiny, I sing this song to the world never letting go of you my girl, you are my world, so I beg of you to watch over The Key To My Heart, never part ways, never leave it a stray, I want no one ever to come and take your place, you take the cake, tried to the jury I rest my case, my

MII: The Return of the King

*love come and take your rightful place, that look upon your face says it all, hanging your pictures all over my walls, infatuated, going through withdraws when we are not as one, you have my soul on fire, hotter than the sun, I can't get enough of your touch, loving you to the tenth power, so much of you I desire, my beautiful flower, not an hour goes past that I don't think of you and what we have, so I say once more, stressing the point, hold The Key To My Heart close, never lose sight of what we both want most, lost at sea in your boat,
in love with you, this I know.*

D. C.

A DIFFERENT WOMAN EVERY NIGHT

I'm starting to believe something is wrong with me, it's all I see, all I think about is making love to the ones who never been loved before, whom never had a real lover, a passionate love maker when I touch and explore, a world of women feed me more, oh how I adore these spices; each and every night, I'm releasing my power of passion, giving satisfaction to all that comes my way, how many have I've had, I won't say, just know each and every one will say I blessed them all in a very special way, pleasuring A Different Woman Every Night, entering their place, that palace, doing things only in their dreams they could have imagined, it's like I have to have it, bringing smiles and joy, destroying their past thoughts of their last, when I get to going deep into their canvas, never crossing their mind, never could have fathomed they would feel the way they feel when pleasuring them with my steel each and every night; A Different Woman Every Night fantasies I fulfill, bringing them to the other side of life, giving it to them Just Right, never have any felt a might of my power before, this love is real, put on this earth to be yours, to make every woman here to at least feel how it feels to be made love to, making the whole night about them and only them, like a movie shooting a film, an hour plus is a must no rush when I'm deep into your guts, making you erupt on que with my movement making music to your treasure chest, giving them the best they ever had, sad when it ends they become, wait, I can't say, I must run, Soul Searching for that number one who will have me stuck like a Cadillac on four flats, my Queen where are you at, searching and searching, going through A Different Woman Every Night, building them up just to break them down, my love game is outta sight; I'm waiting for that right one to come around, I put it down, can give a blind woman back her sight, just for the night until I vanish, hoping and praying their hearts can manage my absence until I reappear, strapped with the right gear, I fear I will be playing this game for the rest of my life, I want to settle down and find my wife. Is any woman right? Is anyone good enough for me? I am King; I need that one who can give it in return, put it on me, put it down take my crown and place

MII: The Return of the King

it on her head, with my knees to the ground, bowing at her feet, this is my dream, until I meet that one it seems, this game will burn like the sun, going on and on, dividing and conquering A Different Woman Every Night, the story of my life, needing my Queen
to come and save her King.

D. C.

SOUL MATE

Hard it is to express how I feel about you my Soul Mate, so I'll keep it short and simple due to me not wanting to wait any longer, to be inside your Pleasure P, you're all I see, your love is getting the best of me, if life had a repeat button, I still would want you by my side, my feelings I can't hide no more, never have I ever been here before, never have I ever cared and adored anyone like I do for you, I never came close to exploring these feelings I have for you my Soul Mate, days, weeks, months, years on top of years has passed without contact and once I've seen what I never had but always wanted came back from my past, a smile came across my face at a single thought of you, thinking about what we could have had, but not living in the past, now in the present, I want you in my future, never have I fronted when it came to you, my heart pumps and moves to your rhythm, your groove, now that you're back, let me prove that I am a show that you've been missing, a real love living inside ready to burst out and give it all to you, my heart belongs to you, I kept it locked away in m safe wanting for the day we came back face to face, I've been feigning, craving this day; come give me your hand, take your place my Soul Mate, bless this day, looking upon your beautiful face, your gorgeous brown almond shaped eyes, down your hourglass with hips and thighs to die for, your palace I must explore, tempting to the touch, but I can wait, there's no rush, trust in me when we get to that Lazy Love you won't be able to get enough, I'm gonna have your body busting and erupting all over the place, with love written all over your face, bless us this day my Soul Mate came back into my life to take her rightful place, ready you are to set that marriage date, horse and carriage to escape the world, just you and me my beautiful girl, you are my world, my everything, I need you in my life, my wife, dream come true, all I want is you my Soul Mate.

TAKE YOU THERE

The things I can do if I was ever allowed to Take You There, going deep inside of you through your mind to your heart past your soul, explode you will once you earn a feel, a touch, a kiss, the way I lick, you will tap, call quits, hold up a bit saying baby you got my legs shaking, backboard will be breaking, filling you up with a different sensation; if I can Take You There, you will call this the greatest love making you have ever been a part of, ever made, the way my kisses, my lips, my tongue will flip your feelings high, going through the ceiling, King's Love is sexual healing, no denying the feeling, opening your eyes to the other side of love, never will you be able to get enough of my touch, when I spread you wide to go deep inside your love, the way I tear it up, back and forth forever I will be your choice, if I could ever Take You There, you will swear that it was a dream, the way I will have you in my kitchen, putting you on top of my counter, blessing you through the midnight hour, glowing you will, my beautiful flower, with my tongue I will devour, will have you dripping wet like a shower, your body whispering louder, burning for my touch as I give off a thrust with my hips pressed in between yours, with my lips adoring yours to the floor we go, but yet I have you floating as I'm stroking away screaming loud you are I have no pillow to cover your face in the morning my neighbors will have something to say, laughing as we kiss and kiss, circular motions in between your hips when I stroke you dip, Team Us on this forever tip, forever trip, this love will never cease, I won't quit as I shift gears, stand up to sit in a chair, you feel every inch, passionate kisses are dished out, seducing my lasting endeavor, I stand to give it to you better, taking control, I will if I could ever Take You There, bouncing high in the air with your hair going everywhere, going deeper in there yes there, screams getting louder I swear, I see I'm Taking You There, but before I let go I lay you across my table to give you a royal show, slow groove inside of you, my love, you will never lose when you allow me to Take You There.

D. C.

CAN'T LIVE WITH YOU, CAN'T LIVE WITHOUT YOU
(INTERLUDE)

I Can't Live With You, taking me to that point where I don't want to deal with you, fussing and fighting about small issues, my heart you're about to lose, beat up and bruised, I refuse to accept the pain, walking out the door, bags in hand, the world I'm about to explore, closing my car door to screams while I drive off, looking in my rear view you holding up the ring I bought, giving me doubts, have I exhausted my love giving you my full amount; I mean I hate this scene, not knowing what to do all jacked up and confused, not knowing what the right thing to do, sometimes I love you, the next moment I can't stand you, but I Can't Live Without You, knowing you are my desire, the way you light my fire, hugging and kissing, thinking about what I will be missing, turning my car around is so tempting, I can't, I can, forget it, spinning around, a real man is what you found, together we run this town, we are bound to be, I can't seem to let you go, putting my keys into the front door to find you crying, laying on the floor, holding my picture near and close; baby, I'm sorry; let's start this show over, your my lucky four-leaf clover, my sun when the storm is over, let the past flow over, I want to spend the rest of my life with you until it's over, my heart says yes, my mind is made over, the wind is blowing, it's the month of October, you have me on a natural high, even though I'm sober, you're My Backbone, every King needs a spine, when looking over my shoulder seeing you there, knowing your mine you wind up my heart, taking me for a spin, forever you will be inside my heart, my soul, nothing can tear us apart, I have enough love for the both of us, Soul Searching I was, not for lust, but for love, in you I have found trust, even though sometimes you make me want to explode and erupt, of your love I just can't get enough.

SOUL SEARCHING

Day and night, night and day, I've traveled this world looking for that one special girl, that one woman who will take my breath away, who will show me love in every way, Soul Searching this earth looking for my Queen that's worth my love that I possess and hold inside my heart, that love I know that will never part, turning my dark days into that shining light, a love that holds the might of angels that are in heaven, spreading your wings wide as we glide flying high above the sky past the clouds; look at what I have found, she stands before me pleasing to my eyes my heartbeat's rate rise, from your feet to those thighs, your hips out wide, that frame tapered Just Right, curves going for miles, ready I am for you to show me what you're about, coasting past your perfectly shaped breasts, my hands ready to caress, love drunk I've become, looking upon your beautiful face until this day I never seen a beauty of your kind, more than a dime a wife in you I find, with your long wavy hair going down behind, gazing into your hazel eyes that are pulling me closer and closer, it is said beauty is in the eyes of the beholder and I want to hold her, hold you dear to my heart, baby you're my Picasso painting on the wall. I'm here to give you my all, going through withdrawals without you by my side, these feelings I hold I cannot hide, bursting out, flying over the moonlight and stars, you don't know how gorgeous you are to me, in you, in us, I see a life together happily ever after, just take my hand and allow me to take you to my Lovers' Land, where I plan to love you like no other once we're under my covers, but know it's more to me than my stroke of love with my mental I will love you tough, making sure you will never get enough; I've been Soul Searching for the stuff you possess, I can pass any test you may throw my way, tell me forever you will stay, for the rest of our days taking your rightful place on my throne, this love will live on and on, my love will perform love acts in many different ways, I have been holding on to my power of love just for you, ready I am to unleash this love for you, my heart is forever yours this is true, your every wish is my command, ready I am to do what you want me to, forever my mind will stay on you my Soul Searching is

D. C.

complete, sealed with your kiss, your touch, those lips, your love rights my ship, sailing in the direction of nothing but happiness, I always dreamed but never did I fathom this, your love is special, taking my feelings to another level, digging deep with your love shovel, never letting go, my Soul Searching has come to a halt, whatever the sacrifice and cost I'm in, I'm lost in your world calling you my everything, my girl, my Queen, I do what I say and say what I mean, you're my Soul Mate, my life has just begun on this date.

MII: The Return of the King

YOUR EROTIC ZONES

Since this morning, you have been texting my phone telling me how you can't stop thinking about the way I played with Your Erotic Zones, the way I made you moan when I stood up to perform, pulling me to the edge of the bed wasn't the norm for me, your stroke was deep, King I still feel you inside, I'm throbbing and dripping wet at work, ready I am to leave, you got me my King, I see you have a few tricks up your sleeve the way you had me weak in the knees making me cum with ease, you please my Pleasure P in ways that I can't even explain, the way you kiss me so softly your lips so soft, going down my neck with your tongue in my mind I'm like King's the one, pleasure at a high when you look me in the eyes, you took me by surprise, I felt the love from inside, you made my temperature rise, touching every base, hitting all of my Erotic Zones as your tongue took place in between my thighs blessing me with grace, Taking Your Time, the way you made my body unwind, I don't think I will ever come to find another lover of your kind, you are a handsome find, when you came up to go inside I caught a glimpse of what was between your hips, well-endowed and fully equipped with an elephant trunk that may make me tap and quit, making my feelings erupt there was no regretting this, when you hit you didn't miss, you took me for a trip the way you flipped the script rotating your hips with an extra dip my heart skipped when you lifted me high, you took me for a ride, a one of a kind ride, my hands to the sky glaring at your arms, mmmmmm, your strength as you perform, I repeat this isn't the norm for me, you took me deep when you flipped me over grabbing me at the shoulders arching my back, sliding in between my cheeks, King you did your thing, you made me sing, shit I'm still singing with a smile here at work, turning me into your fiend, making me go berserk, baby can I come over tonight so I can get that work? I want to show you a thing or two, hit me back boo when you have time, know that you will be running through my mind.

To Be Continued...

D. C.

GAMES, LIES AND DECEIT

Over and over again I play these Games, a different dame, but the Game remains the same, causing pain and hurt, dragging their heart out the dirt just to buried in it all over again, going in with no feelings attached with Lies, making them think I'm one of a kind; Lies, making them think I'm showing them my true colors; these are true facts, blind are they eyes, Lies after Lies just so I can touch them on the inside; in love they fall I make them want it all, even when weeks past, and I don't call their wall of love for me never falls; in me, they see it all blessing them with a love they never felt before, this earth, I was put here to explore them all, looking for that special girl that special woman who can put an end to my madness and all this Deceit, deceive make believing that I'm in love when in reality I'm thinking about the next dove I can give love to, you can call me a fool, trifling and rude for doing the things I do, each new one I play I feel like they take a piece of me as I take all of them, their soul stays in my control, the next man they meet will be treated so cold because of the hold I possess, these things I do to hurt them makes me want to cry; Games, Lies and Deceit will be the death of me; I don't mean to play the villain taking their heart without a gun, a theft in the night, what I'm doing is not right, losing my mind someone call 911 for these crimes I've pulled off, I must pay the cost for using you all, tears I saw so many fall walking away feeling like I didn't do anything, telling my ego it's okay, pride high and I don't know why, my heart on the inside is shutting down locking away for good, I'm no good, I wish I could fly away, far away so I can't hurt another with my Games, Lies and Deceitful ways, lay me down, I've dug my own grave; in my next life, I'm sure I will play the part of a man slave for all the women I mistreated doing my time here on earth, taking their worth for granted, I just don't understand why must I play the fool, breaking all the rules, abusing God's most precious thing here on earth He ever created; I made my bed I must lie in it, consequences aren't prohibited when playing these Games, telling these Lies and being Deceitful, I've hurt so many people (women), it's time for healing, to all I hope that one day you can forgive me for my trials, I know I have been foul, but I am only human; I only do what you allow.

D. C.

TAKING YOU FOR GRANTED

How did I manage to put your heart in this place? Pain is written all over your face; it's nothing I can do to erase my mistakes, running the streets everyday with you being the last thing on my mind, not there for you giving another my time when it's you I should have had by my side, Taking You For Granted, thinking that you will always be mine, I now come to realize and find myself alone calling your phone driving by your home wanting your love, your heart to belong back to me, my eyes weep at night, I couldn't see the light, jeopardizing our love each night when I could have made you my wife, I should've thought twice, I should have loved you better, right when I had the chance, now you're out there looking for another, I need you back under my covers, I want to be your one and only lover, so much guilt I feel when you look at me knowing I let you down, now your heart can't be found, I messed up knowing you were fed up with all the empty promises; I see you can't forgive; we can't press repeat, stop or rewind the beginning of our time; I won't be able to live knowing I was Taking You For Granted, how will I be able to manage without your love, I won't stop until I make things right, each and every night I will send you a kite expressing my feelings, my wrongs and how sorry I am, wanting you to come home where you know you belong; no matter how long it may take, I will right this wrong and make you mine once more, I will always cherish the good times before the bad times I caused; baby, my love is on pause, only you can press play, waiting patiently I am for that day you come and rescue me.

MII: The Return of the King

FILL THIS HOLE IN MY HEART

What have I done to deserve this? Missing you deeply, how could the kiss that was meant for me turnout to be so cold? How could you just let go? Once your touch was so kind and so gentle, you're confusing my mental state of mind, I thought we were just fine, never thought I would find myself in this position, hoping and wishing, fishing for answers, turning my world upside down, calling out your name, but not getting a response, going round and round in circles, I thought we were tied tight as a knot in a rope; how could you be so hurtful? Why must my arms feel so empty? This feeling is killing me; when will this pain stop? How could love be so cold? my heart can't let you go; I feel so dumb, what could I have done to change this outcome? I tried so hard to please you, my love; I thought you were the one, you have dug a hole in my heart that won't be filled unless you come and heal this pain, placing this cloud over my head, everyday it rains, one blink of my eyes my life changed; each night I hold your pillow close; I will never be the same; you took my flame that was burning with the desire to love you whole, the way you escaped and disappeared from my kingdom of love without me ever letting go, I would never know a love of your kind, searching the earth to find Mrs. Right again, so that I can live happily ever after, I want to start a new chapter, but can't start it without someone who is willing to love me for me, real love is what I seek, I don't need your type of love back inside, can't you see, can you hear my cries, long and sleepless nights without you by my side, but I will get through, I will be alright, just fine, I will spend the rest of my days, my time trying to Fill This Hole In My Heart, it's tearing me apart, sunny days are dark as I embark on this new journey without you, I know what I must do, move on alone sitting on my throne, until I can find a new heart to call my home.

D. C.

LOVE AND WAR

I knew every day wouldn't bring sunny skies; lately it's been cloudy nights, fussing while we fight in this Love and War relationship; through War, we have built our walls taller than mountains, steadily climbing when all tears are cleared; the end of the War is near, with no more bombs dropping, waving my white flag just to get back to where we once were, to what we once had without the madness, nothing but happiness, for better, for worse, with no more hurt, no more pain, escaping the rain from the War, we start, leaving a mark imprinted on my chest, when things go left, I feel I'm losing my best, I continue to stand right here, getting through any test; when all the smoke is gone, I will grab your hand to walk you back into our home where we both belong, giving in even when I am not wrong, we can't go on like this clenching fists, when you're losing control banging on my body bringing fire to the skies when you found I've lied with tears in your eyes, we've made it this far sharing each other's lives making up each and every time we fight in this Love and War; no matter what, I will always adore, keeping my vow to never leave, no matter how mad you get at me; we're playing for the same team, but sometimes we become enemies, throwing shots most of them I block, keeping it together, giving it all that I have, all that I've got, our love will get back to the top of that mountain we built, fulfilling our hearts once more even though we may War, as hard as we love I can't place no one above, standing my ground when you throw your bombs and they explode; losing control is not an option; when the fire is put out and we stop the action, satisfaction comes across our face, seeing that we are still here, knowing we both care too much to just let go of this forever hold; our hearts will survive turning the War cold, getting back to Love flying high above the nonsense, it only makes sense to us; in your love, I will always trust, your love is a must have; even when it hurts, I can't deny your passion, your soul, your body is all I know, going through this Love and War with only you, my heart forever yours, these words I speak are a true testament, forever here, just me and you when the smoke clears my only fear is you not standing there,

MII: The Return of the King

*here, near, next to me your King, I will always love you
in this Love and War, my Queen.*

D. C.

OUR CHEMISTRY

Can't nobody love like us, the way Our Chemistry goes, the way I take you down to the floor when your body comes calling for me to explore your passion your love I want nothing more, cruising so that we will last, no reason to go nowhere fast, slippery when wet, I'm not trying to crash my jet, my rocket, deep strokes, your palace is popping, pausing so you can hop on top, Our Chemistry goes non-stop, Tic Toc, Tic Toc, not worried about the clock as you ride, bounce and drop, frozen is time when I'm inside of your box, moving fast, my hands grab your ass, creeping up your back pressing you close, so I can kiss you slow, while stroking from down below in and out we flow, Our Chemistry just goes, in tune with each other's soul, higher we can go, feelings are starting to flow deep with my stroke from down below, moans start to form, singing that song you are as we perform; it won't be long before your love and affection come running down, my love you understand why I wear this crown, I'm not playing around, the way we putting it down you deserve the crown in your possession, I have found my heart connection, placing it in your hands as we do this dance all night long, I told you it won't be long, raising all alarms, singing to the top of your lungs as I plunge deep, you squeeze your cheeks, legs tight and weak, damn Our Chemistry, standing up to give you more of me, we're about to get loose, I'll take you through the roof; my actions are living proof, let me give you more of this truth, feeling real good the way we display the love we have for one another sliding under the covers to give you a taste of my tongue, no we not done, scratching and moaning, screaming out you're the one, top gun, busting uncontrollably, giving you the best of me, all I want to see is you pleased my love, Our Chemistry, breaking you down all night, giving you all of me, sliding up the sheets to go in between with my Royal pleasure, yes baby it's all yours, I belong to you hitting you with my grooves, rocking your body with my moves, my lips to your skin, as I adore you with my love soft, but hard not rough with my thrust, amazing I must say when you're naked, ready to take off, blast off, lift off at any given second, my Royal starts racing, love facing is what

we're making, your palace I'm baking, my legs get to shaking, Our Chemistry is off the chain when it comes to this love making, loving every minute that passes by the hour, your love I have devoured, until the next hour we meet, the thought of our
Our Chemistry will consume me.

D. C.

BLUE DREAM

Blue skies fill the heavens above, Blue eyes when I'm looking at you my love, I can't get enough of your Lesson In Love, not Blue Lust, this is Blue Love, Blue Roses as we lay next to one another, Blue eruption, Blue busting when Blue sheets are pulled to cover your body, Blue light special when we have a Royal Party, Blue Dream of you after we become naughty, enter my mind at my resting time, thinking of that Blue night filled with Blue candle lights, yes that night how you played with my Blue mic, had me singing the Blues all night giving me that Blue delight with your Blue lipstick all over my Blue body, the way you had me excited puts me in a different space, this Blue Dream can't be replaced, can't be erased, your Blue love I continue to chase, no escaping until I awake your Blue love, I can't shake these Blue feelings, breaking down my walls, giving me that Blue healing, your Blue love I desire, my Blue log will put out your Blue fire, I only see Blue y'all, but she shines bright, my guiding light, giving me sight when I can't see, I need my Blue Dream to forever stay with me, Blue lace everything, Blue heels I scream keep them on, I want them in the air when I perform these Blue love acts, Blue love is on the attack, laying you on your back as I Blue stroke, in I go, coasting to the beat of that Blue drum, filling you up overflowing your cup to the capacity, giving you all of me, more than you can handle actually, as I drop to my knees to kiss your Blue palace, soak and wet can you imagine what my Blue tongue is doing, moving in between making you fiend for more of my Blue Dream, this is real, I am King, wearing a Blue crown in you my Queen I have found, putting in down, painting your town with the color Blue, all I want is you, the things you do takes me to new heights, your love making is outta sight, you give me that Just Right, Blue magic all night, stuck with my eyes closed, I don't want to wake before I explode, hold me tight my love in thoughts until tomorrow night, when I can give you more of my Blue Dream delight.

MII: The Return of the King

I GOT A WOMAN AT HOME

In this VIP section chilling with my Kings having a good time while this dime feeds me noise on how she can be better than the next, I stay poised, faded I am, she keeps going, but her words don't take effect on me, see I Have A Woman At Home that gives me everything I need, never could I see me stepping out on her, my stress reliever, my love diva, my heart only receives her, I will never deceive her, the realest I've ever dealt with, my love will never quit, taking a sip of my Henny on the rocks, dapping my Kings saying I must kick rocks while thinking about being on top of my love, leaving this club in a flash, multiple lights I pass, dashing through the speed limit thinking about being in it, inside what's mine, I never thought the day would come when I turned down a dime, but mine is one of a kind, the way we intertwine, speechless I become when our bodies rhythm and rhyme; I couldn't find nothing better, this love I hold, I come to see my gas is low, not wanting to stop, but I must; baby, I'm so close putting it in rush gear; I pull up to the pump, two girls in heels standing outside the car, pretty I recall, words erupt, handsome one says, what's your name the other speaks, you want to come party and play with the two of us we some real freaks, in my mind back in time I would have taken the time to get loose and show them how a King does, but I smile and say, I'm sorry ladies not tonight I'm not that guy I reply you girls have a safe night, hanging up the pump back into my car rushing with her touch on my mind no more wasting time, going home to claim what's mine, thoughts crossing my mind of being in her spine, hoping she's dreaming of me, pulling into the driveway into the house I creep, ready to surprise and give her all of me, taking off my clothes as I walk through the house, item after item, I want to hear her scream and shout, walking in my birthday suit with socks on, happy I'm home, it's about to be on, sliding into the room your smell I consume, pulling back the sheets immediately she smiles and grab a hold of me, eyes still closed, but she knows it is me, saying baby, I missed you replying with a kiss I missed you too, how was the club, boring I couldn't do nothing but think about you and the things I wanna do to you,

D. C.

awakened out your slumber your take hold of my satisfaction, ready to do a number on me, taking action sliding me into your waterfall, slowly touching your walls, grabbing your ass, you dip and pause, twerk and pause, you dip I rip through with a thrust between your walls, fully equipped my heart skips, but not missing a beat, you repeat, faster than slowly switching positions, loving this mission, finding myself on top inside that warm spot, kissing and loving stuffing your oven with nothing but pleasure, moaning as I weather your storm, going on and on as your water streams down my royal vein, in and out, Taking My Time, kissing your mouth, pushing inside, giving you all my love, feeling myself deeper and deeper inside, I can see it in your eyes, feel it through your quivering thighs, that cream filling surprise about to flow, baby let go, express your love that love I can't get away from, that I can't get enough of, making love until the break of dawn, until that light comes through without hitting a switch, no spot goes untouched when I hit, I don't miss, ripping through your walls, freaking you in all, you love the way my royal slide through with a pause, slide and pause, faster motion you call out, leaving you with no doubt, my love game is your kryptonite, for the rest of your life I'm gonna make you feel right, putting it down, King of your town, you never felt it like this wearing my crown as I pound, sweating it out, "Oh My" you scream and shout "that's what it's made for baby", no escaping this touch; oh, how I love you're warming touch, it just fills me up, going deep is a must, as I erupt into your palace of love, I will give anything to have your touch; just the thought sends a rush; this is real love never lust, your love is a must have in my life, until my days come to an end, you will be called my wife.

MII: The Return of the King

FALLING IN LOVE

What have you done? I was once numb to love, but you have found a way to open me up, breaking down my walls; I threaten to call the laws; it didn't matter because you want it all, making me fall deep, going through withdrawals when you're not with me, making me fall deep, deep as the ocean sea, you came into my life completing my very need, what I deserve, you see the hurt that was once there inside, changing my life, doing me in ways that I like, that I love, it's you that I always dreamed of, my beautiful butterfly giving me new life, my precious dove, my Mrs. Right; it's you who gives me that special delight; I tried to fight your powers with each passing hour as I thought this over; I couldn't do anything but think about you and hold you closer to my heart, My Stress Reliever, you made me a born-again believer, catching your love like a wide receiver; can I fall deeper, baby? I become weaker when you come near, setting off my love erasing my fears; you said this is the year of the lover, my heart has discovered that ever flowing passion again, rubbing up and down your smooth skin, deep within your core, feeling good as I explore, giving me more and more reasons to keep falling in love, becoming my drug, wanting only your love; what have you done? You have opened up my soul, pulling on your love, never will I let go, attending your show, going low as my love goes around and around, putting it down placing your X's and O's all over my crown, I have found my Queen, you're all mine and I'm your fiend, wanting wants in between those thighs, your eyes takes me high, what a surprise, never did I think my love would rise high again, never thought I would win, but you came in when I was Soul Searching for that other side of love, for that Perfect Match, our hearts attached as one, sitting here thinking of you; what have you done? Second to None, Team Us, together as one is a plus, my love has rushed to fill your heart and soul, overflowing your cup, making you whole, I have no control of this hold, Falling in Love is what you have done for me, forever we will be.

D. C.

TONIGHT IS THE NIGHT

Your body tells me everything I need to know, the way you smile at the lips, the way you sway your hips when coasting as you walk, Tonight Is the Night, your ticket has been bought, you're gonna march to the beat of my drum, when I enter you with my blessed one, heaven sent Hun, you have found the right one, tonight Falling In Love you just might, your body I'm about to do Just Right, favorite quote, I can back it up, I can brag and boast, let me not get beside myself, back to pleasuring you low, wetness surrounds the sheets, pulling you to the ground, I mean floor, continuing to explore up and down your canvas, never have you had it this way, forever my lady you will want to stay after the way I play with your insides, when my tongue hits you, your body won't lie, doing the things you don't get to do, your last was a fool not to taste your forbidden fruit, juice down my chin, pulling on your crazy sex drive that you have hidden within, getting you off, licking you nice and soft, stroking your pearl tongue, feelings are lost in my world, forever in my world, going slowly so you feel my passion in every lick, no spot in the inside will be missed, the way my tongue twists, I will have you doing flips, crawling up the walls, running like I'm the cops and you broke the laws, slow and easy is the way I love you tonight, standing up to wrap your thighs around my jaws, grapping tight as your passion falls showing strength, going deep within, with you reaching one hand to the ceiling the other holding on to my shoulders, blessing you I am with a different type of sexual healing, a freak under cover, your inner love I have discovered, falling victim to the ways I have your body melting in my hands a lifetime dance is in the plans, forever after tonight my love, ready I am to give and show my might, thunder erupts between the thighs your eyes wide, you seem surprised, "well equipped, strong endowed" is my slogan, yea that's right, no minute man an all-night groove is what I'm about, in pursuit of your love, I'm in motion, entering your love potion, sign says caution, deep love coasting, falling deep flowing into your palace like a tornado, I spin you on top of me, spreading your cheeks as I stroke deep from underneath, reaching your peak I'm hitting spots

MII: The Return of the King

your last couldn't reach, I practice what I preach, flipping the script, you start to throw it back with a dip in your hips with a kiss to my lips, my heart skips. What's this? Is there something I missed? I just fell at the touch of your lips and the groove in your dip, my heart is yours, on a forever trip, my royal tip, I want you to explore, hopping off to go below with your mouth, lips and tongue, stroking my staff, two hands is needed you do the math, no gag reflects, my Queen with the greatest sex, the best love, my everything, oh my and everything else falling from my mouth, I shout, pound, neighbors banging, I'm loud, you deep throat all I can say is wow, what have I found, my one and only, putting it on me in ways I never would have imagined, taking back control, breast sucking, tongue lashing, sweat ass smacking in the summertime love, heaven above has blessed this love, my dove, filling you up with my love placing no one above, never can you get enough of what I have to offer, breaking you off something proper, I am a prophet, after this your love will never quit, watch and see, close your eyes, I will be there in your dreams, you will never ever be able to get rid of me.

D. C.

SITTING HERE THINKING ABOUT YOU
(INTERLUDE)

Closing my eyes just to see your smile, your love takes me on trips, going for miles, bringing a joy that makes me go to the highest mountain point to scream and shout, to tell everyone about the love you give, My Gift, so precious, My Rib I live to fulfill you with happiness and love I can't get enough of that beautiful smile of yours, it brings a joy unknown to those who've never been in love, like a star that shines during the day, my sun when it's night, my everything you bring me such delight, giving me exactly what I need, your love I feed off of my feelings dug deep into your soul, imprinted on your heart, so that you can never let go, eyes still closed, watching the way we flow I want the whole world to know, baby I will go anywhere you desire, you are the flame to my fire, the air to my lungs, my heaven on earth, your palace under your skirt makes me go berserk, you're worth a lifetime of love, and I will be the one to see it come true, I'm just Sitting Here Thinking About You, my Soulmate, my true love, stealing Another Man's Girl turning his world upside down, in me a King she has found.

MII: The Return of the King

ANOTHER MAN'S GIRL II

We both stand in awe; from the look upon my face, you can tell I know who she is; this situation just got real; putting on my shirt to deal with this problem, setting my gun down on the abdomen, I thought it was gonna be the girl's man she was dealing with, but it's my mistress; I'm feeling so much tension in this room, the one I just laid the boom to say, who is this trick King, hold up goes the mistress, I got your trick hoe, ladies, ladies, let's not lose control standing in the middle holding them both back, let me explain, but first my dame how did you find me, I told you we were done a few suns ago, you need to let go, the show is over; go back to your rover and leave, wrapping up her weave saying I'm not going nowhere I declare your heart is mine, I want that one of a kind back, I put a track on your phone; baby, come home where you belong, before I answer the phone rings, Hello she says, it's the man who plans revenge, Damn, what have I got myself in, drunk at the door saying let me in I just wanna talk, he stutters please in a drunken state of mind, she says fine, you're here we might as well kill two birds with one stone, let's tell them what's going on, now it's her, him, her and I seeing rage in his eyes my mistress cries inside, with her and I standing side by side setting them straight, saying we're starting a new life with one another, all is exposed from under the covers, pacing back and forth they are, reacting to the hurt we caused, sorry not cutting it ya'll, he down on his knees begging her please, with my mistress looking at me saying you're all I need, we're both saying it's over between us, through their eyes we can see their souls burst, hearts erupt, fueling with fire in his gut, he stands up looking at me blaming me, all he sees is red rushing towards me trying to knock me over the head, while the girls get to pulling weaves and dreads, he swings and misses, knocking the gun off the abdomen, diving to keep it away, I manage to retrieve it, enough I say letting of a shot, calming the situation, I'm not playing, both of y'all must go and never return, or you will feel my wrath, through my eyes they can feel I meant that, as they walk out, I look back and say to my dame never will I play this game again, I'm with you to the end,

D. C.

but let there be no more drunken men, as we hang and laugh it off,
who said love don't cost.

MII: The Return of the King

ROCK YOU SLOW

I want to show you that I appreciate you and everything you do; tonight will be an Everlasting night, leaving you with memories of the way I'm going to touch your body; from the look upon your face, I see you're excited, no reason to try and hide it; I'm gonna Rock You Slow from all different angles, turning lights down low, music on point, here we go, gazing into your amazing eyes, standing close enough to kiss pulling you in with my eyes, with my hands rising grabbing at your face, my lips take their place, soft and smooth, wet and juicy, but not sloppy, tongue twisting slowly; in my arms, I hold you closely, turning on your passion with my all-night satisfaction, breaking you down like a fraction, your body will be forever asking for my Rock You Slow show, stripping off your clothes at the point of no return, here I go, picking you up just to lay you across my rose petal bed, real love isn't dead, in me I hold that power, your stress reliever, your palace keeper, I'm about to devour for the next few hours, kissing on your curves, touching your sweet spots, hitting them right nerves, feeding all your urges, no spot will be missed, even kissing your feet, but watch this twist as I dip between your thighs, below your waist diving deep in, palace to my face, my tongue is in the right place, sucking and licking slowly, making sure you feel me as I Take My Time; as I take you up without a parachute at the end, you will stand and salute me for my duties; it's my job to please yours truly; signed in cursive with my tongue, your palace starts to quiver, you begin to run, no, no my love I say grabbing at your waist, pulling your palace back to my face, making you explode all over the place, whipping my tongue back and forth, I'm heading north towards your breasts, pit stop for a rest, kissing and licking, sucking and rubbing, hot is your oven, ready to be filled with my stuffing, you haven't seen nothing, get ready for some more erupting, rocking your body slow, in and out I go, teasing your soul, close I hold, feeling your heartbeat against mine, taking my time with each stroke that's so divine, leaving a mark on your mind, I have designed that word "love", look it up, and you will find me your King sitting on the throne as I pleasure you in between giving you what you

D. C.

need as I Rock You Slow, cruising is this boat, slow motion as we go, we continue to float through the night, pushing with a hint of my might, loving that thang Just Right, I'm the one you will want for the rest of your life, after just one touch, you will be scarred for life, my love game is just that tight, just that deep, thoughts of me will consume thee each time you lay and grab your sheets
you will think of me your King.

MII: The Return of the King

TAKING MY TIME II

Picking up where we last left off, Taking My Time Part II, there is some new things I wanna try with you, setting the mood dimming the lights, love passion is in my sights, my Just right, the temptation we can't fight, we will be going for the rest of the night, so baby lay it down for me, racing with excitement, expressing my delight with a kiss to your soft skin, smooth as my tongue begins to stroke your body up and down, doing circles around and around, every tingling spot will be found, Taking My Time with you, let's try something new, I'm so into you; my tongue wants to go inside of you; you find yourself upside down with your legs wrapped around my shoulders, fixing my crown I'm about to go lower, deeper than ever before, you will shout and scream as I give you more than you ever had, not moving fast, but slow Taking My Time in between your thighs I dive without needing any air taking you there, making you float above air, my tongue doing deep circular motion as you stare with love written across your face, down below your waist you're soaked and wet like an ocean, I have twister-like rotation skills, an explosion is what we're facing, Taking My Time Part II is the real deal, my love you won't be erasing, loving the passionate faces you're making, standing up with my tongue still in place, thirty minutes into this unforgettable day; as the night moves on, I look deep into your face while climbing on top going in between your waist, ready to fill your palace place with the touch of my tip, I'm taking you outta space; our love is steadily rising like a cake; I have your hot box oven blazing with warmth, juicy, this isn't the norm as I perform a different stroke pushing up and down your legs spread apart, far out, bringing them high above my head, resting them on my shoulders I'm about to go deeper and slower, so you feel all of me, every inch, your palace is now my fit, no competition when it comes to King working in between, pushing your legs towards your face riding your waves, deep into your pleasure chest, thrusting slowly, sheets are a mess, kissing on your breasts, you're sucking on my chest, get ready my feet are set, your legs are wrapped firm, I'm about to go deep into your treasure hole, with your hands you hold on to my neck, screams

D. C.

out this is the best, Taking My Time with you loving my new grooves and moves, my love has chosen you, pushing you up against the wall making your rain fall, kissing, tongue twisting and all calling you my Lazy Love as I erupt inside, filling your cup taking you up, up and away, never forgetting this day, forgetting me, Taking My Time Part II with my love that's one of a kind, all just for you, forever you will be mine.

YOUR CURVES

The greatest thing created here on this earth is a woman and her curves. If you haven't explored it, then you got some nerves. Let me explain how it works; all your gears will come into play; be careful some will have you steering the wrong way, kissing on her face to those lips, ready I am for this road trip, closing the door starting my engine, so I can dip through Your Curves, doing the speed limit for now going down your neck coming to a steep hill to climb, putting my car in overdrive, teasing your feelings inside as I go around and around your breasts; my car runs off nothing, but the best, coming up on your road sign saying don't speed around these curves, you will crash, it gets slippery when wet, so I can't smash the pedal to the floor just yet, no passing in this single lane, hitting every spot with a lot of tongue lashing down your highway of love, coming out of those hills and curves a straight shot, as I merge left into the fast lane with the way my tongue moves in between, you will have no complaints passing up your waist, touching you in that right place, giving you what you need as I proceed to speed through your highway, overjoy is read across your face, one point five miles before I take my place, filling your space, a half mile until you cum, giving you that A1 until the sun comes up, exiting onto a different part of Your Curves, no blurred lines here, I see your love real clear, entering your stratosphere taking away your fear, hands firm on your steering wheel, deep you feel my thrust going fast like I'm in a rush, nope my tires won't bust until we reach your destination, turning up the A/C, it's getting hot in here like that Greenlight Special or that Until You Climax, Body To Body, pedal down to the max, cracking that two hundred on the dashboard, forever adore Your Curves, breaking your back with how I attack, giving you what you deserve, going hard and fast, you flying high and above uplifting your spirits, shifting gears, your destination is close, we're near, clenching your thighs pushing inside for the rest of the night Your Curves will be all mine.

DRUNKEN NIGHT II

Staring at this ringing phone, text after text saying why aren't you home, what happened to you meeting me, before I reply it starts ringing again, looking at Tracy's face while I answer, hey baby with a shaky tone, I wanted to wait to hear the noise, but I have no choice, you go off saying you were supposed to come home after dropping Tracy off, tell me what happened, I'm blabbering, lying, trying not to hurt you again, but you're not buying in, saying deep within I know you did something. Are you still with Tracy? Why isn't she answering her phone, baby, come on tell me the truth or we are through; looking at Tracy like what should I do, I don't want to lose the love of my life, I should have thought twice, f**k it I must do what's right, baby listen just listen for a second, you are my life's blessing, what I'm about to say will cause stress and pain, oh baby I didn't mean to do you this way, tears as I say, Tracy and I have made a mistake, as you know I took her home to her place, she start telling me about her last, how wrong he did her, saying Kim is a lucky woman to have found you, consoling her as a friend I do, saying you will find Mr. Right, walking her to her door she almost falls as I catch her, she stares off into my eyes pulling me close for a kiss, lips touch, I pull back saying no Tracy we can't take this trip, it isn't right, standing under the moonlight, I started to turn away and she grabbed me pulling me into her place saying if only for one night, I want to feel what Kim feels every night, she talks about it all the time, so I feel it's only right I find out, kissing me, mouth to mouth, her hands started to unbuckle my pants, my royal starts to stand in her hands doing her dance, I don't want to hear no more Kim cries out, I say listen baby just listen you need to know it all, baby don't go, I didn't mean to give her a show, but I was drunk too, that's a sorry ass excuse, but it's the truth, I got loose loving her down pleasuring her in ways I shouldn't have, baby I'm not glad about my act, I wish I can take it back, my love is where your heart is at, you can believe that, this was a senseless act, tell me you still care baby, are you there, yes I'm here and thank you for telling me the truth, I applaud you, knowing I'm still mad, but would have been more hurt if

MII: The Return of the King

you lied, so you stayed there all night? Yes my love I did fall asleep thinking I was waking up to you, baby I'm sorry, what now, what are we to do, I can't lose you, my King I love you come home, so we can work this out, no more Drunken Nights unless I'm in the house and tell Tracy to come to, we got room to make it do what it do, two on one another Drunken Night we about to have under the sun;
wow, I am a lucky one.

GREENLIGHT SPECIAL

Hey love, I say while entering the room, my eyes consumed with your body in sight, laying across the bed past your feet to your legs, thighs, thickness shining from the candle light, temptation I can't fight, drawn to your body up your narrow waist firmly shaped with an ass that can balance a glass, nice soft abs as my eyes pass through your canvas, loving this road trip, adoring this moment been waiting for this moment, ready to slide up on it, coming across your succulent breasts, my tongue wants to caress, we won't be getting no rest tonight, finally arriving to your beautiful face, losing my heart to you replacing it with yours, through your eyes I see us bound, tied, this love will never die, hope you're ready for my Greenlight Special, working you hard, there won't be no issue, enough with the preview, undressing you with my love ray vision stripping you down to your birthday suit, your heart and soul forever I will pursue, never letting go, Greenlight, let's go, not slow my tongue rolls, spreading you low, no time to cruise or coast your boat, high you float as I go low inside with my tongue, playing with your pearl, I've just begun, until that sticky face I'm not done, no yellow light slowing down, I'm about to put it down, with my feet planted firmly on the ground, wrapping my arms around your thighs and waist, putting your legs around my face, as I rise to my feet to service you my Queen, giving you that Greenlight Special, showing you why you're my everything, with my tongue all in between, no red light stopping, back to the bed so I can really get your palace to popping, switching positions, enough of this licking, I feel your heartbeat ticking, are you ready for this sticking and moving, my skills are proven, forever you will be pursuing my love, pushing hard and fast as your nails dig deep, I will outlast your past, with your hands tightly squeezing my ass, I smash and dash through your palace of love, switching to our side, so I can take you higher and above with one leg in the air, this love, my love can't be compared, as I take you there, words from you, I love you, I love this I swear baby take me there, preparing for liftoff, ten seconds until blast off, then let the countdown begin, nine going deeper inside I see it in your eyes that

MII: The Return of the King

I'm qualified, eight has arrived, your passion has come alive with each stroke of the time your body I'm about to unwind, your heart is all mine, flipping you over, so I can hit that thang from behind, fast not Taking My Time, all I see is Green lights, speeding down your highway taking you to heaven once I hit you with number seven, clever strokes I provoke your inner love as I keep taking you up past them clouds going wild inside and out showing you what my Greenlight Special is all about as we count number six, you're throwing it back with a dip in your hips taking all of my fully equipped, loving our mix, call me captain of your ship, slip and sliding to lucky number five, my hands smacking your butt and thighs, loving our night pushing with all my might, your palace so right, celebrating your life my Queen, shining bright in this Greenlight, I'm yours, on to that number four, oh how I adore, wanting more giving you more, always up to explore your world, breaking you down, wiping away all frowns as three comes around, I grab your hair to turn you around, to see your face and love expressions that you make, baking your body like a cake, caution, your oven is hot, but I can't wait, no red lights stops speeding pass the cops, Nascar fast, deep in and out into your abs, you shout number two, baby I love you and the things you do, complete, just us two, keep going baby, right there, don't move, keep hitting me with your tool, make it do what it do, inside of you Losing Control, ready we are to explode calling out that number one, together, the extension of my love can't be measured, my lasting endeavor, pedal to the metal, blasting off into the night, loving my Greenlight Special.

D. C.

A FEELING YOU NEVER FELT BEFORE II
(INTERLUDE)

Opening the door to find a woman standing in her skin tight sundress, removing her glasses asking if she can speak with Renae; come in I say, Renae, I call, the door is for you; we are in the middle of something, but do what you do; with a concerned look on her face, she says, I thought I told you to wait in the car Michelle, I've been waiting, but it's hot as hell, how much longer? Did you break it off? Did you tell him this game he lost? Overhearing the conversation, with no hesitation, I step in saying, what's this I'm hearing, Renae? tell me she didn't say what I think she said, tell me you're not about to say what I think you're gonna say. I'm afraid it's true, looking in my eyes all sad and blue; I didn't want to hurt you, especially after you started spilling your feelings, but I can't lie it's her, Michelle who been healing and mending my heart from that time you tore it apart, she gives me A Feeling I Never Felt Before, if you love me allow us to walk out the door, I will always love you, but her love I must explore, your wish is yours, you go and enjoy, my heart will always play these chords for you, these words I bare are true, my heart is forever yours, that Lazy Love I so enjoyed, you gave me A Feeling I Never Felt Before, closing the door on this chapter, it doesn't always end up as a happily ever after, it's only a matter of time that Beautiful Find comes into my life and give me that real Lazy Love, a feeling that won't make my heart erupt of hurt and pain, but giving that feeling of never having enough, some real trust that I Never Felt Before, opening the door to a new chapter, I will have my happily ever after.

LAZY LOVE

My heart is singing out to you, can't you hear the words soft and sweet, like a blue mockingbird whispering low, as I pull in slowly with your legs wrapped, so that I can't go nowhere, baby right there we stare into each other's eyes, I see love on the other side, that I don't wanna go nowhere my bride; in you, I can stroke all night, that I don't wanna do nothing else type of love, no this isn't a crush, you see nor feel no lust emotion, steadily with my coasting, crushing and tearing down your walls, I want it all, starting with your mind, I wanna be your thoughts, consuming all you have to offer at whatever cost, your heart I know can't be bought, how about we exchange, mine for yours, baby, I'm all yours, falling victim to your Lazy Love, your soul no I don't want to control, but I want to be the one who lights that fire, a different type of brother, he broke the mold when I was created, here to desire your body, I will never leave you lonely, no need for hiding, when away you can just phone me, if only I can have all the above, adoring you I will my precious dove, taking you high when I dug, I mean dig, you know what I'm trying to say, into your palace I play, I couldn't imagine another taking my place, baby there's no escape, you have me for the rest of your days, I misbehave when I can't play inside your cave, I can't go for days without your Pleasure P, that taste to my mouth watering to the taste, when I lick in between your waist, it just takes me to another place, your Lazy Love is number one, taking you outta space, when I touch you cum, your last memories of your last are erased, carving with my tool, making room for the things I want to do, having to take my time with you, dude must didn't know what to do, or else he wasn't equipped with the right tool, my moves will have you running to the news, your Lazy Love is on point, don't get it confused, but when it come to my grooves, well they don't call me King for nothing, the Royal Lover, the best thing smoking, the way I can have your heart, your feelings wide open, with this Lazy Love I'm just coasting, loving the motion, blessing the day you came to me, releasing this eagle, allowing this bird to fly free, love is what I seek, love is what I've found, the way you put it down, I'm giving you the

D. C.

crown, my Queen, you mean the world to me, putting me to sleep waking up to see you lying next to me, means everything to me, your heart I will forever keep my Lazy Love, we belong to each other, just you and me.

MII: The Return of the King

BABY MAKING

I hope it's alright what I'm feeling right now; tonight will be the night with you in my sights; fresh out the shower with water dripping; this next hour, I will be slipping through your everglades, you know where the sun can't go, where it's always stay dark with shade, yea that place; I'm going to Take My Time when downtown, a real Queen is what I have found; in you my heart is wide open, I'm through with that outside noise; I've made my choice; my love I want you wide open, so I can give you what we have been missing, what you been asking me for, a baby boy, a baby girl, I am all yours, you are my world, my piece of Paradise, I don't have to rethink twice; tonight, we start a new life, bringing a bundle of joy into our world, let's start this off right, no keep on the lights, I wanna see the love across your face when I take my place, removing your towel admiring the Queen that stands before me right now, going wild inside, the happiness across my face, I can't hide, as we glide kissing towards the bed, as we lay kissing softly, holding close, one thought flows through my mind, your body I unwind, your stress reliever I am, lay back and recline, as I take my time, spreading you wide, fully erect, so I can go inside, pulling in slow strokes, I begin, real love coming through, I'm with you to the end, I wanna spend a couple of forevers as I hit you with my lasting endeavor, pleasure and love fills the atmosphere, making love is what we're doing in here, hitting on all gears, kissing, licking, whispering in your ear, your passion of love falling down is near, stroke, after stroke, with my hands on the wheel, in control as I steer this ship, splashing through as I take a dip, getting closer and closer to our dreams, as I kiss your lips, I can hear the angels sing, I love blessing you, filling you up, my Queen, from the beginning I saw you as my everything, my wife, my lover, my friend, most importantly the mother of my children, I'm in this to the end, love strokes I send through your palace, all these things I can imagine, did you cast a spell, you're working some type of magic, whatever it is don't stop, staying on top of filling you up staying in control, running the Baby Making show, hitting different pockets, places you didn't know existed, the inside I fix

D. C.

my fit, your stretch, legs you twist, wrap around my waist, a nice soft dip I thrust, crushing with love, I can't get enough, I love you so much, giving all my trust, feeling that rush through my legs, are you ready to be fed with a gift from up above, giving you all my love, looking into your eyes as I erupt, we kiss holding tight, the feeling is just right, a Baby Making night, giving you my love, my life.

MII: The Return of the King

MY PROGRAM

You telling me you want me to put you in rotation, you telling me you want your body in motion, you wanna know if it is true what everyone is saying, floating to my arms, you Can't Resist the way that I stand, I hypnotize your mind when I perform on your stage, sending your feelings into a rage of passion, loving every action you will, I get busy baby, I got skills, call me the real deal, you will never feel this way again, once I get to touching, erasing your thought of lusting, love is the only topic of discussion when inside MY Program, I know, I know, yes, I'm that drug that will have you coming back for more, the way my fingers and tongue explore the inside of your valley, thigh by thigh, cruising up your alley, you calling me daddy, my love, when I fill you up with my royal passion, satisfaction, I'm not lying, will have you flying, you wanna be down with My Program, wanting me to wipe away those frowns, show you why I wear this crown, they don't call me Royal Lover for nothing, I put it down with just one round, you're not hearing me, hot as the sun deep as the sea those other guys can have a seat for you won't need their services any longer; My Program is much, much stronger, going ham when putting your legs above my shoulders, your beauty is in the eye of this beholder, your heart growing warmer from being cold, I hold the key to your treasure, cracking your code, forever I hold your heart close to me, My Program is going to make you want me indefinitely, I know you can't believe how I have you weak from My Program, touching your Erotic Zones, back and forth actions, thrashing and smashing, tongue lashing, you back scratching as I cradle your legs, your hands above your head, you loving my Roller Coaster Ride, taking you high as I drop low, loop to loop, here I go, we coast, floating on air, can you compare me to another, I think not, Niagara falls flowing from your spot, your palace to be exact, flipping you over to the back, your ass I smack and rub, spread them legs, I'm going in, all in, you start to run, screaming I'm about to cum, I pull on your hair, taking you there yes there, I ask again can you compare, baby you say I swear, I never felt this feeling, your love is sexual healing, I got that Lazy Love feeling, forever stay, you hitting my spot, you say King got me feigning, MY

D. C.

Program is the truth, you feel my proof, as I slide through in and out all night long I can go without a doubt you shout I'm cuming again daddy, squirting all over me when I extend with my thrust, making you bust, erupt, loving my touch, going until day break, you know the sunrise comes up, My Program never lies, what's in between my thighs will have your ass surprised, a feeling Just Right, something you've never seen, opening your eyes to me deep inside pushing in between your canvas, can you imagine what My Program can do, all it takes is for you to call on me, and I will come release you from your cage, turning you into my love slave, missing me for days, my loving, My Program, my touch will be the only thing you crave.

MII: The Return of the King

READY, SET, GO

On your mark, Ready I am to start this Everlasting race, your face says it all the way I Set up the place, this date you will log into your memory bank, never will you be able to shake this escapade once I Go, once I float, that undying feeling you feel down below is me when I stroke, devoting my time as my tongue winds and winds, your beauty blows my mind, you're so fine, all mine tonight, open up wide so my tongue can take flight through your palace, Ready you are for that screaming orgasm, as I Set your legs above my head, my tongue goes deep into your land of pleasure, hot as a desert, sweating, calling out my name, professing your love, my rhythm about to take you up, are you Ready for me to fill your cup, so deep that you feel me in your gut, you're Set to erupt, sounds of love making, that's a plus, no rush when I Go pleasuring your palace as I coast, my hands slide over your throat, Ready, Set, Go picking up my flow, stroke after stroke, explode you Go, sliding down my pole, grabbing my pillow screaming out of control, pushing inside of you, letting go of your throat, Ready for another part of my show, Set, wrap your legs around my body like a snake so farther I will Go, giving you an all- night show as I Set my feet you yell, Oh Lord what's next baby, damn, this is the greatest sex baby, the best is yet to come, yes you're gonna cum again and once more before I end, picking you up grabbing a hold of your back end, deep within, taking your love for a spin, a few strokes here you Go again busting while I swim through your river, Mr. Postman yes I always deliver on time when deep into your spine making your body unwind, yes One of a Kind, putting you down so I can hit that thang from behind, Ready, Set, Go, it's almost that time to end my show, pulling on your hair, in the mirror you stare, loving my grooves, my strokes and moves, can't no other dude pull off the things I do, once I'm Ready, focus on your mark, Set at the start with what I need, I will Go on and proceed to take you far, King will bless you, turning you into a shining star, a Queen is what you will be called, if you can take it rough and hard, when I get Ready and Set the mood to Go there on you, only if you're worthy, a lot you would have to prove, follow

D. C.

instructions, obey my rules, show me you can handle the way I groove, when I become Ready steady I am, aimed in your direction with perfection, your heart I Set for my destination, my rocket patiently waiting to let Go, tell me, are you Ready, Set, Go for this show.

MII: The Return of the King

LET ME BE YOUR KING

So many have tried to fill that void, a few caught your attention for a moment, but they couldn't hold it, one came close to peaking your interest, but couldn't overcome what it really means to be called King, not only being called King but being loved by that one and only true Queen, breaking it down to show you what it means, see I'm not your average King, I'm the one who rules on high, sit back my love, I'm about to take your feelings for a ride once I start to slip and slide up and down your canal, you can file all those hurt feelings and bad memories away into your lost and found box, you won't have to call the cops once I take your heart and secure it with my box, non-stop holding your love on a pedestal for everyone to see, beep, beep, fast forward can't you see you and me hand and hand in My Lovers' Land, I hold that master plan, giving you everything you need for my love will supersede your past, I can last, all night I will last while whispering in your ear, holding no fear as our bodies come close and near to be one, taking you all in, rubbing on your soft skin, beauty is in the eyes of the beholder, pulling you closer, holding you tighter to never let go as I stroke your tongue with my tongue, I am that one King who rules on high, sit back my love and enjoy this night time ride, laying your body down, sliding down your side, taking your mind off those clowns, your King is here now watch me, you will feel me Put IT Down, as I show you why I wear this crown and rule this town when it comes to laying my royal challenge down, I hope you can manage what I have in store, pulling off your clothes tossing them to the floor, your body I'm about to explore in the midst of this voyage you will hear your King roar, it's all yours, if you can handle my stroke, allow my tongue to invoke your body as I start my flow, my tongue goes from your lips with a soft kiss to your neck making your palace moist, not wet, wet, just yet, no drip, don't tip, watch me pick up the pace, tongue flowing past your waist, in between your thighs I stare at your palace with a glare that shines from your moisture, sucking on your palace like I will do an oyster, licking you dry, just to wet you all over again, placing your legs up like a peace sign, so I can

*go deep where the sun don't shine, your body I'm craving and it's all mine, so divine, stopping for a second just to admire you, kissing on your thighs as I stand up to unveil what you really want to feel, my royal pleasure, don't try to compare the rest won't measure up to what I'm about to do to your core, I swear after you will want me to be your King as I open you up so that I can flow through your river of love, deep into you I go my dove, no push no shove, nice and slow so that you feel my extension, my love, oh what a heavenly feeling not to mention, taking you higher than the ceiling, up and above the clouds, tonight it won't get wild, I want you to understand why I'm about to Be Your King, with every stroke I turn your feelings towards me, your heart forever I will keep, to never creep with another under cover, your number one lover, as I slide slow, long and deep strokes, running my race at a steady pace, the look upon your face says don't stop, I'm right there I swear you're the best I ever felt King, I feel you King, Be MY King rolls from your lips, as I shift and switch to the side of your hips, uplift your leg your lips I spread, I kiss you as I gaze into your eyes rubbing on your thighs, pushing inside of your love, deep into your sea, soon you're about to see how wet you will become, placing you on all fours, you about to hear my roar, your body I'm about to devour in this final hour, spreading you wide just to pull in slowly giving you a motion picture show, Royalty is what this is called, your love is about to fall, wet, wet you can bet, nevertheless I go and go, your palace talking back with every stroke, you clinch the sheets as you let go, I pause just to move one leg to the floor as your body lays flat I attack with my Everlasting Love, taking you up just to bring your waterfall down, answering all your questions to why it is they say I am the greatest around this town, The One and Only
who holds the crown, King.*

MII: The Return of the King

ROYAL CHALLENGE

Back at it again, yes you know you will win when dealing with King, but I got something new I want to put on your mind, we're going to do this thing a little different tonight, let me take this time to explain my Royal Challenge, my mind works in ways you can't imagine, never seen before, yes I am yours, but I need you to challenge me sexually, mentality, stimulate my soul, so that I would never want to let go, give me that forever hold, Ready, Set, Go, I need you to be me, and I will be you tonight, we're Trading Places, for years I've been telling you, showing you how I'm going to treat your body, make love to your mind and soul, giving you rounds for every second spent away from you, taking your heart to never break, to never let go, I'm that number one under the sun, you do whatever it takes for my Royal Challenge to be all up in your body, to become one, giving me that undeniable show, can't no one replace the things I can do, giving you that Reminder with the moves I possess, yes this is a test, I hope you pass, listen closely, my love is your devotion, so I challenge you not to feel any emotion after all my stroking and teasing, playing with your vibe, you know what I hold inside this lightning and thunder when I give you that royal steel, you feel what I feel that is real my love tingling through your vibes, I challenge you not to look me in the eyes as I spread your legs wide to dip slip inside of your palace, that love deep in your Passion, freaky emotions are flowing in the air, you can't help but stare into my eyes, there lies the feelings through your eyes, so sexy and sensual, seducing, grabbing my full attention while at full attention still stroking with a slow stroke, I go and go, giving you that Royal Show, this my challenge, you have to take these 9 and a half long and thick from the back, watch the script flip, you can't moan or scream, looking at me with that mean sexy face, your body I'm about to do great, wait arch that back your left ass cheek I smack, quick with my attack then I slow it down, passion frowns, love faces, your waterfall is racing you can't hold on to the challenge as I push deep with a hard thrust you let out a loud scream and moan as you bust like never before, I'm giving you a drug that you will feign for, hitting your

D. C.

core, exploring your world, making you erupt, after tonight you will want to be my girl, have me for all time to yourself, my Royal Challenge has been dealt, You Never Felt A Feeling Like This Before, next time be sure you're ready to endure this Everlasting ride, keep me on your mind until next time.....

MII: The Return of the King

KISSING YOU

Dim the lights, setting the mood to Just Right, an Unforgettable Night is about to go down, now that you're here on my grounds in my room where I will consume all of you, your heart is about to become mine, our bodies forever will be intertwined, I'm the last of my kind, tonight I just want you to relax and unwind, as I find all of your hidden pleasures, your treasures that you have buried from the world, tell me do you wanna go where you've never been before my girl, my love let me take you higher than you could ever think of, I'm nothing like your last was, becoming the drug you will need once I start to Kissing You between your knees, I start to please by Kissing You on the lips soft and gentle, slow, easing your mental, showing my affection with these sensual kisses that will have you reminiscing after tonight, I want be hitting you with royal pipe, just Kissing You all night with my X's and O's, taking your heart out of the cold with a hold so strong that it will live on for the rest of your days, as I sway down your neck caressing your breasts, your feelings was once a mess until I passed all your tests, showing you the best you ever had without me pulling out the royal crown, putting it down with just my lips and tongue, twirling down to where no sun can be found, spreading you wide after snatching off your thong, my tongue your palace it's about to be on, Kissing You on your thighs, down to the sexy cave, what do we have here, it is clear that I see a joyous tear creeping out of your eye, never have you had a guy, a King to please you in this way, it's all about you I say, writing my name in cursive, your palace is worth it, I'm about to slay it all night until the day sunlight rise, don't be surprised how I have your legs shaking all night, Kissing You Just Right, you've never been here before as I explore with my tongue, up and down slow and fast grabbing my pillows, clenching my sheets, I hope you can last as I blast through your tunnel of love my fingers start to play, Oh Wee you scream baby right there stay licking in between, rubbing my bald head as I go deep, legs push back baby you're a keeper you scream, doing things you've never felt before, I adore as I explore your freaky emotions, hitting you with the right potions taking you farther than

D. C.

ever before picking you up to give you more, wrapping your legs around my neck, you haven't felt nothing yet, sending your body chills, on a quest I am, trying to make you feel me in different ways, melting your soul, hold on tight my Queen, don't let go as I give you a royal show with my feet planted on the floor hands firmly around your backside, as my tongue slips and slide, you raise high, touching the ceiling loving my kissing feeling, delivering pleasure, three rulers couldn't measure, giving you that forever feeling, healing, putting all your expectations to rest, giving you the best I have to offer, going hard, but Kissing You softer, sucking up all your juices as you cum and cum and once more forever I am yours, Kissing You I adore, putting you to sleep, leaving you wanting more, until the next time I explore your palace of pleasure, remember my Kissing You can handle your stormy weather.

MII: The Return of the King

LOVE TRIANGLE

Crying, calling out King is this why you gave me this diamond ring?, too good to be true, saying you're through, hold up, move, hold up baby, you I'm not trying to lose, what about this other woman standing here in the nude, yea what about me King the other woman shouts and scream, both of you please calm down and sit around my table, I'm sure we are able to handle this royally, just sit and listen, give me three minutes of your time, then you both can decide on what you want to do, stay or leave is the option, sorry I am for having two, but let's set things straight, neither of us are committed, turning my fitted hat to the back , what I am to you miss lady is your Stress Reliever, the man you have is an underachiever, I made you a believer in love again just friends, have I told you I love you, yes I have, but never have we talked about easy math, you know, one plus one equals you and me, I didn't know you fell in deep, through my eyes you see I had my walls guarded up, reason why is cause of this beautiful woman that sits to my left side, let me turn to you and apologize to you my love, two wrongs don't make it right though, you look confused to why I would say that, my heart is true, my heart is yours, real love to the core, did I mess up and explore another, yes, but what did I find out from my undercover, pictures I throw, displaying on the table, you with another girl, here I was ready to share my world, could I have asked what's going on before I went to explore the lovely lady you adore, fearing to hear the worst, you giving up your skirt to a skirt, seeing how you both flirt, it's funny how you both sitting here playing the role of being hurt, you both thought I didn't know you two were together, go ahead and look at the pictures, I see you with her, erase those tears Miss lady, you too played me, so what's it going to be I say, one is all I need to fulfill my needs and expectations, I gave you that ring to see if you would come clean, to start fresh, boy what a mess, my woman to the left stresses she wants us both, we all can stay together, the three living in perfect harmony, my sexy lady disagrees, all I want is King she shouts, that's what I'm talking about falls from my mouth, real love is what I'm about, left side sits with tears in her eyes sliding on her clothes getting

D. C.

up to walk out, shocked at what's going down, banning her from my town, closing the door turning around with you running into my arms, kissing me everywhere, in love with you I am, I swear I will never hurt or deceive you, all I want is you, forever us two, let's make it do what it do, a lifetime of love just me and you.

MII: The Return of the King

COME BACK HOME

Since you've been gone, I have been going nowhere fast; this pain I don't want to last, Come Back Home and save me, I need you with me, my eyes I can't stop from weeping; when I think about the love you gave to me, missing everything about you, from your smile to your perfect teeth, from your sexy style to those beautiful feet, the little sexy comments you used to say are even getting the best of me, needing you I am my Queen, Come Back Home to creep through my sheets, the way you will make me weak is the thoughts I'm thinking of right now my angel from above, tell me I won't be forever stuck in this stuff, in this position of hoping and wishing, seeking for your forgiveness is my life's mission, this love can't be finished, baby tell me we are not through, I need you, I know I do, whatever it may take I will prove, baby I can't lose my home, with me is where you belong, I need you to Come Back Home, come and sit, take your place back on the throne, my love to this kingdom you belong, through it all I will show you no matter how big or how small, I will always show you my all, give you my all, my love falls in your hands, being with you for life is my plan, I can't stand this alone, I want you to Come Back Home and let me love you the way you need, don't stop us baby, you are who I feign, who in which I dream of, the cream of the crop, no one above, you have that number one spot, you set alone at the top, my love for you will never stop, will never cease, I need you to bring your love back to me, bring my heart back its peace, my rose you are the one I chose to love, forever through any stormy weather, ready I am to go all the way, a big house where we will stay, a family, a few kids with a white picket fence sitting on the porch as we watch them play, my heaven sent, you and I are meant, so Come Back Home, patience is a virtue, and I will wait forever if it meant in the end I will have you, sitting on my throne not moving with my drink in hand waiting for that day those trumpets sounds and drums play with you walking back in to take your place.

D. C.

DOWN LOW

Texting your phone letting you know I'm on my way, the things I'm gonna do will make you forever stay, I wanna kiss your face, I wanna touch your body, I wanna lick between your waist, I wanna hold your body close, I wanna love your body licking Down Low doing the most into your world I go, walking through the door, when next to your body I become a freak ready to explore your body, there's nothing like your body, you grab me Down Low to get this love started, swinging on my vine like a monkey from a tree, you can do whatever it is you want to do to me, blowing me away with all I can say is Oh and Ah's, as you take me away, daddy long stroke is ready to take his place, no time to waste, kissing from your neck down to your waist, my tongue wants to take its place, my stroke can wait, I wanna taste but in a different way, I'm going to lick it until you start to shiver, in my Twelve Royal Ways I always deliver, slithering through your river, I felt a quiver, I stand to flip you upside right with your palace in the center of my face, your legs wrapped squeezing tight as I please your Down Low all night, you grab my pipe with a stroke of your hand, filling up your mouth showing me you know how to rock the mic when down south, your juices running from my mouth dripping down my chin, you got my package deep within, touching your throat as we flow to the rhythm of our tune, damn I'm so into you, holding you with strength showing off my might, the delight I'm giving just started, we have a long night ahead of us as you start to shiver, I'm making you bust, your passion erupts, the taste of your love fills my heart up, as I take you up but lay you down, so I can go Down Low and put it down, in me you have found Your Match, the greatest King here on the map, I'm about to show you where it's at, your heart that has been lost for some time, in due time you will find the pillars to your walls will come crashing down, your treasure I will find as I take my time in your jungle becoming a lion, the King when deep in between, soak and wet is the theme, this is no dream, this is the real thing, I have your forest raining, flowing through your woods giving you that good, good, locked up in your cage of ecstasy, your love I will forever keep, going

*wild like the zoo, making love like to heated animals, touching the root of your soul, as I go deep within, rubbing on your smooth, soft skin, to the back I proceed to go deep in, Down Low, beating that thang like some drums, showing you I'm the one and only that can make you explode, cum multiples times, this love was destined, designed for our kind, as the time winds down, I turn you back around to go back Down Low for the rest of the night, pleasuring you with my delight, my tongue, taking you higher than the sun, I am your King,
call me the one.*

D. C.

MR. KING
(BACK AT THE PARTY)

Excusing my way through the party, this Beautiful Find I have spotted on the other side of my Kingdom caught my eyes, making her all mine is all that's on my mind, I see a lifetime with her, and I don't even know her name, this feeling I have I never felt it in my past, I walk up telling the bartender to send two glasses of wine for me and this Beautiful Find, my, my, my I say reaching out my hand saying my name is King, I know who you are she replies, you're the one looking for a Queen, yea that's right and you seem Just Right, my type, I would like to get to know you if that's alright, she smiles with a sigh, impressed with her physique I am, I can't lie watching her walk in front of me looking at that backside, looking to the sky thanking God for this creation patiently waiting I am with no rush, we push through the crowd, I take her on different ground, on a grand tour of my kingdom of many rooms and doors, which one shall we explore, as I start in with my seductive ways, walking through my halls talking about the pictures on the walls coming across one that makes you stop, pause and stare, this picture here is a symbol of my love, waiting patiently I am for God to send me her from above, I have so much to give, through your eyes I see you may be that one, pausing for a second finding ourselves close enough to kiss, lock lips I smile you smile with my hands on your hips showing my seductive ways turning away to say let's finish the tour, holding hands laughing and joking coming to a closed door, you open to explore finding a stage and pole with lights that glow, music on slow, a pretty woman is giving the fellas a show, you smile closing the door saying alone in that room I'm all yours, sipping on your drink walking down the hall giving me a wink, I follow your trail outside towards the pool sparking clear blue, steam rising, heated it is for the cooler nights, I can get used to this oh mighty King, I wonder how you will feel in between, standing close, even closer to the edge of the pool I think I'm falling for you, love is the blood running from the inside out, without a doubt one touch from King your feelings will pour out, are you ready for me to bring your love walls down, to forever wear

MII: The Return of the King

my crown, the rest of the women will wear a frown in this town once they see you on the throne, walking back into my home, embracing you around your shoulders with my arms, love is what we will perform tonight, you whisper ignite my passion, ignite my fire that's burning deep on the inside of my soul, coming upon some double doors, as we flow we go stopping in front of my doors, grabbing you at the face gently with both hands asking are you ready for this dance, an all-night show I wanna show you how far love can go, a lifetime, no tricks this isn't My Magic Love Show, this is the real thing once you open these doors my love you will explore, kissing you on the side of your cheek, ready I am to rescue your love that's trapped, your canvas is my map, following all road signs, forever you are about to be mine, you comply with I'm all yours to have and to hold, to cherish to never let go, opening the doors slowly inside My Royal Room you go, my brother comes rushing up messing up the flow, something important King, sorry baby I must go, stay my love and we will continue this show, off I go, closing the door.

To Be Continued...

D. C.

TAKE CARE OF HOME

Your body is my Home so therefore I'm gonna Take Care of it, make it my own, touch and kiss on it, your body brings me to a familiar stiff, I sit crossing my leg as I sip, you see what you do to my fully equip, your body I'm gonna flip in many different ways, shapes and forms, compared I can't be to the norm, your heart I won't harm, you will see in the love that's about to be perform, grabbing tight by the arms, pulling you close, don't be alarm you're in King's hands forever, your heart will sing and dance to my tune, with the things I can go, making the sounds that lovers do, when I go deep inside of you, in many ways, taking care of your mind first, your mind I work erasing all negative thoughts of that last so called boss, showing you as I caress you stroking your hair showing you how emotionally I can care, taking your mind there, continuing to stroke your hair, kissing on your body, I have mind control now, I'm about to take you there, through your eyes your heart I see, I stare, going in there to bring it back to life, give it air, Take Care, show you what real love is like, that real love that has no fuss, don't bring no fight, strong I protect our hearts hold you at night type, Take Care of Home love you're right, that good love making when in between the sheets at night, and morning, loving you through the bad and stormy weather, I Take Care of Home, nothing or no one can measure up to you, now that I have your heart intertwined with mine, let's start this party, let's groove, show me some moves, turning you into My Love Slave, to my commands you obey, this is Lovers' Land all over again, laying you down to open you up again, nice and wide, the temperature rise, I'm going in, you close your eyes, you're feeling Just Right, I'm swimming through your walls, this can go on all night, pushing deep with my fingers with a light thrust, my tongue giving you a rush, playing with the pearl, your problems I'm about to erase, causing your water to fall like your water broke, pleasuring your palace, my face is soaked, down my neck you roll, pushing your legs back, ass to chest while I lick you like that, Mr. Virgo is on the attack, coming up, sliding into position, your temple is in my submission, giving your soul that royal glow, you're loving the motion, lost in your sea of love as we go, hand and hand, we go, giving you that Greenlight Special show, when I know, I know, from the look upon your face I'm hitting your spot Down Low, my back you're scratching as you moan, taking off, blasting off deep making that feeling come on, your moan is getting deeper, your legs becoming weaker and weaker, Trey Songz Dive In playing through the speakers, making you a soul believer in the skills that I possess, putting all doubts to rest, kissing on your chest, while sticking and moving, flipping you over in one motion, spreading you wide from behind, pulling on your hair, through the mirror you stare at my grooves the way I stroke and move, dip when I hit a certain spot in you, gripping you tight at the shoulders so you can't move, deep inside of you I go making love slow, giving your body what it deserves, cherishing your worth, putting in work, holding you close kissing down your neck to your back deep in with my attack, ready to let go of what I've been holding on to, just for you, showing you this isn't a game, your heart I'm trying to trap, with my rifle I aim, after I fire you will never be the same, taking off like a jet, you explode while dripping nice and wet, satisfied you can bet, I always Take Care of Home, so that no other man can ever come close to touching on my throne.

D. C.

MY HEART IS YOURS

My style is fresh from head to toe, fedora hat, nice slacks with the shoes to match, My Heart Is Yours, I feel so attached, this is the Perfect Match, reach out and grab baby, snatch, My Heart Is Yours, forever, forever to hold, forever to protect and never let go, My Heart Is Yours, I supply you with a lifetime flow of love, My Heart Is Yours, so never place no one or nothing above, hold on tight like a hand to a glove, real love does exist, my love will have your love all in a twist, My Heart Is Yours, are you ready for this? My Heart Is Yours to always keep, to always cherish, my feelings will never perish, erase, break, bend or fold, my love will never go cold, your heart I will never let go, a junky for your love, my pusher girl, I'm your dope fiend, My Heart Is Yours, send your love through my blood stream, My Heart Is Yours, true love is what this means, it may seem it came quick and fast, but my love will outlast your last, he didn't know what he had, he created a path just for me to you, I know exactly what to do, that's why I'm glad to say My Heart Is Yours, you're the reason why I smile, I won't stop loving you, everyday showing you love in little special ways, pleasing you is my life's mission, showing love and affection, incredible when it comes to the sexing, love making on a daily my one and only lady, are you ready to forever hold my heart, it's yours my Queen, my body I want you to explore, hear your King roar, it's yours, placing my heart in your possession, all I need is love and affection to perfection, enduring the greatest sex, the greatest love you ever felt before, you won't be touched by the non-worthies anymore, I'm your King, here to please, show me how bold you can be, giving you my heart here on bended knee, no one else holds the power or the key, but you, My Heart Is Yours, let the trumpets sound, let the crowd gather around so they all know now that I belong to you and only you, My Heart Is Yours I choose you, to love, to hold, to keep warm never to let go, when Down Low giving you a show in between the sheets, love thoughts creep through your mind, forever thoughts starts to form a vine, I'm one fly guy who can having you flying high, will have you reminiscing about each night, oh this is Just Right, it's gonna be a party tonight, blowing you kisses, all my wishes coming true, now that I have you and you have me together we will be, you're my beautiful Masterpiece, come take my hand and explore my land with me, happily just you and me is all my eyes can see, My Heart Is Yours, this love was meant to be, you will forever hold the key.

D. C.

ANY PLACE, ANY TIME

The stage is set, I'm all the audience you need, as you proceed to hit me with your strip tease, aroused I become, pleased through my eyes with the way you move in this club, lights dimmed when I pull you close to touch your forbidden fruit, I wanna be inside of you, show you my groove, are you down to make a move, my hand she chooses, I'm leading the way through the crowd looking back to see your smile, loving how you're down, wild and spontaneous, I've been waiting for a moment like this, to see if you will resist my temptation, pulling you into the men's room, your feelings get to racing, intensifying the situation with a kiss, down your neck I lick, unbuckling my pants, so you can pull out my fully equipped, you're removing your slip, turn over baby I'm in control of this ship, from the back I dip through your soul, penetrating deep in I go, shifting gears, engaged in you, we have no fear of getting caught, I'm all yours, in your love I'm lost, call me your Love Slave as we misbehave, when it comes to you I'm always in the mood, Any Place at Any Time, all day, all night, every day, for the rest of my life Any Place at Any Time, just to be inside of you, pushing deep, you're throwing it back, I arch your back by pulling on your hair taking you there, wet and warm in there, your palace I swear has a hold over me, your legs begin to shake as we creep, moving fast, smacking both sides of your ass, wanting this feeling to last forever, your pretty flower starts to weather, a rain shower, as I bust on que, we're pulling our clothes up trying to get it together, kissing and laughing before we go back to the party, I love how you will get naughty in Any Place at Any Time, my One of a Kind, you're amazing, and I want you for all time, you say you have a surprise, the night is young baby let's leave this spot, I want you to take me to the top of the hill, I wanna feel your steel deep out in the open, with the breeze just flowing over our bodies, show me you're about it, I wanna ride it, you have me so excited, fighting back through the crowd to the exit doors, valet pulling up a Porsche, but that's not mine in due time baby that will be our ride, pulling in right behind, that black on black Challenger SS type, fits me Just Right, a muscle car with strength and might, you better hold on tight, we have one life to live, why not live it to the fullest, shooting to the top of the hill fast as a bullet, pulling up to the spot, the city we're overlooking, your feelings I shook them up with a touch of my tongue, sucking on your bottom lip, hot you become, my button down you rip open, ready for more fun, two of a kind, you are my one, out the car I say let's take this level up to a higher place, your smile right now I could never erase, love is about to fill this place, meeting at the front of my car, exposed we are, spreading you wide to take you far, across the hood, I'm about to give you this good, filling you up with my hard wood, rain begins to fall, our passion starts to go insane, your water starts to fall, wrapping your legs around me to give you my all, as I stand tall with no movement you start to bouncing and grooving, I'm showing strength and balance, I start to get at it, moving my hips, pushing with my royal, your heart flips, into your palace I dip, making your legs shake, your insides I rip with my fully equipped, taking you on this mission, this trip, with each stroke I equip more of your love, taking you Up, Up and Away, through your palace I escape this earth, you're my heaven on earth, my love I know your worth, on the side of my car pressing you up against my Window Pane, your pleasure is about to burst into flames, I'm bringing the pain and love in this rain, kissing under control, you will never be the same, my hold you can't let go, pulling you closer backing up to open my car door, flipping you around so deep from behind I can explore, you're bending over touching the ground looking back with a smile, overflowing your cup with your wetness, catering to your freaky side, Any Place at Any Time I'm willing to swim inside your world, you're special my girl, my woman, my Queen going deep in between making you weak, your palace continue to drip and leak busting all over me, as I get ready to shoot off my stars, loving this night we are, there's no limits you and I can't reach, taking you far as I teach a Lesson In Love, flying high as a dove, until that sunlight I will be giving you my love, in Any Place at Any Time my love, your love, I just can't get enough of Putting A Smile On Your Face, this can never be erased, your love I will never let escape.

D. C.

MY COMFORT ZONE

When I lie down to rest, thoughts of you being in My Comfort Zone comes to mind, in my arms is where you belong, staring at your pictures in my phone, waiting for you my love to come and perform love acts like you never have before, the joy that comes over me when I get to explore your Pleasure P takes control of me, my thoughts, my power for those two hours are rendered under your control, submitting my love to never let go, you complete My Comfort Zone, you put me in a different zone, we're in a whole different lane speeding down the highway, by your side I shall forever stay, my heart is yours, my ride or die, no way this love will die, this love will continue to fly high past the sky, to places unknown to the natural eye, these are facts, my love doesn't tell lies, since my touch has entered your life, your life has taken a turn for the best, your stress Reliever conquering all your quests, passing all of your tests, Putting All Your Expectations To Rest, adoring you to the soul, you have a hold that I will never let go, I'm not putting on a show, these are real feelings I show, My Comfort Zone, my perfect love song, when deep inside your throne, your palace becomes so warm and sweet, kissing you from the top of your head to the bottom of your pretty little feet, your worth goes beyond me, here I am to worship thee, worship you my Queen, pleasing you in everything I do, the things my love will have you do will be brand new to you, not knowing what to do, I'll show you things you never knew before, your friends will start to adore what you have found, this new King has come around and put it down, showed you how love making should sound, rocking steady, while pushing hard, breaking down your guards, making you scream Oh, my Lord this is all yours, My Comfort Zone, your love could never be refused, could never be removed, with you I can't lose, I refuse to make a mistake, I want you for the rest of my days, I can be your Love Slave, we can role play, acting bad when I enter your cave, deep in with a hard thrust when you misbehave, rough until those legs shake, the headboard I will break until your legs shake, through the whole night kissing you, loving you, I'm not through until you're through, I can't get enough of you, of your world,

MII: The Return of the King

the dark hole has me all in a twirl, wrapped around all your fingers, your smell lingers when you leave my room, your heart, your soul, I consume, flashing lights and sirens pop on when I lay the boom, my stroke will have you flying to the moon and back then to the moon again, I don't play when it comes to me going deep within your treasure, there's no limit baby, my love you can't measure, I will always take you to a higher level, hard as steel, tough as metal, showing my skills when digging deep with my shovel, giving you that Can't Resist, filling you up with my fully equipped, making sure you never forget, after this for life you will reminisce on each time I take time to show you a royal time, For Eternity, you will always be all mine, completing My Comfort Zone, my heart is yours to have to own, I want this love to live on and on.

D. C.

RELAPSE

You don't know if you're addicted until you Relapse from detox of love making with that one you have been forbidden to touch, missing that rush, that chill, just to feel you going through my veins, it's not the same, but you're so bad for me, so bad that you feel so good all in one, knowing we're not supposed to be doing this finding each other in this hotel room, pause how did we get this far, the room spins, my phone rings, it's you on the other line telling me to come and find what's yours, let me, make you mine, you know I got that One Of A Kind Relapse, spinning in circles rolling some of the earth's finest purple, sparking to put it in the air, the high won't compete with what I'm about to give to you, a natural high that will give you the love jones, back to the phones as I reply I'll see you tonight get ready for this ride, back to the inside of his room, here we go, your lips I touch with mine a soft kiss with a whisper, saying we are not supposed to be here doing this anymore, the last time you Relapsed, I was deep in your core breaking you down to the floor giving you this remix, touching every inch as we reminisce on the times before as I explore your curves each and every time I come to your city I make you Relapse, your head falls in my lap curling my toes your love rushing through my veins taking me up as I fill you with more than you ever had before even with time passing us by no one who has touched you came close to filling my void, I am that one who can pull on those cords, your strings that lead to your best, opening you up is so priceless, art, holding your body in the air, suspended as I stare into those beautiful brown eyes, drawing me in closer and closer making me Relapse more and more, you see my sin I can't lose, but I can't win with you either is that crazy, maybe, feel me, just feel me when I'm in between your thighs giving you that royal surprise, tonight will be a long night.....

To Be Continued

MII: The Return of the King

I CAN'T LET YOU GO

Please don't go, I know what I've showed you so far, finding numbers in my car marked with a star, baby let me pled my case, you're slamming the door in my face, in my car not trying to let no tears come down, calling your phone, standing in the rain saying baby just come home, please don't leave me alone, listen to me for a second, you are my life's blessing, hanging up in my face not allowing me to plead my case, outside your home begging from the night until the day trying to find the right words to say, please don't take your love away, tell me forever you will stay, fellas listen to me it's not worth seeing that one cry, it isn't worth killing your home finding yourself alone, jeopardizing our love, what the hell was I thinking of, I should have never placed another above, not thinking it will ever end like this, your heart I will forever miss if I can't get you back, please don't go, I should have loved you right before you had the chance to slam the door, now you're looking for another to adore, I'm writing you this poem to let you know what I have in store, what's on my mind, now that you have some time I want to express what I hold deeply inside, you have opened up my eyes, my heart is racing faster than time to the other side of love, floating high above ground, taking me higher above the clouds, I can't get enough of what I've found, I love it when you come around, I just want to love you down and go places where there's no sun allowed, I think we should be down for each other, if you agree show me a sign, I want you to be the mother of my child, you are One of a Kind, I Can't Let You Go, my heart aches when that thought crosses my mind, tears starts to roll down my face, no one can ever take your place, it will be a mistake somewhere in the book of love if you're not at my side, standing in your rightful place, your love I can't escape, you take me there, where I don't even care, all I know it's where I want to be, your love lives deep within me under lock and key, your love I seek, never complete until your next to me each and every night, I don't know how I will continue to go through life without your touch, my baby I need your love, it does something to me, sends a rush through my body, I love when we become naughty the life of my

D. C.

party, I couldn't find another Mrs. Right, the way you put it down when serving your delightful pleasures, temptations becomes hard to fight, the way you sing into the mic has me going strong all night, ecstasy is given when switching position, repetitions when those hips start their engine, pleasuring your love is my life's mission, riding fast, then slow, I Can't Let You Go, sliding down my pole, swallowing whole, you're in control making me Lose Control, your love making touches my soul, this is a forever love, I Can't Let You Go, a lifetime I will take to show you my love is here to stay, with my hands on the sides of your pretty face, sliding down to the small of your waist, these feelings can never be erased, emerged in your pleasure place, dripping all over the place, smiling from ear to ear, across your face, your love takes the cake, nothing else matters after today, I will cherish you each day, deep into our own world I'm your King and you're my Queen, I choose you to represent what that word means, you give me what I need, I'm your fiend, high I become when deep in between, my soul on fire like the sun beaming down, hot bare feet to the ground, forever knowing your worth now, a real love is what I have found, never will I Let You Go, you opened my eyes, never closing these curtains to this forever love show.

MII: The Return of the King

MY HEART FOREVER YOURS

These words I speak to you are from my heart, they are true, nothing can ever tear us apart, forever I want to be with you until my dying day, you will always have a special place in My Heart that's Forever Yours, growing apart, being lost can never happen, your love is everlasting, burning deep in my soul, I can never quit, I will never let go, willing I am to show how strong my love is, how far my love can go, this is no act, I'm pulling back the curtains to this real life show, breaking down all of your barriers, tearing down your walls, moving mountains, your feelings shall fall, with you I belong, I couldn't fathom going through life without you along, come and turn my house into a home, My Heart Forever Yours, with you I belong, reaching for my phone to get a glimpse of a picture of you my love, I adore your beautiful smile so much, it takes me to a different realm, blessed I am to know your name, to hold and kiss you, my feelings haven't been the same since you came into my land, since you took my hand, I want you to understand I am yours to have and to hold, you are mine to forever adore, your touch I crave for more, you have opened my door, My Heart is Forever Yours, growing through the laughter and pain, I will still be yours, you are my sunshine after the rain, I have no complaints when it comes to your love, my heart erupts with nothing, but joy, deploying love in your direction, filling the room with romance, passion and affection, caressing your every desire, baby you have lit my fire that has been out for quite some time, I never thought I would come to find my One of a Kind in this lifetime, I was blind, but now I can see, you and me living peacefully, on bended knee, presenting this ring with me I want you to be, I close my eyes and it's you I only see, there's no me if you are not with me, there is nowhere else I'd rather be, my feet are planted firmly, there will be no uprooting, for life I will be doing whatever you may need me to do, proving in me you chose the right dude, the right King, my life's duty is to see you pleased, walking to the rhythm of your heartbeat, following passionately, your heart forever mine, this love is meant to be, I want us to forever be, I can't see no one else beside me, nobody can be you, My Heart Forever

D. C.

*Yours, these words I speak are from my heart,
they are forever true; my love is your living proof.*

MII: The Return of the King

RUN AWAY WITH YOUR LOVE

My mission is simple, my plan is set, I'm a different type of individual, ready to Run Away With Your Love, taking off faster than a jet, the moon and stars are set, in store a freaky night you can bet, Ready, Set, Go, I move in slow grabbing your hips my lips to your lips I catch you as you dip, through my lips I hold the power to make your world do flips, your palace will become wet like the mist on a Sunday morning, making you horny, making you want it more and more, we will be going until the morning, tonight I'm all yours, Losing Control of your legs, my kiss, my passion is that strong, putting you in a daze, carrying you over to the bed where love will be made, I'll dig deeper than a six feet grave, my nine and a half will consume your thoughts, making your body play the part of my love slave, moving to my commands, thoughts of your last man will be removed, gone forever, after I'm done, we've just begun and already I have you saying I'm that one, we've just begun and already I have you blazing hot like the sun, I've just begun licking you from your neck to your breasts, as I undress your bottoms, your legs I got them in that V shape, ready you are I say to escape this world of misery, your King I'm willing to be, going underneath to please your pleasure, I can't be measured to none, I've just begun and already you're about to cum, I've just begun this all night voyage of love making, hot as an oven, I have you cook, baking, legs shaking, pillow facing, screaming, biting my pillow case, feigning, your past can be erased, Running Away With Your Love I am today, I've just begun making you erupt, I'm about to do work, staying in control, moving up your thighs slow, sliding in my pole, staring into your eyes, those eyes make my insides glow, those eyes I can't lie makes my heart go, I continue to flow through your palace, filling you up with lasting endeavor, yes I am the clever, exceptionally better at this love making game than those lames you allowed to touch your palace, going deeper I am than you could have imagined, in and out, in and out, Slow Strokes, my King rolls from your mouth, passions and passion strokes going through changing gears from the coast, faster down south I go, my love making is an art, showing you what I am

D. C.

about, I moan, you shout, I go deeper, you scream King you are a keeper, with your nails back scratching, your lips and tongue showing my neck some action, your palace is soaked and wet, showing that response of satisfaction, I keep thrashings, mashing through, riding your river of waves, exploring your cave and hidden treasures, no one can do it better, my love will become your daily need, your everyday fix, your drug, you will never get enough of this, my royalness you Can't Resist, I will be here to fulfill your every request, your every wish, no spot goes unturned, I don't miss, I flip you to that back side, to go deeper inside, look back baby, I wanna see those sexy eyes, those love faces you make when I take my place with a stroke between your walls that I break, spreading you wide, taking my place into your space where the sun doesn't shine, hitting you from behind, forever you are mine, our hearts intertwined, deep into your spine, extending this pleasure as I recline back and forth with my attack, you will never find another of my kind, those others was jokers and jacks, this King will Run Away With Your Love and never give it back, your love will be where my heart lies, entrapped, in safe keeping, I'm the only one you will be needing.

LOVE AT THE END OF THE TUNNEL

Searching high and low my love has gone cold, locked away in an ice box; When will this pain stop? Somebody dial 911, I need the cops, my love has been stolen by that one who holds that number one spot, you never know what you got until it's gone, I must repeat that, I said you never know what you got until it's gone, I must stay strong, you stay coming by my home, stay blowing up my phone, saying you are where I don't belong, walking away on this far and long journey back on my own, love doesn't have a home in my heart at this particular time, will love ever find its way back to my soul, this I don't know as I stroll through this dark tunnel, trying to funnel my way back to love, speeding going fast, I lost love from an angel I thought it was going to last, now I'm leaving my past I want something that will last, that forever love I want to grab, I'm not looking back at what I had, moving forward I am waiting for my real Queen to come and please a true King, you fumble my heart and tore it apart into pieces, will the next be able to put it back together, I hope so, if not I will never love again, I hope there's Love at the End of the Tunnel for me, happy is what I want to be, I did anything you asked of me, I wore my heart on my sleeve, I thought you would never leave, but you deceived a King, I thought I was all you would ever need, someone come put my heart at ease, come Fill My Empty Space, when it comes to your love I must erase, I don't wanna close my eyes and see your face any more, when it came to you I did nothing, but adore, but what did you do when it came to me, crumble my heart like it was paper, throwing away our love, not taking me up, filling my cup with hate, doubt, you know nothing about real love, true love, I gave you everything you ever wanted, I'm the one who built you up, you're bad news, my feelings have erupted into a ball of fire, you're no longer the one I desire, with that being said you don't win, you lose, careful I will be to choose my Just Right, a love that will be there through thick and thin, each and every night, you had everything under the sunlight that you could have ever asked for, my heart is torn, I need someone out there to come and perform, not like the norm, take my heart out this ice chest, make me

D. C.

warm again and never let go, I have yet to get any rest, this is a true test of my will power, with each passing hour your love I lose, making moves, true love come play doctor and heal my bruise, revive my soul, I want love to go back through my veins, I don't want to feel this way, lost and weary, I can't eat or sleep, hard it is to breathe without love living inside of me, bring me loyalty, honesty, love and affection, that's what I'm professing until I get to that real Love at the End of the Tunnel, love me internal as well as external, my eyes see this heart shining bright, with your light whoever you are I want you to fill my soul for the rest of my life, where are you Mrs. Right, searching high and low, to the mountain tops I go swimming down river for your love, I will deliver until your next lifetime, where is that One of a Kind, you will never find a loyal King of my kind, walking this tunnel of love until I find a woman who is worth my time that I can praise high and above.

THE LAST TIME

My love, we have been here once before, your body I have explored over and over, but you have a man and I have a girl at home, tired I've become of sneaky around this town, OMG if these walls can talk right now, I am lost, but you're loving the way I stay putting it down, we have found ourselves in a mess, feelings are starting to progress, starting to form, your man, my woman are starting to catch on, following us around, ducking and dodging just so we can be around each other, hiding because we are undercover, but the storm is coming, I can feel it, so let me mention this will be The Last Time, baby no you say I can never find another, don't leave me this way, I am deeply sorry my love, my heart belongs to her, she doesn't deserve what I'm doing, if she finds out my family will be ruined, I must let you go, there are no hard feelings, don't let them show, from the get go we had an understanding, no catching feelings, now you're demanding my attention, calling my phone at all times of the night, wanting me to sneak out and give you that royal pipe, with the way I can go all night pushing your body to the limits, when I'm up in it never am I finished until you're finished, in the beginning it was fun, but now I need you to forget my love, just become numb to how I make you feel, I want you to know that each and every time it was just as real for me as it was for you, lust I must say, no love coming from my way, these words I say are true, I'm in love with my Queen, NO you scream I was your Queen the other night, yes you're right, but that was just for the night, when I close my eyes to rest it was her I was holding all night, this just isn't right, don't get me wrong your love game is Just Right and it's taking all my might, my will power to fight, to swallow this pill, but I must be honest, let me be for real, I'm not in love with you, it's her to whom my heart belongs to, please don't cry, if I could I would have you in my life, so for The Last Time just for the night you will be mine and I will be yours, after I will be shutting the door on this chapter, going back to my Queen so that I can live happy ever after, I hope that you can adapt to not having me at your beck and call, I will miss being inside your walls, but it's time we put a halt to the mess we have created, I

D. C.

know my love can't be rated, faded you become when I pull in with my shotgun, blowing your mind away for The Last Time you will remember me for the rest of your days, sorry I say this is the way it has to be, for you don't really belong to me, and I don't belong to you, so let's enjoy tonight and move on with our lives, we must right our wrongs, who knows maybe next lifetime we will find ourselves back in each other's arms, tonight will be The Last Time I performed these Lessons In Love making, back breaking with the headboard shaking, with your legs shaking, juicy I'm making your palace, can you imagine a lifetime show between us two, my heart will never forget you, but it's time I am true, sorry I have to hurt you, but I rather it be this way, than to see those tears down her face, so let's escape for The Last Time, our bodies intertwined, I'm taking my time, breaking you down like a fraction with my actions, satisfaction all the time, if only this was another lifetime.

MII: The Return of the King

FILL MY EMPTY SPACE

When it was you and I, hanging with the guys I sacrificed, knowing you could not last one night without sleeping by my side, I should have seen this coming, from the look in your eyes I should have been smarter, it was you creeping at night around town, it was me the only one putting up a fight for our love, even with the way I put it down I see it wasn't enough, no love was found in the depths of your heart, you fumbled my crown, my love making is priceless art, meanwhile I loved you, you were my Queen, putting you before any and everything, I adored you with all my being, but you weren't ready, love you professed, no more love beating inside my chest, I say, love you don't know what that means, it seems you wanted your dinner and dessert on me, with me paying for your plate, today is the last day you hold any power over me, in my heart you can't stay, I need a real woman to take your place, for her to come and Fill My Empty Space, for the rest of your days, you will be facing sleepless nights, crying nonstop, praying, saying why, how did I lose this special guy, knowing I loved you, wanted you for life, but you weren't ready for what I had to offer, so know that you don't have to bother with calling, for I won't be there on the other end to answer, it's okay girl cause I'm gonna be alright tonight, I'm too young of a guy to be wasting my life sobbing all through the night, I'm going out with my fellas, there's no more us, single I am, I can give a damn about your feelings now, cruising around town celebrating a new life on the hunt for a real one I can wife, someone who can Fill My Empty Space for the nights to come, that one, look at what you have done, damn I loved you and adored you, but you weren't ready and willing, I'm in this party looking for some Sexual Healing the way I'm feeling someone is gonna get the business, doing what a single man does grooving to the rhythm of the night, my phone is out of sight, tonight is the night I take my life back, was lost in you, now I'm found, your words doesn't penetrate my sound barrier, I can care less about her, about you, there's nothing you can say or do, infected with a tainted love I was, no more, my love is ready to explore a new venture, someone worthy of this royal King, fulfilling

D. C.

all my means, I can hear your cries and screams through my voicemail, torn and hurt you seem to be by what you caused, I applaud your Grammy act, you should win an Oscar, but here are the facts, you should have cherished what you had standing right before you when you had the chance, listening to your friends, playing me for a fool, I rule this world, you must have forgotten, my people saw you in that spot with that guy, I can't lie you hurt me, stabbing me with a dagger to my side, but it's okay, I will be alright, live your life and I will live mine, In Due Time my Queen will arise, come and find me to Fill My Empty Space for the rest of my days, you played a good game, you made your bed, now it's time you lay in it, we will be forever finished, my love knew no limits, you weren't ready to get it, someone else will reap the benefits, waiting I am on my heaven sent, I'm sure I will be deeply missed, you will never get to feel my lips again.

MII: The Return of the King

CAN I HOLD YOU CLOSE?

Yearning I am for your touch, your kiss sends a rush through my body, from my head to my feet, I love having you next to me, Can I Hold You Close, I wanna do the most, fulfilling your every request, I can pass any test given, I'm willing, only if you knew my feelings, better than the rest when it comes to that Sexual Healing, you will call me the best you ever had, adorning the time we have right now, taking off my crown, a King is what you have found, laying you down, Holding You Close, never letting go, as I coast through your love inside your tunnel, taking you up away, face to face, there's no escape, my heart is taking your pain away, with each stroke no extension, as I hold you close we float on cloud nine, diamonds and pearls you are One of a Kind, deep into your mind I go, diving in, slow motion, body rocking, roller coasting into your heaven, releasing your passion, giving you that Lazy Love, placing No One Above You, as I Hold You Close, hot as an oven, sweet dripping all your stuffing, cuming down my vine, Taking My Time with you, my beautiful rose blooming bright, tonight's the night you feel my strength, all my might, picking you up holding you close, chest to breasts, legs in my arms, as I perform these love acts, slow and deep into your palace I attack, kissing your lips, making your body tilt, grooving to my rhythm, each time I will deliver when I Hold You Close, your body makes me do the most, laying you back down turning you around, laying you flat, spreading you eagle, chest to back, I start my attack once again, swimming in and out your waters, in that deep side of your pool, oh the things your body makes me do, Losing Control as I stare through the mirror looking at the way we groove, with the way I move pushing slow and hard, breaking down all your walls, no more needing to guard, I will take you far, farther than you've ever been before, doing it until your legs shake, making you scream with that love look in your eyes, making you love me from the inside, making you love the way I ride from that back side and the things I do, you and me forever crew, I love being inside of you, making me change all my rules, just for you I will do anything it takes to please your special place, forever remembering this day,

D. C.

whispering in your ear to say, I love you babe, that time is near, but have no fear I will always be here, making me climax to the fullest, shooting out shotgun bullets, taking it all you are, your body in my arms, our hands, fingers are interlocked, as we fall to sleep waking up to you is the best thing that could ever happen to me, easing all my pain, your love has rained down on me, when holding you close love is all I can see, your heart will forever be tied to me.

MII: The Return of the King

ANYTHING YOUR SOUL DESIRES

You call me sire, but tonight I will be playing the part of being submissive giving you Anything Your Soul Desires, setting fire to a hundred candles, my love I hope you can handle my freaky love emotions, floating over two dozen rose petals, from the floor to the bed, poured wine, drinks in hand, making a toast to you for being everything I could ever ask for in a Queen, you always seem to please your King, but it's my turn, I yearn for your touch, but it's no rush, finish your drink let it set in, with your smooth skin a massage comes into play, I say my love lay on your chest with your back exposed, my hands begin to Lose Control, up and down your back, slow, lower I go down your hourglass to those hips past your perfectly shaped round ass, on to those thighs making my royal rise, to no surprise it's gonna be a long night, rubbing down your feet, you are so wonderful to me, flipping you over so you can see me, my hands start to creep back up your thighs, spreading you wide to slide my finger inside, looking you right in your eyes, you tell me it's all mine, I want to feel your tongue inside my palace, Anything Your Soul Desires my love I can manage, diving head first, you burst with a scream, I've just begun and already you're flowing with cream, tasting so good, so sweet, I'm doing the damn thing, doing circles around your pearl ring, another loud scream, while I indulge into your palace, making you wetter than ever before, King of your jungle I roar, I'm all yours, here to stay, blessing you in many different ways, coming up with that sticky face from being down below in your cave, ready my royal is to take his place, there's no escape, no getting away, no breaking out, I'm about to service you my Queen, giving you Anything Your Soul Desires, she says baby lift me high, I wanna ride while you stand inside, Your Wish Is My Command, wrapping your hands around my head, with your legs wrapped around my waist, Up, Up and Away we go, my feet planted on the floor, as I lift off into your palace, you scream I love you in Spanish my King, in French this love is meant to be, I stroke deep so you feel every inch, all of me, with your head falling back, as I attack, you raise up to kiss, our tongues twist while I push up in it, it feels like

D. C.

the room is at a spin the way we're going and going, my love I will continue to show it all in different forms, you know I'm nothing like the norm, you say baby lay me down and perform for me, I want you on top of me, laying you down gently, giving you all my loving, stuffing, filling your treasure up with my goldenrod, pushing inside, gazing deep into your eyes, giving you that Royal Therapy, all of me, your King is here to please all that you need, guaranteed to have you weak in the knees, I aim to please Anything Your Soul Desires, lighting your fire, taking you higher with ultimate satisfaction with my love actions, back and forth, in and out, south and north, landing deep into your ocean of heaven, legs wide open, eleven past seven, opening your eyes to the other side of love, I'm your eagle, giving you all that you can think of my beautiful dove, Losing Control, faster I go and go, doing you right, your everyday lover all through the night, this passion you can't fight, these feelings are oh so right, lasting until the sun comes up, making you erupt nonstop, freaking you on top, making your juice box pop, I have you handcuffed, call me a cop, your sirens going off loud, high above the clouds I have you floating, your Pandora box I have opened, soaking, raining wet, this is the best you've ever felt, giving you all that you desire, now you can go back to calling me sire, your palace I have devoured for the night, putting out your fire, turning out the lights, as we sleep the night away,
my love is here to stay.

THE PLACES I WANT TO KISS

I've never seen something so beautiful here in front of my eyes in a very long time, tonight you will be all mine, I send over to your table a bottle of Stella Rosa Black wine, with a rose attached is a note stating, talking in a club is not my thing, tonight I want you next to me, signed your King to be, you're stunned, your girls grab the note read and scream, girl do you know what this mean, you have been chosen by the one and only King, he never chooses, it seems he see something in that ass girl, y'all laugh, before you know it your hand is grabbed, hello at last, are you ready I ask, a blank stare is passed, you smile, stunned, a sip from your glass as you pass it to your girl saying you will meet them later on, putting on your leather coat, I say let's go, clearing a path to my ride opening up your side, you slide in nice and tight, we're in that XK Jaguar type, we dash in a flash, out of sight, fall in love you just might, your prince, your knight, nah your one and only King once in between, sliding in putting my thang in drive, green lights after green lights, flowing through traffic, admiring your flesh, tonight I will show you nothing less than the best, the greatest love you've ever felt, pulling up to my kingdom gates, open are your eyes wide, your smile is wide as the ocean, out of the car your door I open, leading you to the way of ecstasy, I'm gonna make it so you never forget about me watch and see, double door open to a sea of white roses and candles leading the way to my land of love, seducing you with a glare from my eyes, with my lips I lick as I say would you like a drink or would you like to follow the trail up the stairs, you roll those eyes with those hands on your hips flipping the script saying I'll follow the trail you make my drink, I hope you're ready for me, you cross my path with a wink, I say do you wonder why I chose you, I'm about to dive in holding my emotions in going to the kitchen you continue on your mission up the stairs to My Throne, opening those doors knowing it's about to be on, a fresh scent of oil hit your nose, filling the room, rose petals across my black silk sheets, you undress quickly, leaving your bra and sexy thong on, lying across my sheets as I stand with your drink, when I saw you I didn't know how to rethink, you smile, wink and sip, I drink,

D. C.

yes killed my glass alone at last, The Places I Want To Kiss, no spot will be missed, I begin my trip from the top of your head my lips are led to the side of your cheeks, you kiss, I'm weak, taking my breath away, I'm in to deep, to your lips where my heart sinks, time has stopped without you, my heart won't beat, nibbling on your ears, this is no track meet, Taking My Time hurdling through every obstacle, giving you a King treatment show, from your neck to your shoulders I go, holding you close, never letting go of you, I see us growing older, rubbing and sucking on your breasts, your palace getting warmer, we're about to perform love acts, your stomach I pass pulling off your thong, moving along, down your thighs you spread oh so wide, reading my mind, ready to dive on in kissing until the end, down to your calves and feet, you mean the world to me, forever we will be, proceeding with my tongue up your inner thigh, lighting your fire I am, I can see it in your eyes, in record time you will feel that quiver down your spine, that undying I can't hold it no longer power of my tongue getting stronger, pushing deep playing with your pearl, you squeeze tighter feeling weak I stop before you complete, roll you over to finish my kisses, down your back I make your canvas my map, with my lips massaging, with my hands showing I am that one from your head to your toes I have your feelings exposed, your passion ready to explode, spreading you low wrapping your legs around my neck, I stand and go on an everlasting expression show, you start to shake, rattle, bust and flow and that's just my lips and tongue show, The Places I Want To Kiss to make you let go, imagine if I would have pulled out and gave you that Royal Show, next time you will feel me deep, I will make you weep when I creep through and through, in and out, putting you to sleep as the lights go out, this is just the beginning of what I'm about.

MII: The Return of the King

YOU GIVE ME WHAT I NEED

I just love when I'm with you the things you do the things you make me feel, baby It's Yours, yes only yours, nobody else can explore that's for sure, You Give Me What I Need when you explore my passion when our tongues get to lashing back and forth, you hold that Olympic torch, you have me, my feelings racing faster than that new Porsche, but there's no rush when you touch my body all night deep inside it, inside you, your palace makes me do things I thought I would never do, my love is true, I was put here for you and you only, special I feel when you hold me, no more of being lonely, you changed the old me, love is pouring, flowing all through me, together you and I we're flying high when in between those thighs my Mrs. Right doing everything right I like, I love, taking the cake my heart please don't break, I wouldn't be able to take the pain and rain, it's plain to see with you beside me I am a better man I hope you can understand this is God's plan, hand and hand we go this is no act, this is a real life show, I will go where no man has ever gone before, loving you more and more with each passing day, sparing no expense, you were heaven sent, oh my, my, my you have showed me the other side of love, I will never place anyone above, you have allowed love to take its place in my heart as we embark on this life journey as one we become, my precious number one, I cherish, I vow to never perish from this love your love gives me peace of mind, gives me so much, all it took was time for a woman like you to find me, a lost island I was, now I'm sky diving deep into your heart of gold, our love is all I want to know, flowing slow as a river we coast, you always deliver the goods when pleasing my royal wood, if I could I will live inside your mind, creating nothing but thoughts of me all the time you close your eyes you will see nothing but me, You Give Me What I Need, free as the fish at sea to you forever I will be, to your love I defer, my beautiful angel here on earth, you are my worth, my blessing, teaching me lessons on love, my heart I give up to you I will prove my loyalty is true in everything that I do when it comes to you, as you continue to Give Me What I Need, my heart will forever feed off your love, digging deep as

D. C.

a grave, turning me into a loving slave, willing I am, whatever it may take, for the rest of my days I want you by my side, look past my eyes go into my soul and you will find that I will never let go of this love that I have found in you, oh my, my, my the things you make me do, taking over my mind as I speak, your love is all I will ever need, You Give Me What I Need, my Greenlight Special freak, the way you tease me when down low, oh my, my, my, is all I can shout when you float on and on until the break of dawn, you take me far and beyond the skies pass the stars, landing on My Love Planet, this love will never vanish, can't no one compare, can't even challenge my thoughts, when it comes to you there's no limit, no matter the cost, I will pay just to spend one day, one night inside your love, baby You Give Me What I Need, continue to take me Up, Up and Away, each day is special to me when you're near I have no fear, opening up my wings to fly you have entered my life and made me love you babe, made me love you babe, you made me love you babe, with your power you have conquered my heart and soul, You Give Me What I Need, I will never let go, this is a lifetime show, my love will never go astray,
beside you is where I will forever stay.

MII: The Return of the King

MY ROYAL BED

When you enter my room, the scene will consume every one of your thoughts, no cash needed, your ticket has been bought, love don't cost a thing dying to get in between, but I'll take it slow, there's no limit to where we are going to go, where I'm going to take you, giving you a feeling that will last for seven days and seven nights, can you handle the might from my royal pipe, we shall see, I start to creep, my love will seek and destroy your walls, deploying all my passion into your Erotic Zones, it's about to be on, moving along, it's time to perform, my love making is nothing like the norm, sexing you in many ways and different forms, don't be alarmed when I start to bring your love walls down, in me you have found a real King, welcome to My Royal Bed as I proceed to go in between teasing your treasure, my tongue will have you busting forever, my sheets appear to be going through a stormy weather, wetter is better, sweet and tasty, your heart is racing, face to face, sliding in that hot and warm wet place, giving you my all, a tear falls, neighbors banging, knocking on the walls, I hear sirens, the laws racing past the house without a doubt you scream and shout, giving you what you need, I am your King, taking you farther than ever before, each time I stroke I score, you hear me roar, love is what I pour into your soul, filling your cup, making you erupt, deep into you is a must loving the touch, feeling that rush through your body, on top I am being naughty, welcome to my part Royal Party, My Royal Bed, your legs I spread, setting them on my shoulders, your beauty is in the eyes of this beholder, kissing on your neck and shoulders, I become stronger as time progresses, hoping you can pass this test, My Royal Bed is a mess giving you my best, yes, sweat dripping wet, soak in need of a rain coat from the showers you're giving, loving you to the core your heart is my mission, I must please, never taking any intermission, never finished until you're finished, representing this crown in me you have found your King to be, this is what it is, you and me will forever be, this love you have sought for so long now you can call it all your own, it's on in My Royal Bed, love is what's being made, your palace I slay, inside of you each and every day, love is all I can say, my love is yours as your legs shake, screaming oh baby you're hitting my spot keep that flow, Greenlight never slows, never stops, that red is a no go, I evoke your spirit, giving you that special feeling, making your love come down, leaving my mark on you, you are my world my piece of paradise, I will sacrifice it all, when you call I drop whatever it is I'm doing, this is the start of a union, a beginning never knowing an ending, My Royal Bed has your feelings doing things they've never done before, your love I explore, more and more I give, touching your ribs, I live to please your every desire, you scream out sire, my King you giving me all I need, plus this is real love, never lust, your touch is a must have in my life doing you Just Right, this love will be going all night celebrating a love like no other, underneath these covers, you can't find this love in a store, this is tailor made, from the very first day I knew the love we would make would last for the rest of our days, giving Lessons In Love, taking you high and above, never will you be able to get enough, making you erupt once more, touching you deep past your core, your heart I will forever explore loving you in ways that you never thought was possible, there is no place I won't go, your love is all I will ever know, I will never let go, giving you a show each and every time you come close, My Royal Bed is no joke, I will go until I can't go no more, you I will forever adore.

OUR HEARTBEATS
(INTERLUDE)

In tune with one another we are no matter how far apart we may be, no matter if we haven't talked for days, Our Heartbeats stay connected, creating a wave through our bodies, closing our eyes at the same time to find each other, holding each other close never to let go, able I am to smell your perfume that consumes my thoughts, forever my lady no matter what ocean I have to cross to get to you I will do, whatever it is I need to do just to be touched by you I will do, all I want is you, do you feel that thump in your chest when our lips are pressed together, Our Heartbeats stay in sync, we are linked, chained with a lock and key, you are never getting away from me, my heart smiles when I see your face, these feelings can't be erased, my world is yours forever in a day, I want to explore, you give me more than you could ever know, my sweetest love song, to you I belong, addicted to your love, the more I get, the more I want, placing no one above, when we're apart Our Heartbeats perform their symphony, just you and me, forever we will be, all I can see is you next to me, no other can compete, I adore everything about you, from your head to your feet, your love is all I will ever need, Our Heartbeats will go on until I'm Wide Open, you have filled my cup, my love is yours, ready I am to erupt with passion, you give me more without me asking, satisfaction, Everlasting, from the beginning never knowing an ending, you have me, my heart is yours to keep, please stay in my life, your love is all that I seek, my all or nothing, all love, never lusting, busting with love, never will I give you up, you have me, I'm Wide Open.

D. C.

I'M WIDE OPEN

Lost I've become staring up into the sun, blinded by your love, what have you done to me, you are the one I seek, the one my soul's been searching for high and low, I just want to adore, my heart has risen from behind my walls, a ghost is what you can call me, Before You Came Into My Life no love was right, my Just Right, you have brought sunlight into my dark world, oh how precious you are to me my girl you are my world, my everything, my queen, I'm Wide Open can't you see what you do to me, isn't it obvious, all that I want is you, can't nobody come in and take your place, you give me what I need, I want you for the rest of my days, you make me misbehave when wrapped in between the sheets, you just don't know what you do to me, all I can see is you, Perfectly Blind, I will follow your lead, never take your love away from me, I even want you in my next lifetime, I will do it all over again times five, you're all that I need in my life, I live to love you, I'm Wide Open, your beauty blows my mind, your kiss is just that divine, your lips soft as rose petals, intoxicating without a sip of wine, your touch makes me lust, but you know it's love, I just want you so much, I can't get enough, I'm Wide Open, my heart is pouring, soaking, all my devotion is aimed your way, come stand by me and take your rightful place, you have erased my past pain, with you I will remain forever loyal, my love seed is planted in your soil, the world will watch us grow into a beautiful flower, blossoming like no other, when tangled in your web, in those covers, my love rises to another level, I am a lucky fellow to have stumbled upon you, a Queen, for the rest of my days I will fiend for you, your touch just takes me Up, Up and Away, no other can sway my feelings, my thoughts, my love can't be bought, you already Own It, my heart is yours, no more prolonging, let's do this thing right baby, I want you to become my wife, I have so much to offer, life partners is what I want us to be, softly you whisper yes, holding you close never letting go, you have me so, you have my feelings so open, I'm Wide Open, my heart for you will never close, forever I will love you deep down to your soul, this I know, I speak nothing but the truth when it comes to you and the things you do to me, damn babe sometimes I even weep about how deep I feel for you, your love I never want to lose, Your In Control, handling my heart with care, I swear to never leave you alone, I will always be there, here to console your every feeling, giving you that loving healing when I touch in between your thighs, I can't lie you take me high past the sky, past the sun, you are my number one love, I'm Wide Open my dove, you have me soaring through the clouds, in you I have found my one and only, my everything, the way you put it on me, words can't describe, my love has come up from that hiding place, you take the cake, I'm Wide Open, your love I never want it to escape my grasp, my hold, when touched by you I Lose Control, your love is all that I want to know, forever we will be one, remain close, you are the star of this Never Ending, Everlasting, Lights, Camera, Action show, I'm Wide Open, I will never let go.

D. C.

EASY

I'm trying to catch your vibe, so I can take you on a natural high, through the skies your feelings on rise, my hands slide up your thighs, gazing deep into your eyes your body has already decided that you want me inside, taking your feelings on a ride, your heart coincides with mine, intertwined when kissing you softly, gently, chills start to cover your whole body, my love you will never get enough, wait don't bust just yet as I tease your soul taking away your stress with pleasure, my royal you can't measure, I keep growing and growing when pushing inside of your love, touching your ribs, My Rib you are taking your mental far, your palace wet like the dark skies, shining bright as a star so fine you are, your beauty taking me to another level, it's getting hotter in this room, your love I consumed through my veins like a drug feed me more, give me more, make me roar, my pole is your stage, take me deep into your core, do the splits down to the floor, pop, pop, pop that ass make me want more, sitting up, as I take you up, coming to a stance while I cradle you in my arms, my love this is Easy, watch me perform in these arms I hold the power to the tenth, I won't stop until I devour and knock down your towns, flying my plane right into your window of love, you erupt as I take you Up, Up and Away, making you say Papi, oh Papi this is your palace you can have it On Repeat holding you close and tight, pushing with all my might, giving you that all night long, your song On Repeat, I'm giving you multiple On Repeat, you see me, the only one of my kind, the last King to reign supreme in between these sheets, showing you a real love when I go down with my tongue you twitching with every touch, every lick sending a rush through your body, my party will never quit until you tap, pause as I sip my drink, you turn over while giving me a wink, starting to move to the beat soft and Easy, giving me a show with a slow twerk of the hips. your ass jumps, skips, I pull the sheets, tossing them to the floor, my passion is about to creep through your soul, in I go spreading you wide pulling on your hair to kiss your lips as I stroke in and out looking in your eyes, giving you the One Of a Kind Love, that I Can't Resist your touch love, filling up your cup, overflowing with my love, my beautiful dove erupts with passion all over my crown, I'm in your town only for tonight, giving you the best you ever had, with every stroke I'm getting closer and closer to unlocking your hidden treasures, trust I can weather your storm, I'm nothing like the normal you're used to, my way, my groove, my mental is just too different, I'm heaven sent here to show you your worth here on earth, love making is Easy when you know how to fill one's void, even if it's just for the night, I will always be the one to show you that King version of that Just Right, leading you to My Royal Room where I will consume your love.

D. C.

THE PERFECT MATCH

Where do I start, how can I explain, where do I begin to tell you of this special dame, this Perfect Match, my heart forever is attached, latched on to hers, my beautiful girl I have traveled this world going from zodiac sign to zodiac sign making love until I stumbled upon this One Of A Kind, all mine, my sign, Virgo, oh my Virgo how I can't let go, stuck I have become, my body goes numb when you come near, my heart starts to race, but I have no fear knowing I found exactly what I've been searching for, for so long, I call this Virgo my home away from home, the way she performs when entering her palace where it's warm, bringing on that stormy wetness, I never can forget, I Can't Resist your sticky softness, it's her body, the effects I feel are unreal, possessing the same skills to make me feel as if there's no better love, minus the glove when I dig taking me high and above, relaxing my mind as I unwind, in and out of your spine with nowhere to go, Taking My Time, you're extra fine, the truth, my Virgo, The Perfect Match, showing me proof in everything you do, pleasing to the touch when deep inside of you, stimulating my mind you are One Of A Kind, putting my thoughts to sleep about the next, I can care less about the rest, you pass all the tests the way you caress not only my body, but my heart and soul, giving all control to you, that hold you have over me I know will last a lifetime, I'm Thanking My Past for at last I've grasped a real one, the right one for me, she gives me what I need, nothing even matters to me, she's all that I see, all that I breathe, the only one who can fulfill my dreams and needs, you are my Perfect Match can't you see, you are everything to me, feeding off the love my Virgo throwing my way, forever in a day my heart belongs to you, I will always stay by your side my ride or die, my heart doesn't lie, I can't spend a night without you lying next to me, I wouldn't be able to sleep, you keep my soul at peace, I become weak when you are not next to me, you are my strength, My Back Bone, my love you will forever own, here is The Key To My Heart, we shall never part, until my final resting day I am here to stay smiling from ear to ear across my face, opening my eyes to more than I could ever dream, this love means so much, I couldn't bare living without your touch, I can't get enough of what you offer, I counterpunch with something much softer, a kiss to the lips, my hands on your hips pushing slow, I love to go and go deep into your love, it takes me Up, Up and Away, you have me flying for days the way you make me misbehave just isn't right, this is the life I choose, to be with you and rule this earth as King and Queen, The Perfect Match, you mean everything to me, no blurred lines here my love is in top gear, racing with no fear whispering in your ear that we are The Perfect Match and I will always be here next to you, my love will forever stay true, I want nobody but you, completion is what you bring me, my life now has a meaning since you came into my life, no thoughts of thinking twice, I will forever adore you, my wife.

D. C.

ONE MORE TIME

If only I had One More Time to makes things right with you, to make things work I would show you that I could be that man, the rightful man by your side, my heart doesn't lie, I have made some wrong decisions in my life and letting you go the way I did was just not right, look into my eyes my love you will see the pain and hurt, knowing I caused you to be sad know that I am mad at only myself, the pain I dealt lusting and flirting after another, hiding secret tails under cover, you were the closest thing to real that I've seen, baby, love, I didn't mean to put our relationship in jeopardy, your heart is my home, it's where I want to be, remember how it was just you and me, kisses, hugs and beautiful words, nobody else's, just his and hers, forever was our word, but now it's gone because of the wrong I've done, I know you were the one but I wasn't done playing around, running the streets going from town to town breaking hearts, taking your love and making art with others, blessing them with what was yours, oh my Lord I need your help, I call upon you to give me strength to get throw this agony and heartache, your walls I want to break back down, I know somewhere in there my love is still stored and can be found, I can't even come around without feeling ashamed I am the one to blame for this pain, can someone tell me when will this rain stop, nonstop around the clock a cloud, a dark cloud is hovering over my head, walking the streets as my feet lead me on a path to nowhere, my love I swear I declare you to be my Queen, if I knew what I know now I would have been that faithful King, reminiscing on the things we used to do, the way I would hold you close, oh what I wouldn't give to kiss you slow, lips to lips oh my, my, my, I now know your worth, they say only when it hurts you fiend for what you used to have, somebody build me a time machine so I can go back to the past and change that last act, these words I speak are facts, I wanna make it work, I need you back, your love is where I want to be at, baby come back into my life and show me that love that was Just Right, oh so right, you are My Light, MY Love At The End Of The Tunnel, your heart I did fumble, broke into little pieces, I can fix this, we can make it work, we were so down in love, remember how you couldn't get enough, damn I could have love you so much better, with all that I did, with all that I caused you never walked out on me, you gave me chance after chance, maybe I thought I was exempt and you would never get tired of my mess, oh boy was I so wrong, now I am all alone, you won't even answer my calls, leaving messages after messages on your phone, driving past your home just to see if anyone has taken my place at the dinner table, I know that I am able to give you all that you ask for in me, damn I am so weak, I can't even eat, I get no sleep, haven't shaved in two weeks, do you see what happens when I don't have your love next to me, can't you see it won't be the same if I was with somebody else, how it won't be the same if you're with somebody, knowing I made many mistakes before, baby do you hear me roar, I promise to never hurt you anymore, I got all that you need plus more, missing your voice, oh how I adore, if it were my choice I would rewind to that time I was exploring your canvas, damn my love I just have to have it, I just want to rewind the time, but keep the mind that I have grown to have now, knowing what I found in you would have been my proof that my love for you will never cease, if I can get you to see what I see just you, me and our mini me's, One More Time baby I am on my knees, you have exactly what I need, you feed my soul, I don't want you to let go, I don't want you to run away, my love do you think of our love? I know you don't need me, I know you don't want to see me, but I want you, my love is all for you, I didn't mean to baby, I didn't mean to turn our happy home into something so wrong, with you is where I belong, if you let me back in I will sure enough never let you go again, foolish not to realize what I was looking for stood right before my eyes, the grass was not greener on the other side, baby I need you, what we had when our love was true nothing could stop us, fixing my days you did when I was feeling blue, damn I need you what do I have to do to get you back, I lay on my back screaming out Ohhhhhhhhh with tears in my eyes, not able to take this pain, my girl I'm about to go insane, you are my sun, the only one who can stop this rain, I still want to spend a couple of forevers with you, my heart is plain, I will never be the same, knowing that you are gone forever and ever, I don't blame you for not wanting to give me another chance, I want you to know you have made

D. C.

me a better man, I will never place no one above, I dug deep within my core opened up and told you things that are very dear to me, you're all that I will ever need, from the first time I saw you I knew you were it, I just didn't know how to keep it, knowing what I want, but kept putting a twist in it, I should not have lied, I could have been blunt and upfront with you, I'm asking you for One More Time, let's go back to the beginning when it was smiles, frowns no, without the ups and downs, happy sounds, a joy to be around, just One More Time, don't you hear the crowd screaming loud, I stand here not proud about how I feel inside, I want you to know you will always have a place inside, I will love you for life.

MII: The Return of the King

I WILL DO THE THINGS YOUR MAN WON'T DO

Opening your eyes and doors to new experiences that you have never felt or seen before, your love I will put to the test each and every time that I explore not only your body, but your mind as well, in me you will find heaven not hell, In Due Time your heart will tell what it really feels when I come near, erasing that fear of having a dose of the same thing you had before, never will I let down my guards I will always adore, hitting you with new pleasure that you will forever enjoy, once I deploy my love, this blessing from up above will dive deep into your soul never letting go I'm gonna show you things your man couldn't, you shouldn't settle for less, allow me to take away all stress that you may have, putting your last into the past, broadening your horizons, taking you high through the sky and putting love back into your life, I will make you my wife unlike the man you have, I wouldn't think twice, in my hands I know what I have, a diamond in the rough, I will make sure you will never get enough, loving you in different ways and different forms, your last showed you what the norm will give you, but you deserve more than the norm, you're a Queen and should be treated like one, come sit beside my throne, my heart will be your home, I'm just a phone call away, your love displays across my face when I smile, thinking about you makes me want you now, right now as I write these words, traveling your canvas making it my earth, my love I know your worth, you are a One Of A Kind woman, I submit to you, just allow me to take you to new heights, come and float with me, I want you each and every night, the way your man does you is just not right, taking you for granted when you should be the apple of his eyes, he treats you like a second place prize when clearly you are number one, your heart is broken, look at what he has done, I can be, I mean, I am that one who will put those pieces back together, I know you never thought this day will come, for someone to show you real love, to give you exactly what you have dreamed of, exactly what you need, I am a different breed, I want you to feed off the love I am going to give, showering you with my love, I told you once before that I am blessed

D. C.

from up above, I'm writing your name across my heart so that whenever we are apart you move to the rhythm of my heartbeat, all you can think about is me, I swear I want to be near your love now and forever for all time, no more of being lonely, holding you close, holding you tight, close to my heart and soul, this I truly know, I Will Do The Things Your Man Won't Do with each day and every falling night treating you Just Right for the rest of our days this love will remain tight. P.S, come home where you belong.

SECRET LOVER

When will enough be enough, my lust has grown into love, kept as a Secret Lover pleasing you underneath my covers, your palace I murder in my special way, calling me your King in that special way, love is written all over your face, but at the end of the day, you go back to his place, leaving me until that next day comes about when I can make you yell out it's yours when I start to adore your heavenly body pushing down south working you out, putting you to sleep when I freak you in my sheets, pleasure written all over your face, ready I am to replace this Secret Lover title, my signs you should follow, I'm swallowing my pride, setting it aside so that my true feelings can't hide any longer, you make me pause and wonder when I think about how you make me feel inside, this, your love has taken me by surprise, treating you like a Queen when my tongue flows inside, giving you more than what you came for, giving you more than what you can handle, I know you like for me to feed before I enter with my extended pipe, Everlasting all through the night, rocking your body until the sunlight comes, filling you up as you bust, damn I pause feeling a rush through my body while your palace warms my touch as I go in and out, round and round, lifting you up just to break you down in this bed rolling around, putting it down so that you will never forget about me your Secret Lover times four, hoping and praying you will come back for more, ready and willing, Anytime, Anyplace, dropping everything to please you with my sexual healing, just call my phone, and I will race right over where I belong loving you down , "OMG," the way you kiss and lick me, calling my body your pleasure throne, your love is just too tempting, I Can't Resist with evidence of what we have done on the couch to the kitchen floor, picking you up to take you to my Royal Room so that more passion can be explored, how did I forget to mention when I gave you more and more, spreading you wide deep into you is a must, I love it when you erupt, start flowing down my vine when I'm deep touching your spine, pleasing you with what I have in between my thighs, Our Chemistry is Just Right, fine is what you are, our minds stay in sync, I really think we could be, just you and me, together we can be, forever wanting you with me, don't you see how I

D. C.

feel, my love making skills is just the tip of the iceberg, Love is War, and I will fight for you with all my strength and love here on earth, my heaven's worth, deferring to what you have to offer, being your everything, I was placed here to please only you my Queen, my Lazy Love, placing no one above, as the doves cry being your Secret Lover I will until the start of our new life.

MII: The Return of the King

FOREVER I WILL ADORE

Since the first time that I explored your love, I knew way back then that Forever I Will Adore everything about your love, with that one single touch from you, feelings rush through my body, this passion I can't hide it, each time I pull inside it, inside your love you take me up and above, I can't get enough of those lips, each kiss takes control, my heart does flips when I sit alone thinking of your love I've grown to love, the best love I've ever had, I erupt with joy, no more days of being sad, Forever I Will Adore your mind and spirit, this is the beginning, no need of fearing, I'm putting my trust in you, my heart has begun its healing, your love takes me through the ceiling, exploding through the roof, my love I will show you love is real, I will be your proof, for each day that passes, I will show you something new, Forever I Will Adore you, it's you I seek, I want you standing right next to me, at my side, I want to be inside of your love for the rest of our lives, opening up the door to your heart and allow me to come inside, let me show that softer side of love, the love that will fill you up, over running your cup, let me take you to a place where you can never get enough love, I want to give you a couple of forever and ever, together until never, never ending, we will be stuck in the beginning, this love can never be finished, you are my life's mission, to please to adore to forever explore your soul, to keep you safe to never let go, protect you I will not let no hurt or harm come your way, I will protect your pretty face, your doubts you can delete, go ahead and erase, you are getting a real King here on this day, I don't play when it comes to your love, not afraid to speak of your love to any of my peers, all I want is you near, my only fear is being without you, I wouldn't know what to do, my life I will lose if I couldn't adore you, I want only you, my heart pumps for you, Forever I Will Adore you to the core, I want more and more each time I explore your palace, you give me more than satisfaction, the way you swing it back and forth, the rest is just candles to your torch, the spark to my flame, you keep taking me higher and higher, I will never be the same, my number one desire, this is not a game, you are my fire, you can call me sire, when I acquired the inside of your love, filling you up with my well-equipped, making you fall in love with this real life movie script, hitting you with all the right tools, pulling out all the right moves to show and prove why Forever I Will Adore your love, without placing nothing or no one above you my Queen, ready I am to drop to my knees and give you that ring, In Due Time you will come to find out exactly what I mean, forever you and me, King and Queen.

MII: The Return of the King

THANKING MY PAST

I would like to dedicate this one right here to my last, right now I feel the need to Thank My Past women for teaching me lessons on what a great woman shouldn't, a Queen is what I have found, lost I was wondering trying to deal with the hurt and pain, down and out I never thought love would come my again, I didn't think anyone heard my screams and shouts, never will I reroute in choosing the wrong lover, the woman I have now had made me rediscover what true love is really about, I had my doubts going into this one, but something about her told me that she was the one and only one who could restore my faith in love once again, first she was my friend a true friend there to listen to my problems uplifting me without a problem, becoming my problem solver, no she is not a rebound, in her I have found my worth, I will cherish this woman until I'm down in the dirt six feet under, I now don't have to wonder if this will work, there is nothing in the back of my mind saying it won't, there's not a don't, a won't, can't in sight, all I see is the delight that is being giving to me, a true love unconditionally, you would think it was me playing the part of the bad guy, but that wasn't my life with my last, my past, they had hidden agendas that came to pass, that came to the light showing me all I needed to see, none was worthy enough to have pleasure for this King, I mean what else could they have wanted, a roof over their heads, cars, money, trips, a stallion in the bed, foolery is all that can be said, they didn't know what true love really meant, it's not all those things I had, it's not what's in those jeans or what's in between (even though that counts) hair hanging low, it's the look in one's eyes and how they glow when you touch low inside, it's like now how real love is flowing through my veins, knowing that this feeling will forever remain strong never the same it must grow, for if it stays the same then the love will never evolve and will always remain stuck in the same place, a strong love can never be erased, misplaced or dealt out to another, I have uncovered the true meaning of love, so I'm sending this out to my past, Thanking My Past for allowing me to run into this beautiful woman at the right time in my life at last, I will always treat her right, giving her

D. C.

the best she could ever ask for, plus more, my lady has restored my faith in love, my heart beats to the rhythm of her drum, she is my one I want forever under this sun, under the moonlight, each and every night I recite these words to her my Queen, if it wasn't for you I wouldn't know where or what I would be doing, my heart would still be confused, there's no way I will ever lose my heart to another, you are my wonder woman, I thank you for uncovering my soul and for bringing me out of the cold, forever my love I will hold you close, lock and key, forever just you and me.

MII: The Return of the King

PUSHING INSIDE OF YOU

Over and over again, for so long you have dealt with the wrong lovers, giving up your precious, it's time you discover what really awaits for you in my Kingdom, your palace has been locked away, it's time I set you on a pathway to freedom, blessed I am when I crawl in between those thighs, in between those covers, my passion so strong you will pause and think about it when alone and wonder how everyday will feel with a real King such as myself, you Never Felt A Love Like This Before, I'm going to uncover your pain and expose your heart, filling your cup up to the rim with my love, we will never part, flirting with these words playing games is for the birds, I know your worth with my hands sliding down your back, ready I am to attack and give your body, heart and soul what they deserve, loving your sexy curves, I'm about to rock your world when these lights go out, I have no doubt you will shout out my name King, the way I please your body and soul, an uncontrollable hold I gasp once I enter your pleasure hole, deep into you I go Taking My Time, my stroke you will never find, yes I am One Of A Kind when pushing inside there's none you can compare me to, I'm a different type of King when in between your world doing the things that I do, never letting go my girl, all I want is you, my passion seeks you, my love is true, my heart pumps and beats to your movement, my heaven sent, My Beautiful Find, now that you're all mine I'm going to Take My Time part one and two, I hope you're ready for what I'm about to do to you, showing you your worth once I start Pushing Inside Of You, there's nothing you will be able to do, your limbs will become weak, my love will overtake thee, once my missile is locked and loaded out to seek your pleasure chest, erupting on impact showing you why I am the best, the greatest at what I do when I'm Pushing Inside Of You, staring into your big brown, hazel eyes, Pushing Inside Of You as the level of passion rises, no foreplay tonight, I'm feeding you nothing but this long, hard and thick pipe, giving you what you like all night my Just Right, blowing your mind with each stroke through your spine, beautifully divine, rolling you over to push slower inside from behind, in front of the mirror we find

D. C.

ourselves with each push your heart melts letting out passionate moans and sexy love faces, these are the Sounds Of Love making, Oh and Ah, my King, damn I love you my Queen right there, I swear your tones take me there over the top, keeps me going nonstop, feeling and knowing when that eruption is coming on, pulling on your long black hair, taking you to another level as I hit you there, pleasuring your special gift, your right and left legs I lift to pull in deeper, no spot will be missed, taking you on a never-ending trip as I Pushing Inside Of You making you explode on cue, I value each time I get to explore you, your soul, my love I want you to never let go, allow me to be your Hollywood, Vegas show, every night I will go, take you there, my love knows no limits, I will always be here when in need, ready and willing to give you all that you need, I'm all yours, you can have all of me when Pushing Inside Of You I know no other love but you, my heart is forever yours, I will stay true, I could never get enough of Pushing Inside Of You.

MII: The Return of the King

ON REPEAT

The first time I held you close, we raised our glasses to make a toast, I don't want to brag or boast, but I did the most to your body, I had you feeling some type of way, at first you weren't trying to fall, you didn't want to stay, you curved it all, until I unlocked that hidden treasure, digging into your soul, going places no one else can go, you tapping my butt whispering go baby go, make me explode, putting my groove into overdrive, your water fall has arrived, On Repeat baby as I Turn you to your side, lifting your thigh so that I can slide through your puddle of love, oh what have I done, sprung you are going to become, I am the one who can have you On Repeat in one session, I'm giving you a Lesson In Love, putting it down in so many ways. I have your body doing the wave, as I stroke your everglades, this love, my love will sway your feelings my way, yes you are going to want to stay in this place I call my Kingdom below my waist, this taste I'm giving is like none other, drowning in your puddle under these covers, I am that lover they call King, making you fiend for my drug as you scream out number two, I'm giving my best to you, none can do you like me, I told you I can have you On Repeat in one session, confessing your love you are, smiling brighter than the stars, far from done, hard and stiff, come climb my mountain, place, slide my fully equipped into your palace, cruising slow, hitting every wall, making them fall as you quicken your pace, faster with your flow, yes baby go, popping that ass and dropping it low, showing me that freaky side, reverse cowgirl, damn is that right, you're letting your inner animal free, out the cage you are, looking back at it, you getting it I say while smacking your ass to your motion, at the very moment you explode, I told you I can have you On Repeat in one session, this here was your lesson, Putting All Your Expectations To Rest, tomorrow you can call your girls and tell them I'm the best you ever had, my Royal Love will never leave you mad, dissatisfied looking through your eyes past your heart to your soul, anytime you want me to hold you close, all you have to do is give me a signal like batman, I am that man who can have you On Repeat on any given night my love is just that right, oh what a night.

D. C.

MY BEAUTIFUL FIND II

Oh my, my, my how time flies, at the blink of my eyes, we come to find us intertwined, joined at the hip this love will continue to exist from here on out, my love for you I scream loud, I shout it proud, I give you my all, I give you my crown, my heart was once lost but now it is found, you are the cause of my happiness, Perfectly Blind I am, filled with bliss, I can give a damn with the next has to say, their opinion I dismiss, a single thought of you makes me reminisce on that first time, oh what a time that was, from that day, I knew I wouldn't place no one above you, my words are true, the things you do make my heart beat to the rhythm of your love, the others I gave up, they can't touch me in ways that you do, I'm lost in the middle of your love, my heart will forever stay true, this is My Beautiful Find Part Two, I can never get enough of explaining my love for you to the world, I want everyone to know that you are my girl, my special lover, I've walked this world Soul Searching knowing I'm deserving of a love of this magnitude, the other dudes couldn't do the things I do, and I'm not talking about when I'm in between those thighs even though I know they couldn't make your temperature rise the way that I can, from here on out I will be your man, here I stand with my heart in my hand ready to put it in your box with you holding the key, you belong to me, and I belong to you, there's nothing no one can do to change us, together forever, never lust, my passion you have made erupt, love is what I will be giving, dishing that real so that you can feel how it feels to be loved in return, oh how I Prayed For A Love Like Yours, you have made me explore the other side of love, my eyes are Wide Open, wishing and hoping this feeling never passes, Thanking My Past for allowing me to be loved by someone that's real, her love making skills is mmmmm, I can't even put my thoughts into words, her canvas is my earth, I travel from her sea to her lips, taking a trip when I pull it out to rip through her palace, Anytime, Anyplace she can have it, I never thought I would be with My Beautiful Find, the time has come, we both have aged, I want you to always be my one, today is the day I give you my all, for so long I had up my walls to the world, Perfectly Blind only seeing you my girl, My Beautiful Find, I will be crazy to substitute, never will I find another of your kind, of your stature, these hands of mine need your guidance, ready I am to express how I've always felt about you, I'm not fooling around, in you I have found my Everlasting, igniting my passion with your fire, my only desire is just to please you, not allowing a day to pass me by without showing you love in different ways, I will always and forever be Your Love Slave, you are my wish come true for the rest of my days I will make you say my name King, hashtag the word love next to me knowing that I know what it means when it come to a real thing, a real love, you have dug deep to my soul baby, never letting go baby, I think of only you and the things we're going to do My Beautiful Find, I see us in the future living that good life, at night when we find ourselves in My Royal Room making love is what I want too, Taking My Time with you, evolving I am, damn looking at your physique I say please baby give it all to me, your face, my hands on your thighs, I want to showcase it all taking you high through the sky, going up and down like an elevator dropping your clothes to the floor, ready I am always to explore what's been mine for so long, My Beautiful Find, spending the rest of my life loving you indeed, with you inside my world, my heart feeds off your love, my world has come alive since you came into my life, my wife, since the clock passed seven I've been stroking into your heaven here on this earth, you are my worth, you deserve the love we will share, I want you to give birth, be the mother of my child, yes I want to take it there, diving deep into your palace, I've always imagined, dreamed of having this day come true, face to face, me on top in between your waist giving you that Royal Love, filling you up making you erupt, loving your touch My Beautiful Find, I will never be able to get enough, I will keep you running through my mind for all the time I will love you and only you, My Beautiful Find.

D. C.

A CRAZY NIGHT

I must be honest with you babe, I cannot lie on my love, for tonight there will be a change, please don't take me strange, but if you know me by now you know that I am a freak, first I'm gonna turn the lights down low with candles in place, just Follow My Lead so that I can see all your reactions when I start to lay down that satisfaction from every angle with the mirror up top, cameras in every corner spot, I want to enjoy the aftermath, nonstop, seeing you watching me when I'm hitting all your spots, your palace I will make wet and hot, in my Royal Bed, you are the crook, and I'm playing the part of the cop, putting you in handcuffs making your pleasure erupt, bringing nothing but pleasure with the pain I'm giving as you rain down my pole, Losing Control, uploading your soul, this video won't get exposed, it's just for my pleasure, measuring how far you can go, my tongue evokes your feelings, howling to the moon as I dig deep inside turning my Royal Bed into that jungle atmosphere, I am King my love there is no need to have any fear in this lion, there is no denying that I am hung like an elephant trunk, once we are stuck together you will erupt even more than before, stroking you to the core, your passion rises from the floor to the ceiling, love is in your heart, yes that's a real feeling that you been feigning, kissing you gently, soft as my tongue twists giving your breasts a twist, uplifting your soul you're forgetting about your past, letting go as I go and go downstairs, no my love can't be compared to another, real passion is what's being delivered, real love is what's being discovered with the way I give you my all, making you moan out oh, oh I can't deny you King, it's yours to have and to hold, I want this to be an everyday, every night show, I love you so much, confessing with your tongue that I am that one and only, telling me I am everything you will need and want under the sun, damn baby I love you, you call out right there make me bust like a gun, don't stop my King you rocking my spot, stroking deep while Pushing Inside Of You slow making your waves flow shifting your boat as I climb aboard to give you more, exploring your seas, weak you become in your knees, Breaking You Down I am that man, that King who holds the power to

MII: The Return of the King

bring down any walls that you may have, my tank is on full, I will outlast your last, never running out of gas with your nails in my back tearing at my flesh, giving you the best that you ever had, the others will be mad since you have had King, they will never be able to get back in between, giving you what you need, what you desire, making all your fantasies come true, I can relate, as we lay the night away in my Royal Bed, I play with your pearl letting you know you will always be my girl, the way you're taking all my inches I did forget to mention no one has ever be able to handle what I've been dishing, coming with the strength of ten men as I swim through and through, giving all my love to you on this Crazy Night being Body to Body, it's a party in your palace box, I told you I won't stop, the neighbors complaining about the noise threatening to call the cops, nonstop, they're not doing anything but making me go harder, making you get louder as I take it to another level, hotter than the devil in this room, I'm laying down that boom, boom, clap, giving you instructions to turn that ass around, so that I can tap that apple bottom from the back, spreading you wide so that I can slide in with a fast thrust, not in a rush but not Taking My Time at the same time making your love come down as you unwind, I grind deep pulling on your hair, so that I can stare into your eyes when you look back at it, hopping fast like a rabbit, but this trick isn't for kids, I give you My Rib so that you can live, pleasuring you with My Gift, touching you in ways, so that you will never resist the temptation of this King, making you explode is the theme, pleasing you because you are a Queen, you're letting out that scream, that scream that lets me know that I am deep in between touching your soul as you let go, this was A Crazy Night, my love making has taken you to new heights, I got that Just Right, anytime you need my might, just give me a call and I will be right over to make your love fall.

D. C.

I WANNA BE

Thoughts of you ignite my fire, consuming all my desires, which makes me want to do nothing but please you in ways you've never been before, your heart I want to explore, inside your mind I go wanting to know more, deep down to your soul is where I Wanna Be when I perform and go into your core, in between your thighs on top of my sheets, damn already baby I have become weak, what are you doing to me, you got that Lazy Love, soon as I get in it, I just want to erupt, just thinking about how we have become each other's love freaks taking my tic, tic, tic, time when I'm underneath your naval as my cable cord grows longer than those norms, I will be able to perform in ways that will have you misbehave, turning you into My Love Slave, once I enter your cave, the music will start to play to the rhythm of me, your palace is where I Wanna Be giving you all of me, deep sea diving, dripping wet, your body is my island nobody could find your treasure, they couldn't measure up to the challenge, but I have found all your hidden secrets with my tongue being the key to unlocking your treasure chest, playing with your breasts, no rest tonight, we're going all night, blazing outta sight, blazing to the moon as I zoom, zoom through your walls making your water fall as we fly back to my room, your palace has me performing love acts like never before, I'm Wide Open, it's impossible to ignore, I want you more and more, each time I stroke your spine our love becomes more divine, In Due Time you will be forever mine, My Beautiful Find you have me suspended in the air, I tried to compare you to another, but none came close, these passion strokes has me on float, it never felt better to me, what are you doing to me, you're giving me all of you doing what you do, I'm swimming through your body with my hands pressed tightly against your hips, sending me on an Everlasting trip with a kiss from your lips, my heart skips a beat or two, I Wanna Be with you, I know what you are looking for, you don't have to search anymore, your body belongs to me, babe I crave your waterfall waves, flowing in and out splashing down south, moans crawl from your mouth with a shout, King that's what I'm talking about, a little deeper baby you're a keeper, my dream Queen, I love to be in between turning you out so that I'm all that you think about forever and always, I Wanna Be with you without a doubt in my mind, you are all I will ever need in this lifetime.

D. C.

GOOD GIRL TURNED BAD

Ever since I saw you, I just had to have you, knowing that we both are involved, but I know you can solve this problem to my equation, your body is banging I'm saying each time that I see you how I could love you better than your man, baby I'm just saying can't you feel this attraction, satisfaction when you deal with me a King, I feel you about the creeping, but I need you next to me, my love runs deep, just try me and you will see that I am all that you will ever need, late night sessions you will be professing your undying love to me and only me, just watch and see, you say you talk a good game, I reply, but it's not a game that I am playing, for me this is real, soon you will believe, just think about what I'm saying, a week passed and look who's lying next to me saying I see why you wear that crown, I want you to be the King of my heart, I don't ever want to part, cruising over to your crib, I sit outside and park as you try and let him down easy while packing your bags, A Good Girl Turned Bad, not caring about his feeling, with him in the doorway looking sad, you're smiling, I'm glad, dashing off into the sunlight, I finally have my Mrs. Right, together we will be for life, taking you on trips, places you've never been before, I am all yours, your body I will adore, those curves I explore stick shifting slow, there's no place I won't go, my love is all you will know, the good side will be all would you know, no hurt will go on here with me, unless when in the sheets rough passion strokes when dealing with me, but it's a good type of hurt, I'm going to have you going berserk, you can call me Captain Kirk for saving you from that simple life you once lived before, this time next year you will be my wife, is that alright? Our future together is bright, you're My Love At The End OF The Tunnel, funneling some of that good, showing you how to treat my wood when on top pleasuring with your P, giving me all of you since being with me you know now exactly what to do, I'm giving you all the game, making you rain at the very thought of my pleasure and love, filling you up, exploding, bursting into flames, now it's real love that you claim, your mind, body and soul will never be the same, we will always remain, playing this game for keeps, happy I am that you chose to be with me, your love I have sought for so long, now that you're here I know that my heart belongs to you, I will always show and prove that you made the right move by allowing me to turn that good side bad, this will last, putting our past in the rearview, all I want is you, together we will rule, side by side, this love will never die, I will see to it that we will never cease, my feelings will never tap or quit, I can admit to the world that you are that one, my only Queen, you give me all that I need, I will continue for as long as I live to feed off the love you give, there's no ifs, ands, or buts, your love is enough for me to love you into the next lifetime, blessed I am that you are all mine, I love you my One of a Kind.

D. C.

OUR CONVERSATION II

Hey my love, come in and have a seat, Tonight Is All About You, standing stunned at what she sees, a single flower is presented with rose petals and candles leading the trail, my love says, my King is all this just for me, yes baby let me pour you a drink, don't you start to weep the best is yet to come, I've been running through these thoughts over and over in my head, my Queen says baby what is this all about, there's no doubt that you have my heart from Our last Conversation there will be no replacing, you already have given me all that I can wish and hope for, I'm all yours forever and more, my darling your love I do adore your core that I have explored for a few years, now that we are blessed to have a bun in the oven my loving has risen to new heights, I'm on a different level, we have found ourselves deeply in love, I Can't Resist your love, I want to show you how dear and special you are to me, baby wait, my King is this what I think this means, jumping out your seat to hug and kiss, I say baby with a smile just listen to me, calm down, I know you are excited to know what tonight may hold, all I know is that I want you forever close, your love has me floating baby, I'm floating on clouds with you, you better go boy do your thang she says as I say I want to give you the finer things in life, I want you to have all that your soul desires, all that you deserve, my baby I don't need all that you say materialistic stuff here on this earth, I have you who brightens up my life every day, I know my love, but you're worth so much, my passion erupts when thinking about the things you do, when thinking about the love you give, My Rib, we are destined to be together, this has already been designed before the hands of time, you were mine and I was yours, heaven has opened up its doors and sent you, my angel from above, oh how I could never get enough, my heart you have pieced together like fine art, you just don't know how you really make me feel, I couldn't live if I didn't have you, we were put together to do the things we are supposed to do, just you and me plus one, our life has just begun, here under the sun I want no one but you, my words are true, you say I believe you, I feel the same my love is plain, I haven't been the same since Our last Conversation, patiently waiting for our next one to come, moving closer I do with you looking up at me I drop down to one knee, you say you hold all the keys to my heart, I start to plead my case on how this love is not a mistake, today will be the day I make an honest woman out of you, this is what I want us to do, I never want us to part and with this ring I want to lock this union between us two, I place no one above you, no one can even enter my zone, you are where I belong, from here on out I'm making this decision without any doubts in mind, My Beautiful Find of mine, some say I should Take My Time, but my heart says otherwise, I know what I want, look deep into my eyes baby and you will find a true heart, so tell me baby are you all in, what do you wanna do? With tears in your eyes, you cry out yes baby, yes my King, I want you for the rest of my days, sliding this carrot on you across your finger, I say with this I promise to never go back on a promise, I will always be honest, forever I will be true, baby just me and you against the world, fast forwarding to the altar where we're both in agreement say I do, I will always love you this I know, your love has been imprinted on my soul, I will never let go.

SECOND TO NONE
(INTERLUDE)

In this club feeling alone on my own, yes on my grown man tip, at the bar taking a sip of this royal passion, smooth to the taste, I turn to see your pretty, beautiful, sexy, gorgeous face, I see no one else in this place, watching you dance, catching your eyes, we glance taking a chance putting my drink down taking my stance, sliding in on point, moving to the beat of how many drinks by Miguel, not wasting no time you welcome my kind by pulling me and turning yourself to show off what you have behind on that backside, grooving closely, seducing me with your hips, twirling with a dip, my heart skips, holding your hands high twirling you to your front side, eye to eye, swinging side to side, Second To None you're not tonight, moving Just Right, DJ slowing it down, he's on point tonight, in my hands I found a Queen holding you close your ass I squeeze, your palace I want to please, whispers of you coming home with me from you, as we groove staring into each other eyes, those brown eyes shine so brightly, lighting up this club, Second To None, precious you are dancing the night away loving the way your hips sway, your heart I hear it say, please hold it near, a fear of love I have, I want nothing more than to give you all that I have, as we dance our way up out this place, racing to my place so I can take my place, listening to what your soul says, place me above the rest, I'm your match, King, the best at what I do, I want nothing more than to please you, kiss you I do, crossing through my doors, love, real love is about to be expressed, hearts our hearts are beating through our chests, pleasuring each other in ways we have never explored, bringing so much joy, making so much noise, we don't have a choice, it's just that good, that great, from this day you will belong to me as I will belong to you, just us, just the two, Second To None, I only will and forever want you, always adoring you, showing you what a real Royal Lover can do.

MII: The Return of the King

ROYAL LOVER

Listen my love, mic check one, two, is this thing on, excuse me ladies may I have your undivided attention, all I need is a few minutes, a moment of your time to explain why I am that guy, that one you should know, why one night with me will be an Unforgettable Show, listen to my flow, can't nobody do your body like this King could, Royal Lover is what they call me, you would too once you feel the way I rip through your palace in between my sheets, there's a lot of things that I can't do, mistakes, I have made a few, but there are two things I can do better than the rest, writing poetry hitting you with my word play putting you in the mood, putting your mind in that rightful place is one, rocking your body with my weapon of mass destruction, yes I will have your body erupting with the tools that I possess, my only worry is if the one I choose can pass the test, you won't lose, loving you gently and smooth, I will be light as a feather but hard as rock pleasuring your body nonstop from the top to the bottom pushing your love to the limit, going until that sun shines I will be light as a feather, but hard as a rock, I will be going nonstop, you will be whispering your pleasures are hitting all my spots, thundering down with my raining weather, my tongue to your pleasure palace, soaked and wet you will become and I've just begun, your wetness will start flowing down my chin, you will scream out King you are the one while I'm gripping your thighs, ladies do me a favor and just sit back and relax take a sip of your drink and close your eyes and just watch me, can you see me, can you feel me close, as I start to raise you high, your thighs, legs locked tightly, showing you my might, my love making will last all night, you will bust twice before I even come close to hitting you with my long-lasting strokes, to the sky you float, I lay you down to pull you inside, we're at the point of no return, forever you will yearn for my touch, do you feel that little tingling rush, with just one thrust no rush, feeling all of me is a must, Take My Time you say, hitting those unknown spots I will unlike your last, he couldn't find them, I climb deep in with my vine, love is running through your mind, One Of A Kind that I am, putting your body on a pedestal, making you feel like

D. C.

you never have before with the way I explore your canvas, no spot will go untouched, I never miss, flipping you over grabbing your hips putting that arch in your back before I dip back in taking your mind, your body and soul for a spin, you never will want this to end, rubbing on your nice curvy body, loving your smooth beautiful skin, I proceed to go in pulling on your hair, into the mirror we stare, my strokes you cannot compare to another the way I dig with emotions to uncover your true passion and love, very fluent I am in this language your hips speak, the way you are calling for me, I'm totally aware as we stare into the mirror, I am taking you there, farther than ever before you scream I roar, I have more, turning you around so you can explore my strength, legs, knees are bent, grabbing your thighs with my arms, I perform better that the norm, lifting you high I slide right inside moving away from the bed, deep into your cave your love I crave, we're celebrating love every time you find the time for me to enter your spine, killing you softly, making your palace my fit, your next will not fit, I pack a heavy punch with this fully equipped, having your feelings all in a twist, pressing you up against the wall with a kiss, locking lips, quick strokes as I'm deep in moving fast in between your hips switching gears laying you back on the bed where passion strokes are made, slaying all your demons, no more feigning, I'm your pusher baby, call me when you are ready for your next fix, supplying you with what you need, I will fulfill your fantasy and dreams when you come to see me, you can open your eyes now ladies I thank you for your time, all through your mind you will remember me your Royal Lover, until the next time.

MII: The Return of the King

SLOW STROKES

The scene my Royal Room with candles that gloom with rose petals shaped balloons all over the room, actual petals on the bed and dresser just for you, with a mirror on my ceiling hovering over my throne, so you can look up and see, not just feel my Slow Strokes, I want you to look up when I get on, turn off your phone, no interruptions when I start to perform, the First Time I told you I'm nothing like the norm, here's a pause button if I get to deep while moving fast as I creep, just sound the alarm, and I will hit you with my Slow Strokes, you have summoned me, Your Love Freak, when I perform with my taser tongue, your legs will be shaking, my sheets you will be clinching, hot you will become like the sun, dripping sweat, wishing on a star, yes I'm the best, the button has been pressed, I'm in too deep, let me Slow Stroke while I creep through your palace, you say don't stop I just have to have it, I got you smoking good as my wood pleases your soul, you're high off me, ready you are to Lose Control, I'm giving you what you need plus more, Pleasure my love you have scored, with me licking and sticking, with you quivering and shivering, giving you what you been missing, willing I am to go where those others couldn't reach, my love making will have you preaching to the choir, calling my name out loud, Sire you're giving me that fire, burning my soul with all that you have baby go just go as you please give me that Greenlight Special but in those Slow Strokes, I go Pushing Inside Of You deep spreading you wide, so I can make you reach your peak, there's no one like me, your King is here to show you the other side of love, gazing into your eyes as I hit you with My Rollercoaster Ride, cruising to the side as I slide back in with your left leg up, deep into your guts is a must, I won't stop until you tap and quit, my love making is the shhh, I want to have a little fun with it as I flip the script, sliding out to rise to my feet pulling you closer to the edge of the bed, flipping you over, so I can give you something new instead, grabbing at your legs, lifting them high wrapping them around my shoulders and neck, so I can taste your palace from behind, as you hit me with Slow Strokes to my vine, I can do this all night,

D. C.

there's no time limit, like I said before I'm not finished until you're finished, this is just the beginning, yes you are winning when you indulge in my passion, laying you back down on all fours so that I can give you that back and forth actions, satisfaction is, well you know the slogan says it with me, guaranteed, I'm all you will ever need as I feed your insides with more of this Everlasting night, hitting you with my long and hard pipe, Taking You There, this I swear you will never want another under covers, my love you will discover that it has a hold that will never grow cold, as I go and go with my Slow Strokes, I pull out so I can invoke your spirits, I have some more sexual healing to give, just follow me My Gift to my balcony, in tune with each other we are, taking you far as I raise the bar, lifting you high towards the stars, howling at the moon, the button has been pushed, Slow Strokes baby she says, but keep doing what you're doing, yes that way, as we resume I have you in that explosive position the way I'm giving it to you, putting it down making all your love come up as you cum down, crowning me the King of your town, in and out, in and out, you shout from the forty-second floor, with each passing second I'm giving you what you will adore from here on out, you shout again as I moan, I'm feeling that rush coming on, so I hit my on button to give you those Slow Strokes to prolong this feeling, falling victim to that Lazy Love I'm giving and teaching, that love you've been missing in your life, hitting you with my Just Right, that real deal, no way you can doubt my skills, the way that I bring those feelings back, lost but now found, I'm on the right track with the way I'm putting it down, Slow Strokes from a real King is what you have found, precious as lost art, you didn't know coming into this scene that you would lose your heart, now we can never part, attached at the hip, you loving my well-endowed, my full equipped, that's in between my hips, making your heart skip a beat, Slow Strokes baby I'm gonna continue to give, so that you will forever think of me, your one and only.

I'M WHAT YOU NEED

I just want to Take My Time, even if it's on borrowed time, after you will come to find that I am One Of A Kind, once I enter your spine, thoughts of me will stay running through your mind, he's who you are with, he's who you are with, but rest assured I'm What You Need, one day you will be all mine, baby can you hear me, I'm What You Need now and forever, I will feed your soul with a love that will go on for all time, once I let it out the box my passion will never stop, it will never cease, I can be soft and gentle, but also I can turn into a beast once we start rocking in between the sheets, I'm What You Need, perfectly blind when you see me I'm What You Need, can't you see, I will never leave you be, can you feel me in your heart, the way I have you weak never reaching our peak, I'm going to make it so that you can't live without me, your love is what I seek, baby I'm What You Need, all the air you need to breath, everything you are to me, he's who you are with, he's who you are with, but I'm What You Need that's a guarantee, that's why you are now at this very moment here with me, it's plain to see he can't love you like I can, he tried for so long, now you need to come home where you belong in my arms, I have a master plan, I have the key to your heart in my hands, come and dwell in my royal land, my Kingdom awaits, if you want freedom come and take your place next to my throne, your heart is my home, on and on this love will live on after we are dead and gone, even in death, my love will press on, it's time you sing a different song, I'm the drugs in your veins, let go of that pain, he's who you are with, I'm where you belong, giving you everything that you could ever need, your past can't compare to me, your King I am willing to be, I'm What You Need, I see it clearly, we can have each other, we can take it from there, once I take it there you will swear there's two of me, why don't you just allow me, allow us to spend a couple of forevers together, I will weather any storm, nothing formed against us shall prosper, I am the author of our book, you came in and took my heart from right up under my eyes, I am surprised how you came into my life and shifting my feelings knowing that you're dealing with another, it doesn't even matter, I'm What You Need here under these covers, I will climb the tallest building just to prove my love for you, I'm a different type of dude, the others had you confused, I'm here to untwist your wires, baby I desire to love you more than you ever know, this is a lifetime show, this will never end, I'm gonna keep doing it, and doing it again and again, I can call you my best friend, I'm here until the end, swimming the deepest of seas, walking the dry desert just to show you I can last forever and ever, no one can do it better than I can, I am that man, that King, I'm What You Need, let me feed your soul with the passion from my fruits, I just want to show you how real love is supposed to go, there it goes that smile that makes my heart flutter, I just pause and wonder how can your last be so blind, never mind he didn't know you were One Of A Kind, but I'm not blind a different breed in me you will find, I want you for all time, I want you here with me, I want to call you all mine, with each stroke love will twinkle down your spine, never stopping, time don't wait for no man, I told you I have a master plan, I just want to sweep you off your feet like a broom, take you from that lonely place, I can brighten up your days, never leaving you astray, in me you have found a love that will love you better than the previous day, coming up with new ways to show you how precious you are, my shooting star, I just want to take you far, far away from here, opening your eyes and show you the light, you will never find a love this right, I'm What You Need, with each passing night I will make you believe in love all over again, in my arms you win, there will never be an end, I'm What You Need, just take my hand and follow me.

MII: The Return of the King

MY PARADISE

Opening my eyes every morning to see you My Paradise, you excite my world, precious you are my girl, adoring the very ground that you walk on, I will never leave you alone, I'm all yours, lost in your love island where no one can find us, you bring a positive plus to my life, from that first day I spoke your name I knew right then and there I would never be the same, you are the one to blame for me regaining my lost love, my heart was torn until you came in shining like the sun, you have given me that sense of really finding that one, that one and only, never again will we be lonely, I am here to be all that you will ever need, you have restored that love inside of me, the apple of my eye, My Paradise here on earth, without thinking twice knowing your worth I have found my Just Right, my Mrs. Right, My Paradise, for your love I'm willing to put in hard work for the rest of my life, overtime, so that the rest of our days you will be forever mine, never reaching our climax, this love will continue to climb on high to the top we go, never will I let go of you, My Paradise, your pretty brown eyes, hazel when the sunlight beams off them, God has brought us together for a reason this is the season that I will settle down, in you I have found a woman that I can place my crown upon, with The Key To My Heart in the palm of my hands, this will be a lifetime dance, there will be no chance of me going back on this promise I have made here today, with your name tattooed down my arm, you are here to stay, baby you take the cake, you can't be replaced, I will never try, knowing it will be a mistake, no one can compare or even come close should I say, I knew from that very first time I laid you down, that night you were all mine, forever imprinting on your heart, taking you away from those fake paintings, those clowns didn't know how to make real art, there are rules to this love making, never forsaking your soul, you have a hold that I can never let go, this is the beginning of our show, our movie, a Hollywood script, I want the world to come take a look at this trip we are on, I'm in heaven's arms when in your arms, it's you, wherever you are at I belong, taking my heart from out that cold, once I was frozen stuck in time, until you came into my life, My

D. C.

Paradise, my wife, my Queen, I've never seen nothing, no one of your stature, I will do anything just to please you, before you I was looking to my left, looking to my right, up and down, round and round, until I spotted you and those pretty brown, hazel when the sunlight beams off them eyes, you are my One Of A Kind, I know I couldn't find another like you, I love all that you do, we will fight through any stormy weather, we can get through whatever, we will make it work as long as we have love nothing will be able to stop us, you're my fresh breath of clear air, when you walk in the room and appear, my eyes and focus you command, forever I want to be here in this place call you, My Paradise, all I can do is think of you when we are away from each other, thoughts of how freaky we get when under the covers, I thank your mother for giving life to you, thanking your father for blessing me for what I'm about to do on bended knee all I can see is you in my life for the rest of my life, I will have my very own Paradise.

UNTITLED LOVE

You say you want it, but I don't think you really do, My Program will have you acting a fool, the way I get down when I'm doing my thang, you better ask somebody, I don't play no games, you won't be the same when you leave my sanctuary, I bring the pain, slaying your palace making you rain more than you ever have before, so tell me are you ready, do you wanna take a trip on My Rollercoaster Ride, once I lock my bar across your thighs there's no turning back, be sure you're ready to lose your heart to me, safe I will keep, you will love the way my tongue creeps, without you telling me your secret fantasy, I already knew what will make your body weak, just give into me, making your mind go so far away with no words to say, just moans as I grown, screams come on, ringing your alarm this is just the beginning so don't be alarmed when I start to perform unlike the norm, changing your world my sweet baby girl, beautiful to the touch, the more I give the more your feelings will rush through your body party, the way I have you acting naughty when I go deep inside baby I have you rising high off this Untitled Love, my angel, my dove, twenty-seven licks it took to make you cum, no baby don't run from this love escapade, I'm invading your space, I'm ready to take my natural place in between your thighs with my rough surprise, OMG slides out your mouth, oh what a night, off that Moscato, deep inside of you I go, I feel like I have hit the lotto, anywhere you go I will follow, I'm drunk off more than that Moscato, legs weak as I follow your passionate road signs so that I can find your ecstasy, working in the middle of your love is where I will forever be, with you saying OMG you have all of me, going crazy and wild, deep into your jungle, I want you to bare my child, hitting you with all my Twelve Royal Ways, turning you into My Love Slave, as we creep the night away, deep in you I want to stay, allowing me to call this place, your palace my Untitled Love, I will never place no one above, you have gave me all that I can think of with how you consume all of me, taking all of me, the deeper I go, with your legs pushed back just to show you what I'm made of, taking you to new heights, higher and above, giving you more than just love in all

D. C.

this back and forth action, it's more than just passion that's being dished, this love will have you reminisce after the fact when I'm gone searching everywhere hoping one day I will come back and hit you with my royal attack, with nowhere to run, wrapping your legs around my back so that I can push deeper, I know baby I am King, yes a keeper, making you a believer with each Slow Stroke as I coast and coast, you will brag and boast to your girls when the sun comes up rushing to call them on the phone to let them know you have found your home inside my heart, together we will be to never be apart, even in death this love will be an amazing piece of art, continuing to take you far, farther than ever before, I am yours and you are mine, I want this to last three lifetimes and even then that won't be enough, starting to give it to you rough, with passion bites to your neck and shoulders you can't get enough, the way I'm making you erupt, you're putting all your trust in me your King, making you sing at the top of your lungs, I have brought your love walls down with this Untitled Love, giving you what you deserve and much, much more, forever we will explore Sounds of Love making, patience is a virtue and all I want is you to be the Queen of my throne, my home is your heart, where I will always and forever belong.

MII: The Return of the King

YOU ARE IN CONTROL

Tonight, I'm in your hands, I want you to command my body, You Are In Control, I won't fight it, lying back to enjoy the show, your ride, I close my eyes as you climb on top seducing my feelings, taking me high as the ceiling, baby show me you understand how to make me feel, show me that sexual healing, show me this feeling is real, make me believe my Queen that I am the only one true King in your life, the only man in your world, curling my toes as your tongue twirls up and down my chiseled body, from neck to my chest your lips caress my soul, holding you tight as my royal pole grows and grows, give me that Queen all night Everlasting show, give me that feeling I've been searching and asking for, do the unthinkable, you start to slide slowly down below you go, with both hands you stroke my royal pole teasing me at first with a lick to the tip, then a kiss comes making me ball my fists, you're hitting every spot, not missing as I tell you not to stop keep going you got my rhythm flowing, you not even knowing what you are doing to me, making me feel light as a feather free as a bird as your tongue swerves up and down, around and around you're putting it down, lost but now found, You are In Control, I'm letting go, you start to move slowly giving me more of a show, clenching my pillow as you go putting me under your spell, your name I yell out, yes my love give it to me I shout, my Queen of my sanity, you put me in a place where I forever want to be, deep into your pleasure as you keep stroking me, picking up the pace, removing the hair from out of your face, so I can see that look upon yours, those last thoughts of my past you have erased from my memory bank, I am all yours, you are taking the cake I say, you say dripping that sweet nectar from your lips, flipping the script, climbing on top sliding my royal pole into your warm hot juicy box to make those hips pop, lock, dip and drop, my fully equipped is hard as a rock, stiff as a board feed me more my Queen, you're giving me everything that I need, plus, with each thrust sending a rush through my body, just as I imagined your palace is wet as ever raining like a storm with you on top I'm watching you perform, grooving slow my hands wrap around your curves grabbing low at

D. C.

your ass pushing the limit, I will last, moving fast, screaming and moaning putting it on me times three, reverse cowgirl, deep into your palace sea, you turn around to give it all to me, making me weak, almost reaching my peak, you don't know what your palace is doing to me, clearly Your In Control, the faster you go bouncing up and down, turning your head around to look back at me, so sexy you are, taking me far, giving me A Lesson In Love making, backboard is breaking, the neighbors we're waking, my legs start to shake and contracting tight, deep into your palace I explode with all my might, kissing you softly as I stand to give you an ovation for your royal Queen show, that was one performance that I will never forget, the way you controlled the show, a memory that I will never let go.

MII: The Return of the King

HOLDING YOU CLOSE

This right here goes out to you my love, I want no one but you in my future, I hold our love, you take me up, up and above where I wanna be, look through my eyes, so I can give you that release, I'm What You Need and What You Need is me Holding You Close in my arms, I hold the power and control, my love will grab you so tight, will hold onto your heart and soul with all my might, filling your body up with slow strokes, teasing you with slow kisses as I go and go, baby the way I flow up your river of love when I deliver when my vibrator tongue enters that spot, giving you that number one, sharp as a knife, I just begin to cut up, real love making this is not lust, I don't rush when it comes to laying you down on my Royal Bed where love making is made, intoxicated off you as the night fades away, screaming as you say you love the way my royal pipe slays your palace, swimming in you all night, giving you what you have envisioned, giving you what you have imagined, this love making is outta sight, I know you just gotta have it, King gives you that delightful touch, feeling that rushes from your toes past those thighs, sucking on your breasts while looking deep into your eyes, you stare back looking at me, yes you have won that number one prize, Holding You Close all night I will, delivering my skills, pleasing you I will, filling your heart with love real love as I build you up, overflowing your cup with my passion with each thrust, ecstasy in every touch, making sure you will never get enough of me, you will be calling me your Dream Catcher when you sleep, hunting your thoughts, so all you think of is me Holding You Close, there's nowhere my love won't go, with hurling winds, rain or snow our hearts will always flow, sticking close when I'm Holding You Close, our heartbeats and coast, in sync, in tune with one another, in you I have discovered my one true Queen, you mean the world to me, you're everything I will ever need, you feed my soul when I'm Holding You Close, all I can think about is never letting you go, this love I want to know for the rest of my years here on this earth, you are my worth, as I am yours, forever we will be exploring this mood that we are in, I'm a unique type of dude that can never be created ever again, this

D. C.

love is coming from deep within, while Holding You Close doing the most when our tongues touch my heart just explodes with love, feigning for your touch every second on the hour, my Queen you have conquered what I thought can never be conquered in this lifetime, forever you will be mine, I can't sleep at night if I'm not Holding You Close to my heart, my prized position, lost in your beauty, so natural, a work of art, you're the reason why I live, you are My Rib, My Gift, the way our bodies twist I just can't get enough, you take me up, up, up and away, with each passing day another level is reached, to the world I preach about the love I hold so dear to my heart, never in this lifetime do I want to see us part like the red sea, all I can see is you and me, King and Queen, no jacks, no jokers, you have me Wide Open, I've Prayed For A Love Like Yours, forever this love will be in motion, never at a standstill, I will always be true, staying real with you when Holding You Close, your love just flows through my veins, when Holding You Close I know our hearts will remain together forever.

MII: The Return of the King

ONCE UPON A TIME

A love of a special kind entered my life Once Upon A Time, but now I'm lost trying to find my Once Upon A Time, left with visions of you roaming through my mind, my One Of A Kind, I need my Once Upon A Time back in my corner, back in my life, I need my Just Right again, I feel as if there are nails deep within my skin, I can't win without you by my side, standing on the outside looking in, I need my best friend, my love, my Queen, the one I placed no one above, my Once Upon A Time, I need you to be all mine, on the outside I'm doing just fine, but on the inside I'm dying a slow death, lying to myself and others when they ask if I'm doing alright, trying to cope, believing in hope, wanting your boat to float back my way, dropping your anchor to forever stay, I need you to take your place back on my throne, back by my side, I lay with your picture at my side each and every night, with you staying on my mind, hoping you find your way back home, my life has come to a halt, a stop, to a complete freeze, my Once Upon A Time I need you, baby come cure my disease, each day I become more and more weak, dying on the inside, needing you to come and revive me and restore what is rightfully yours, my heart, my Cherie Amor, I will always adore you to the core, Once Upon A Time I used to explore your core, your mind, your body and soul, your Palace Of Pleasure, I can't handle this stormy weather, I reminisce on how we used to do it whenever, wherever, never will I come to find another love like yours this lifetime, praying that one day you will come to find your way back and be all mine, I will wait five lifetimes just To Feel Your Touch Again, I will do whatever it takes to have you back again, swimming the deepest seas, walking the hottest deserts, I'm willing to do whatever it takes, praying for that one special day that you come back my way, balled and chained to your heart, even though we are apart I feel that we can never part, no matter how far we are, the distance will never stop my love from existing, no other woman is even tempting my thoughts, I only think of you and the things you used to do, the way you used to make me feel, I now know that love you gave was real, you gave me all that I could ever need, all that I will ever want, I don't

D. C.

want another, you have my eyes perfectly blind, I need you under my covers, come back my Once Upon A Time so that I can rediscover that love you gave me from deep within your soul, your heart I will never let go, your love is all I want to know, I need you my Once Upon A Time to bring that show back to my life, I should've thought twice, I should have made you my wife, I could have stopped you that night from leaving me, but I allowed my pride to get in the away, when I should have set it aside and married you from that first day I laid my eyes on you, missing you deeply, I need you back my love to complete me, spiritually and mentally needing you with me for the rest of my days, I will never be the same until you come back and remain at my side my Once Upon A Time.

MII: The Return of the King

FOLLOW MY LEAD

Take my hand and just follow me to my Royal Room of ecstasy, I hope you are ready for me, I just want you to Follow My Lead, watch you will see what I can do, once my hands begin to creep up and down your body, my tongue will put you in a groove, a mood that you wouldn't want to lose, when it comes to this love making I will have you singing a different tune, headboards we will be breaking once I pull inside your womb, your palace, my heaven on earth, I just have to have it, enough of this explaining, let's get to this love making, lights I roll down low, as I strip you naked Usher seduction is the music you hear playing, laying you down with a kiss to your lips as I stand giving you a little dance taking off my shirt, next are my pants, I start to move slowly up your legs, your left and your right I spread, kissing and licking with your hands on my head, Oh's and Ah's is what my ears are being fed, making love with my tongue, soaked and wet is the bed, the night is young, you haven't seen or felt why I am that one, that only King of Kings, sliding up your stomach, kissing at your breasts as my hips and thighs take place in between yours, looking into each other's eyes as you reach in between my thighs and say oh my, what have I gotten myself into with a smile to a kiss with a stroke down south, you turning me over so you can feel him in your mouth, your tongue licks around, up and down, you Following My Lead, I read, turning you into a Queen, you're making me moan, I'm going to make you scream, you have skills, but let me do my thing I whisper, Taking Control I stand licking over your whole body, flipping you around now your back is exposed, biting you at the shoulders, getting you even more excited, loving on your body, I grip both of your thighs, holding tight I lift with enough might wrapping your legs around my head, Pleasure, yes, Pleasure is about to be fed, shakes and shivers are going through your body, weakening your legs as my tongue goes deep inside it, becoming weak even more, your waterfall starts to fall, with me in between your walls, slowing down to a pause, laying you down so I can fill your walls up with my fully equipped, hot and moist you are, King I am the right choice by far taking you up higher than the stars, into another planted, my seed is about to be planted into your mind I will stay, deep into your heart is where you will keep me safe, holding me close to your soul, after tonight you will never let go, never will I steer you wrong when you ring my phone, just be prepared for the way I'm about to take you there, sliding in as I stare at your love faces, my love erases any hurt and pain, each stroke is never the same, never dull and plain, as you scream my name and continue to rain down on me, through your eyes I see you are happy that you Followed My Lead, Taking Control, proceeding with giving you all these inches that you need in your life, doing you Just Right, as we are Body To Body, there's no question we're loving, hot in this room, baking your body like an oven, changing positions you role reverse, on top just like we have rehearsed, all aboard my pole, deep into your cave I go, you're rocking your boat back and forth, floating to your rhythm as we coast, you start to move fast like a speed boat, I slow you down spread you low so I can go and go fast from the bottom to your top, you feeling me deep, I sit up with you grooving to my touch, to the beat of my drum, I lock your legs with my arms and stand to my feet, I want you to feel me deep, all of me, slow is the first couple of strokes as I steady my feet, your arms are wrapped around me, you're yelling what are you doing to me baby, putting that arch in your back, you're loving my performance, your head falls back, with the way that I'm attacking your pleasure chest, pressing your back up against the wall we are now chest to chest, kissing filling you up, your hair all over the place your palace is about to erupt, overflowing your cup, you start giving that bounce I say yes just like that, higher I mount as you throw it back, we're running sprints, running laps, you gonna need a map for how deep I'm going, you cuming again is what you're showing, release, you just keep it flowing, I'll keep it going, on and on to the break of dawn, my gorgeous swan, this night will forever live on, never wanting to leave and go home, the way that I perform, laying you down I still have a few miles left in the tank, take this passion that's being dealt, never have you felt this way, opening your legs wide, deep I go when I pull inside, love falls through your eyes as I press your legs and thighs back towards your face, I rise going deep into your special place, my love making can never be replaced, Blessing You I am on this date 2016, taking the cake, this day will forever be with me the night we spent here in between these sheets, my legs becomes weak, at my peak, for the rest of the night in my arms you lay sleep, dreaming about Following My Lead over and over again for the rest of your days, becoming My Love Slave.

D. C.

OTHERS AFTER YOU

I wish I can take back that one day, oh my that one day I did that act that caused me a lifetime of pain, never will I be the same without you, Others After You only fill that void in my heart for a short period of time, searching and searching, trying to find another love of your kind, exploring and exploring the realms of this earth, this love, that love, but no love, none I can place above you, forever you and me is how it's supposed to be, thinking about each and every time we will creep in between the sheets, just thinking about it makes me weak, I begin to weep, I'm playing wolf and you're the sheep, your love can't be beat, each night I weep missing you, missing your love, I have dug my on grave, even with this dame on my side, it's just not right, she isn't you, not the same, I miss the way you walk and the way you move, the kisses you gave and the way you would misbehave with that tongue of yours, my number one love, I place no one above even though we are no more and I explore different fantasies each and every night, it's your love that lives deep inside of me, your love is where I want to be, these Others After You can't compete, they can't compare, I pray for the day you come back to me, until then I will sit on my throne waiting patiently for my Queen to return to her King, if you can hear me I need you my everything, screaming these words from the top of my lungs at the highest mountain, come back home so that we can spend a couple of forevers, you're the only one I want to be with together until never, we can get through this stormy weather, together we can just float high through the sky, come back into my life and break my heart out of that ice box, I tried reporting to the cops, that my heart has been stolen, but there was nothing they could do, they laugh leaving me on my own as I try and find you, I need you and only you, come back baby, I'm tired of these Others After You.

MII: The Return of the King

I CAN'T STOP LOVING YOU

Without beating around the bush, I'm going to come right out and say it, I can give you what you need, I can fulfill your fantasy and dreams, close your eyes and visualize the things I'm going to do as I tell you why I Can't Stop Loving You, from the first time I saw you I thought to myself heaven may be missing an angel tonight, I hope and pray my heavenly father doesn't mind, as I begin to express my delight, express why I could never find another of your kind, you always stay on my mind, I spend all of my time thinking about the life we share, never will I compare you to another, none even comes close to your stature, I see no one but you, you are my air that I breathe, you are everything that I need, I love your motherly qualities, it's more to you than what's in between your hips and knees, even though your palace pleases me, I Can't Stop Loving You because of the love we have built up, expressing my affection for you is what I want to do with one touch putting you in a groove, giving you my heart, I know I want lose, time and time again you have proven to be worthy enough to wear that Queen crown I have given you, in you I have found my everything, loving the way that your independent, how you don't need me, but you want me, feed my soul baby, never let go, allow this to be a lifetime show, there's nowhere my love won't go, all I want to show you is true and honest love, a loyalty that you will never be able to place another above, giving you that compassion that security to never fear love again, with you by my side there will never be an end, this is a love the world should know about, walking hand and hand with paparazzi popping out snapping pictures trying to figure out what this new love I have on my shoulder's all about, proud I am to say it, I Can't Stop Loving You, forever me and you, to the top of the highest mountain where we still wouldn't reach our peak, my life is now complete, having you with me brings a joy like no other, I have discovered that other side of love, through your eyes I see our love going up to different levels, digging deep with a shovel of love, I thank the man above for blessing me with one of his angels, to hold, to cherish, to love, never will this perish, here for all time, for the rest of our time I

D. C.

will love you through the good and bad times, I want you to always be mine, that's why I Can't Stop, will never stop,
Loving this you My Beautiful Find.

EMOTIONAL

So weak I have become, I can't eat, my thoughts won't let me sleep, I close my eyes and it's you that I always see, those happy times just you and me, Emotional I have become, baby I'm so weak, it's hard for me to breathe, you were my air, no way can I compare the love we once shared, needing you back in my life, I need you back my wife, I believe in our love, there's nothing I wouldn't do, missing the small things you used to do, missing your voice when you would call me your boo, the way you would kiss me to put me in the mood, oh how I need you bad, I can't take this pain, I'm about to go insane, hating the mistake that I have made, so Emotional, feeling like I'm lost somewhere in a cave alone, come home, it's like I'm lost deep into space, come back baby and take your rightful place, letting me back in I will show and prove never will I lose sight of what's right in front of me, but I was searching for all the wrong things, when all I could ever want, all that I could ever need was right in front of me, baby come back and feed my soul with your love once again, foolish I was to leave your side, my eyes played tricks on my mind, since then they have yet to be dry, I've told lies, played games and deceived the one and only one who was always down for me, not realizing I had my Queen all along, staring at my phone wishing it would ring with your number and tone, so Emotional, no matter how long I will have to wait, I will give anything for that day to come, wanting you back bad as a heart attack, sinking I am like quick sand, come back and take my hand, I need you back in my life's plans, come fulfill my Wonderland, I will do whatever is needed to have you back in my world, you are my girl, I'm wanting you so bad screaming at the top of my lungs, no it can't be true, wake me from this nightmare, I need you, you mean so much to me, I know this now that you're not around, so Emotional, I'm going down, so Emotional I've become knowing I can't live life without you, my one true Queen.

D. C.

WINDOW PANE
(INTERLUDE)

Staring out my Window Pane as the rain impacts the ground I start to reminisce, to the sky I close my eyes, I can only see you, Perfectly Blind, a Queen I have found, I miss the things we would do, wishing I can go back into time to change your mind, placing those sweet thoughts back on me, I need to be your King once more, I can assure you that your heart has never been explored with a soft, but hard real love down to your core, my heart is always yours, never placing no one above you, never giving what is yours away to a stranger, defending you in any type of danger, that always loving what you do type of love, loving you from all different angles, chained together like Django, my love will have you weak, sleep on the floor, waiting for me to come home with you sitting in front of the door, wanting another man, nah, nah, not anymore, give me that thang once more, come and remove me from this Window Pane, save me so that we can always remain in each other's arms, I will do anything to have the chance to show you this love is nothing like the normal, you are so wonderful, the only audience I need when I perform, safe I am when inside your home, your world, I need you in my life, this is a must, what I wouldn't give To Feel Your Touch Again, to hold your hand, I miss your kisses and all the freaky places they will land, come back to Lovers Land, come feed my soul with your energy, without it I will continue to be weak, blink after blink through this Window Pane hoping you will pass by so that I can grab a glimpse of what I have been missing, reminiscing on A Once Upon A Time, laying you down when you were all mine in between my sheets just you and me, listen baby to me speak, hear my cries through this Window Pane, I'm dying inside, each and every night I lay on your side with your pillow, it still smells like you, soft and smooth, oh how I need you, staring out my Window Pane wishing things can go back and be the same, us as one, as I see myself through the Window Pane saying there's only one who can come and Take Away Your Pain, will she ever, well that question remains.

MII: The Return of the King

TAKE AWAY YOUR PAIN

Watching from a distance, waiting for the right time to strike, the way he treats you just isn't right, you're not even knowing that I have you in my sights, call me a thief in the night, taking your heart to places of loving you the right way, trying to be your knight in shining armor throughout the rest of your days and nights, your King, my lady, my Queen I won't bring any harm to your heart, I'm ready to push start with my love, filling any gaps in your life with my love, if you've ever felt you ever went without someone loving you to the core, I am here for you to explore, I'm going to show you a different type of way to score, in the bedroom I'm all yours, that's too easy, trust baby believe, for what I have equipped in between my hips is nothing but a plus, yes, oh yes you will erupt when I fill your cup, your palace, I didn't even mention my tongue lashing, satisfaction guaranteed, I want to embrace your body in my arms and give you what you need, let me release you from his shackles and feed you my recipe, these eyes, my eyes sees Your Worth, a beautiful woman, best thing created here on earth, cherishing the ground that you walk on, bowing at your feet, your smell is so sweet, with rose petal like smooth skin, the hunt begins, catching you alone is the plan, time is ticking, enough of that hoping and wishing, I have you caught up in my web, love has led you here, I know you have another, but he doesn't do you right in between these covers, amongst other things, the little things, those everyday things, I miss you today type of love, your hair looks good baby type of groove, letting you know how much he loves you type of guy, take away your stress, holding you close each and every night type, don't you want that Take Away Your Pain with the force and might giving by the man above, giving nothing but that type of King Love, I have all the tools to give you what you need, allow me to enter your life and open your eyes to the other side of love, I will never place no one above, loving you with every touch, making sure you could never get enough, let me erase all those rough times, I have exactly what you need, in me you will find a love like no other, you will never leave, believe in me, step out on faith, let real love take its course, riding off into the sunset on

D. C.

my Clydesdale horse, turning your last relationship into a corpse, I will keep you under my spell, in my arms you will dwell for the remainder of your days, sometimes I will play the part of the Love Slave, when I hit you with My Twelve Royal Ways, you will be singing my song for the rest of your days, with me you will forever stay, to me you will always belong, treating you like the Queen you are, sitting next to me on the throne, fixing all your wrongs, turning that upside down frown into a smile, taking every bit of your pain away, from here on out you will never be the same since you have allowed me to Take Away Your Pain.

BLINDED BY YOUR LOVE

Blown away I have become, baby you are the one under this sun I need next to me for the rest of my days, love is written all over my face, my body loves your body, you know when I enter in between your waist and pull inside, taking my rightful place, before you I was in a place where I thought love didn't exist, it wasn't until I tasted your lips, taking me on a trip, it felt like a love scene from your favorite movie script, but this is real action, not fiction or fake when it comes to this satisfaction vows I do take, ready I am, I was a mess ready to break, I was sick of love, but you might be my therapy, Ray Charles to love you see, you have put that back inside of me, Blinded By Your Love, closing my eyes only to be guided by your touch, by your sweet smell, suspended in the air I become when you come near, I never thought I would love so deeply that I fear the day I will lose you, I will never be able to see another love, my heart only wants you, my eyes are Perfectly Blind, your smile unwinds my spirit, takes my soul for a ride, I hold you deep inside of my world, into my life, I want you to be my wife, Blinded By Your Love forever, this feeling is oh so right, filling my cup, overflowing, this love will keep you going, and going when I'm loving you through the night, we're never finished until morning, the way you perform makes me want even more, it's you I will always adore your love and your passion, I will forever explore not only your core, but your mind as well, finding new ways to make your body misbehave, your love I crave, my heart is at a steady pace with the love you give, you give me reasons to feel great, with these words I say, know that you hold the key to my most prized possession, without question it's dear to me, my heart, my heart is yours Blinded By Your Love thanking the heavens above for sending my angel, my dove to find this lost treasure, never can I compare or measure the next to you and the things you do, this is true, with these words I say, always just the two, just me and you.

D. C.

LIGHTS, CAMERA, ACTION

Welcome, please come in and have a seat, once again welcome to my private movie premier, while I get everything in gear, my movie will, is going to steer your feelings into my direction, without question I'm going to show out, give more than enough to talk about with your friends, coming up with a plan in your head to keep me fed, keep me close, after this show you will know real love, let's make a toast to never looking back at your past as we just float, I'm going to coast through your palace, through your temple, real love is very simple, sexy when you smile, I love your dimples, this will be the best love you ever had, I ask, are you ready, you shout out Yes, I call out Lights, I'm about to take away your stress, It's about to be a long night, are you ready for this test, you shout out Yes, I call out Camera rolling with a kiss from your lips to your neck with my hands feeling on your breasts, even in this dim light I can still see your silhouette, I'm on stage craving your sex, ready and set to give you this Oscar winning performance, equipped I am with an enormous package, here comes my Action, walking over to your seat, ready to show you satisfaction, taking you gently by the hand, now you stand close to my body, excited you are about my movie, kissing you slowly as you whisper out baby she's wet, I want you to do me baby my body is ready, I set and I go, pulling back the curtains, pressing play I'm about to show you why you will forever stay in my life, pleasing your soul all through this night, but enough with the dialog, blazing this is about to be, outta sight, marry me you just might, my movie is just that tight, putting your body on a pedestal, I'll show you that Just Right, making all your dreams come true, with all the freaky things I do, check my moves, as I lay you down and undress you with my caress, with my lips hitting your surface, the wait was well worth it, with my tongue giving your canvas a lick, my hands move and twist, feeling all over your body, from your neck to your breasts, when I'm done you will call out the best, past your navel to those hips my hands have a mind of their own, placing them on your nicely round curve, the others you deal with will be pushed to the curb, saying I'm that one you need here on this earth

MII: The Return of the King

while spreading your hips, I am the director and producer meaning I can flip the script at any given time, there's nothing I won't do to make you mine for all time, deep into your spine I will go, but let's take it slow, strokes with my tongue down where no sun can shine, I have you open wide, with two fingers pushing inside while I'm licking, licking while I'm pushing, moans while I keep dishing that love with my hurricane tongue, your legs becoming stiff, numb like symptoms, pleasuring you with My Gift, as I hit you with a twist from my tongue to your pearl, making your toes curl, your hair on the back of your neck rises, just wait until I pull out my royal surprise, I proceed with showing you what my movie is all about, leaving you with no doubts, I hope you can handle what I pull out of my boxer briefs, tonight I'm something like a thief, the way I'm stealing your heart, taking you far, beautiful is what you are, shining bright, my number one star, watching my every move you are, feeling my grooves, all I want to do is be with you is what you're showing through your eyes, as I enter your spine, it is time I give it to you Just Right, I will be your superman, I'm here to save you from the ones that are not worthy, you deserve that Love To The Tenth Power, stay with me, I will make love to you on the hour each and every hour, your body I will slay and conquer, dealing you no craziness, you're falling for a real King, I give you my everything, my all in all that I do, kissing you while pushing deep, slow and hard with my strokes, bringing down any guards that you may have up, touring your palace, up and down your halls, around and around your walls, deep into you I fall, your loving I hear is calling, your waterfall starts to falling, back scratching and all, nails deep, my name you call, King you're the best you shout out never will I be the same, I hold no complaints about your Lights, Camera, Action, hitting you with my stamp of approval, past satisfaction, we on that everyday double level, dug deep to where you can't let go, I know what you want, I'm What You Need, very aware of you wanting my lips right there and my body yeah right there, those hurt feelings you once had have disappeared, this love will live on for years and years, you will never fear my movie, your love runs deep through me, flowing fluently, bringing your stream down, a real King is what you have found.

D. C.

MISSING YOU

You never miss a good thing until it leaves you, what am I to do, going out of my mind, running out of time, wishing I can turn back the hands of time, press that button rewind, I can be the man that you deserve, searching this earth for you so that I can change your thoughts, no matter the cost, my heart is yours, you told me before when you are gone you will want me back, I didn't believe you then, but I believe you now, my pillow is soaking, it's hard for me to stay focused, needing you, I want nothing more than to please you, wishing and hoping that you arrive at my door, I want to hear that knock once more, I should have listened to you before this point, sitting here in my sorrow, drinking and rolling trying to ease my pain, my life has not been the same, going down like a captain losing control of his plane, sitting in flames, crashing and burning, I'm yearning for your voice, your touch, your smile, my hair is growing wild, I haven't shaved, I have been walking for miles with no shower, no sleep, hours and hours go by, and I can't think about nothing more than having you by my side, with no food gracing my stomach, I won't eat until I see you my woman come back into my life, I need you back my wife, Missing You like crazy, I should have thought twice, I wasn't loving you right, my last impression was that fight, you storming out the house with bags in tote, crying, while I punched the walls with all my might saying just go, thinking it was just a hoax, bragging while I boast, saying you will be back, days, months passed and no contact, what have I done, ignorant I've become, just dumb, thinking I can do the things I do and get away with it, looking up to the sky to plead my case with tears rolling from my eyes, sorry I am heaven, you sent me your angel and this is how I repaid your grace, no one can take her place, no more coming home to a hot plate, I miss my X's and Oh's, trying to get through my days, hitting my phone with I love you followed by a smiley face, your love can't be replaced, I can right this mistake, I'm Missing You baby come and take your rightful place, I want to feel you one more time, Missing You until I find your love once more, forever I am yours.

MII: The Return of the King

UPS & DOWNS

Our Ups are lovely, we smile, we are a joy to be around, I love you from the ground Up, we mess around talking about all kinds of stuff, showing each other that softer side, when looking into your eyes I know I have my Mrs. Right, with having no one else in sight, you're all I want by my side, laying by your side is what I want for the rest of my life, you do me Just Right, when we're Up late nights, I just can't get enough, pleasuring you is a must, I love it when I make you erupt, that look upon your face says you can't get enough, your moan takes me to another level and the heat turns Up, pleasing your every need, my heart pumps and bleeds for your love, everything is so right when everything is Up, kisses and hugs, oh baby I can't get enough, what really brings it Down, what is the cause of that bad stuff, the no smile, you start to see those frowns, you really don't want to be around each other type of stuff, now you're starting to think too much, is there another person in the bunch, oh it's going Down, your mind is in a rush, making things Up, when Down your frown becomes deeper, you start to watch them closer, any sudden move that will indicate someone else is in the mix, you will flip, but your mind is playing tricks, when things are Down they are lined with a tall fence, no laying close in bed, you don't get to feel that kinky twist, feeling stranded on dry land, somehow we have to fix this, you are my life's plan, but can you muster Up enough fight to weather the storm, no need to be alarmed, I know sometimes jealousy and feeling a little insecure for a moment will come around, reassuring you is what I will do so that we won't have to visit this Down not knowing its none of the above, I know it's normal for couples to go through the fire, but you take it to the extreme dragging me through the wire, cutting me deep when all I want is for you to be happy, for you to always wear that beautiful smile of yours, I know Your Worth baby, I am all yours, no one else will ever adore my love, you are the one for me, you have everything I need, I feed off your soul, I could never let go, even with our Ups And Downs I'm willing to go through a little pain for you even when in our Downs I'm still very much in love with you, for I know when we are

D. C.

Up there is nothing like that love inside that makes me erupt, the things you do take me Up, higher than the sky, overflowing my cup, so I will go through the little bitty stuff just to keep you around, I love you that much, I want you to forever remain the Queen of my heart.

MII: The Return of the King

BEFORE YOU CAME INTO MY LIFE

Alone in the world I was, that was until I met you, snatching my heart, changing my views, opening my eyes to something new, the other side of love, showing me the real you, a lost puppy I was, a stray looking for the right place, the right woman to keep for the rest of my days, with The Key To My Heart under your control, blessing me with a hold I can't let go, Before You Came Into My Life, my outlook on love was insane, wild and on the go, I was touching everything under the sun, every weekend I was on float, not knowing my own worth here on this earth, rocking dames' minds as well as their boats, hopeless I was I know, playing Russian roulette with my heart, before you became a part of my life I couldn't find that right one, that right fix, no one will mash and mix, it's just wouldn't click with anyone, my heart says you're that right one, Before You Came Into My Life there was no sun, no joy, I knew no happiness, feelings were missed, not feeling at all when I would Lay down with Ms. Jane Doe, my heart remained numb and cold, closed off to the world, not allowing anyone to break down my walls, not settling, needing not half, but whole, needing it all, before you came alone, Before You Came Into My Life, I wasn't ready to settle down but now I want to make you my wife, adoring you with all that I have until the end of time, forever you will be mine, I couldn't find another of your kind, searching and searching, blessed I am that I have stumbled upon my worth, my heaven on earth, the best thing God has ever created here on earth, thanking the man above for you when I go to church, I have found My Rib, see you came from my passion, this day was already written, I prayed for this day to happen, coming together to stay forever, you can see it through our eyes that our hearts are intertwined, Before You Came Into My Life I never thought I would find my never ending love letter, my One Of A Kind.

NO ONE ABOVE YOU

Seeing true love for the first time, wiping my eyes to make sure you're not an illusion, there's no confusion, I see you as my angel, my goddess, my heart rate is rising and I can't stop it, my heart is drawn to you, I am floating over to you as I stare into your beautiful eyes, hook on you my drug, those thighs, connected to those hips, my heart beat takes a skip, flipping the script on you, hitting you with words you've never heard before, your pleasing smile sends chills through my core, a junkie for your love, placing No One Above You, your love, my heart, My Gift is all for you, this is true, I will do whatever it is you want me to fulfilling your every desire, setting your soul on fire, setting your mind at ease, as I take you higher, cooling your body down with whatever it is you need, ready I am to feed your soul with a love you never had before, my blessing you are from the Lord, with my x-ray vision staring right through your core, your insides I will, I want to explore, spiritually through your mind, getting right with that love mentally, I go through finding out exactly what it is that makes you the happiest, what makes you the saddest, avoiding all that foolishness, I am the realist you never had, baby just give it all to me, I place no one above thee, all of you, love defines you, my love is true, I see no one but you, my eyes are Perfectly Blind, you shine with the brightness of lights, you give me the strength and might to go on, forever you will be the lyrics to my song, this love will live on, your heart is my home, I will never place No One Above You, your love is where I belong.

MII: The Return of the King

GIVING YOU ALL THAT I HAVE

Our time is coming to an end, I feel it in my soul, ready I am to let go, I have been Giving You All That I Have, but I see our love will not last, trust and honesty aren't enough, you want more, the world is what you want to explore, loving you like never before, material things I do not own, but I'm Giving You All That I Have, ready you are to go back to your past, my past when I was getting that money fast, coming and going, just flowing quickly, it's very tempting, but the inside of those jail walls I can't see anymore, my world is falling fast, your bags are pack, my love acts can't keep you here, I fear I will be in the grave on the streets, in a casket I will lay trying to please your happiness, but I will not revert, I will not repeat the same steps, baby hang in there with me it's not over just yet, not listening like a jet you're ready, set for takeoff, this love is lost she says you pay the cost to be the boss, pulling off with another in that 750i, I can't lie the BMW was hot, but that's just it, that thang was hot, later that night I heard a few shots down the block, walking up on the scene I see that 750 thing, a man and a woman slumped over, blood from their heads to their shoulders, saying to myself, baby you chose the wrong lover, not knowing what was under that cover, wish you would have discovered peace with what you had like I have, life and God, praying that your soul is at peace, forever you and me even still now that you're just a memory tatted on my sleeve, I can't believe it happened that fast, that fast life doesn't last, I was giving you all that I had, changing for the greater good, I wish I could take back the few hours and show you if you were to go down that road where your life would end, I need you back my friend, I'm sorry this has happened in the end, all that gleam and glamour for the night, life is worth more, important it is, heaven I'm hoping you get to explore the golden gates and roads, your heart is mine, I will never let go, may you rest in heaven,
my lucky number seven.

D. C.

I'VE PRAYED FOR A LOVE LIKE YOURS

I've prayed and prayed, time and time again, Oh Lord send me my angel, send me my Queen, send me My Rib, My Gift so that I can cherish her, so that I can give all this love I hold inside, I need someone by my side, on bended knee, closed eyes head bowed at your feet, just sit back and listen to me sending nothing but sweet music to your ears, lady have no fear, I was put here to fulfill your every need, whoever God shall send me I will live my life showing my Queen why I am that right one, never shall she need anyone or anything, I will provide cash, I will be your dream reality, this love will last, fulfill all your fantasies, I give you complete control, send me that one I can hold when my bed grows cold, I need that warmth here on earth, a righteous woman, a woman who is about something, a friend, a lover, someone I can take home to my mother, I have yet to discover that true love, I look to you my God above, I'm feigning for that drug, I don't want to give up on love, not when you have so much to give, this is my last chance, I want to live the rest of my life with that one, my wife, I've paid the price of being alone, coming to an empty home, no one calling my phone, invisible I've become, my Lord send me my one that will be there through thick and thin, until the end of time, someone I can wine and dine, My Beautiful Find, I pray and pray until you become mine for all times, I am waiting patiently on that one and special day even if it takes me a lifetime.

MII: The Return of the King

IGNITE MY FIRE

Ignite My Fire baby, Ignite my love, no one can ever do me the way you do me, opening me up and fulfilling my every desire, Igniting My Fire you have, setting my soul to a blaze, going round and round, I'm trap in your maze, turning me into your Love Slave, fulfilling all my fantasies, bringing out the best in me, especially when in between your knees, I hear those undying beautiful screams, you are my dream come true, I want no one but you, I will do whatever it takes just to keep you, I never want to be without you, special you are to me, through your eyes I see as my wife to be, nothing more will make me happier you see, you have set my soul to a blaze, you have me doing things I never thought I would, I never knew love could feel this good, I love the way you play with my wood, Ignite My Fire baby, show me you can give me all that I desire, with me pushing in deep and you screaming out Sire, hitting you with all power, your palace I have evaded and stormed your walls, breaking down your walls, making your water fall, giving you my all, picking you up to place you on the wall, now you're climbing the walls, with my hands around your throat and with our faces jaw to jaw, your face says it all, you're in awe, I'm breaking you down like a fraction, I'm all about action once you Ignite My Fire, I don't wear this crown for nothing, you scream out Sire once more, as I pull you to the floor with you landing on top, pop, lock and drop, give me what you got, deep in with a twist, work your hips, make my toes curl, I want my heart to do flips, lift my mind to a different horizon, my fire is steadily rising, my love has come out of hiding, it feels like I'm gliding through the air, I will follow you anywhere, to the ends of the earth, I know Your Worth my Queen, you're so Royal, you stand for everything that word means, it seems all I can do these days is think of you, think of us, the way we touch sends a rush up and down my body, you're the life of my party, love it I do when you become naughty and naughty, Igniting My Fire that was put out some time ago, this I know, forever we will grow, the things I will show will be Unpredictable.

D. C.

YOUR WORTH
(INTERLUDE)

All I ask of you is to do me the honor to always giving me all of your love, I'll do all the rubbing, knowing Your Worth I will go to the end of the earth just for your loving, Placing No One Above, your skin is soft as dove feathers, with you I will weather each and every storm, this love, my love acts will perform in different ways, you can be my puppet master and I will be your slave, I crave your touch, your kiss, your love is just enough, oh how much I need you my worth, wanting you to give birth to my child, in you I have found what I've been searching for, praying to the Lord above for My Rib, My Gift to you is my heart, never will our love be apart, shooting high in the sky, shining bright as the moonlight and stars, this love will go far, beautiful is what you are, precious as a rose picked from the garden of Eden, proceeding with surrendering my love to you, my words I speak are true, I wouldn't know what to do without my worth, I know Your Worth, here on this earth, an angel, my angel, loving you from different angles, this love I will forever hang on to, just me and you, forever my lady I will worship you, Your Wish Is My Every Command.

MII: The Return of the King

YOUR EVERY WISH IS MY COMMAND

Tonight, I give you my crown, go right ahead and put it on as I kneel to the ground to kiss your pretty feet while saying I am your servant, I will give you all that you need, Your Every Wish Is My Command, displaying your hand, I grab and kiss you gently before I stand, your first Command is for me to undress myself slowly, Taking My Time so that you can stare at my perfect shape, muscles all in the right place, chiseled body, with a smile coming across your face, you start to fan yourself while saying Oh My God with your eyes, I start to pull my pants and boxer briefs past my thighs, your eyes grows big when you see what's in between my thighs, tonight is about to be One Of A Kind, one of those nights, invading your mind, so that I can love you for the rest of your life, instructing me to dim the lights and come over to the bed where nothing, but sweet love is made, Your In Control, I'm your slave, Commanding me to undress you from your head to your toes, you say wait leave my heels on and grab my Forever Rose Petal body lotion, so that you can perform a massage and get this thang in motion, I comply and begin to rub you down Just Right, up and down your back towards your butt spreading your thighs, you look back with that sexy glare in your eyes, I turn you over, so that I can massage your front side, making your passion rise when I pass over your perfectly shaped breasts, your body curves to my touch, loving my caress, Ready, Set, Go, you're Commanding me to go down low with my tongue, ready you are to bust and cum, I can feel your water starting to stream down, wrapping your legs around my neck with your hands on my head, so that I don't move from this position, we're on this freaky mission, you got me deep sea diving, I'm swimming through your river, you respond with a quiver, love is what I am going to deliver, you begin to sing clear and loud, shouting proud, I've been down for a while, your feelings I'm driving wild, a King you have found, you say baby enough of that foreplay now, climb on top and give me your love, come and put it down, I stand up catching you staring at what's between my thighs, standing tall ready to hit you with

D. C.

all this might, from that look I'm getting I see that I qualify to enter your palace, moving towards your palace opening your legs and thighs so that I can pull inside, tasting your lips with a kiss, interlocking our hands first, gasp you do as my royal slip through and through, not giving you all just yet, up and down, long strokes, you call out you're the best, with a passionate pound bringing all your walls down, you hold the crown, my crown, Queen of my town, taking you up as I fill you up with my royal endeavor, what you're feeling right now can't be measured to this fella, to this King, you let out a scream baby keep giving it to me, wrapping your legs around my waist, so I can go deeper in between your special place, your past I have erased, your palace is mine after this day as you Command and say, my King show me your strength in these arms that I'm rubbing on, I want you to raise me high as you perform, working you ten times better than the norm, hold on tight my love we are about to take flight, up and away as I slay and conquer your love, not playing as I fill your cup, overflowing you are, shining brighter than all the stars in the galaxy, I am your Dream Catcher, forever your reality, going deep, enjoying my moves, giving my all to you screaming and back scratching as I do what I do, Commanding me to put you down even though you're loving this satisfaction, I'm your Co-star tonight, I'm about action, turning around you say this is why I kept my heels on so that I can stand with balance as you perform, bending you over, so that I can get back into that warm place, love is written all over your face, you grab your ankles as I pull in teasing you with my tip, its beyond hot in here, my sweat begins to drip and drip from my chest, tonight has been the best, the greatest for us both as I coast you feel me low, hitting you with power, making you bloom like a flower in the springtime, smacking you from behind, fine as wine you are, your body bent with an arch, this is poetry in motion, divine, I keep stroking and stroking, picking up this Rollercoaster Ride, you Command me to turn you over to the front side, Why? I reply, I'm doing just fine, I'm almost at my peak, you say I want to look you in the eyes when you and I explode inside of each other, we switch, I open you wide pushing the covers to the side, making sure you feel me deep, you pull me closer, I'm feeling weak, giving you the best of me, making Your Every Wish

MII: The Return of the King

My Command, making them come true, I am King of your Lovers' Land, completing this night with a kiss to your frontal lobe as we cuddle the whole night away falling asleep in each other's arms, you will never be able to get enough of the way I perform.

D. C.

I WON'T SETTLE FOR LESS

I know what I want, I'm putting my foot down, I Won't Settle For Less, I want nothing but the best, no ordinary love, I Won't Settle For Less, I need someone who can take me up and above, an exceptional love is what I'm looking for, someone who can fill my soul with joy, exploring my every thought, true love can never be bought, all it costs is your heart, two becoming one, not allowing nothing or no one to come in between, I Won't Settle For Less, I need that Everlasting, inseparable love is what I mean, my one true Queen, no I Won't Settle For Less, love is ready to burst out from my chest, where are you my love, my life quest is to find that one who will make me put these foolish games to rest, where are you at for real my love, I Won't Settle For Less, I will play the part of a fool just to find you my treasure chest, I will show and prove that my love can move mountains, I only want to drink from your fountain, with me you will not lose, I choose not to settle for plain happiness, I want that I Can't Live Without You type of happiness, read my lips, listen to my words, I need a lifetime partner to come and fill my cup, to come and forever go on this trip of love, I will never quit, my love will continue to fill you up, enriching the love you already have, making it evolve so that it will last, so many from my past had their chance, but I don't play, I am not a boy, I wear grown man pants, no time for games, I'm taking a firm stance, beauty is not the only attraction I have to dames, it's your mind, personality, your curves, how the inside your palace makes me feel, will I forever be, loving, a professional woman, that's such a turn on to me, see it's other things I need, caring, compassion a love that's satisfaction guaranteed, turn me into your feign, give me what I need, I Won't Settle For Less, make sure your love making is at its best, someone who brings no stress, a love that will never rest, I Won't Settle For Less.

MII: The Return of the King

MY SWEET LADY

You're my lady, My Sweet Lady, without you even knowing, without me even saying it, I dreamed about you My Sweet Lady, ready I am to enter your world, to you I defer all my love, precious you are as a dove, you take me high and above My Sweet Lady, there's none I can think to even compare, you are a rare breed, I want to forever feed off your love, come take your rightful place beside me, allow me to take you Up, Up And Away, my love is here to stay once I place my heart in your hands this will be a lifetime dance, oh My Sweet Lady I want nothing more than to be your man, drown me in your love, I'm falling fast like quick sand, baby take my hand I have that master plan, let me escort you to my Lovers' Land, saying My Sweet Lady as I kiss your hand without you even knowing you have my love flowing, My Sweet Lady you don't know what you have done to me, your King to be, I see you with me, in my arms is where you should forever be, holding you closely so that our heartbeats become one, become in sync, you're my lady, My Sweet Lady in my mind we're getting X-rated, love is what we are making, with passionate kisses, all your wishes come true, the things I can do will blow you away, forever you will want to stay by my side, my ride or die, look deep into my eyes, now close yours, can you feel my touch, do you feel my warmth, sending a rush through your body party, you will love it when I get naughty My Sweet Lady, such a beautiful lady, I am ready and willing to give you what you have been waiting for, ready I am to give you what you have been missing, showering you with a love that is deep as the ocean sea, all I see is just you and me, you open your eyes and to your surprise you still feel me running through your veins, my love will make you sing to the heavens, I am your blessing, your angel in disguise, My Sweet Lady I am in this for the long ride, are you ready to be filled with nothing but pleasure to your flesh and mind, deep inside I will go to find your hidden treasures, my love can't be measured with a ruler, I am King, the ruler of your town, now that I have found what I have been Soul Searching for, ready I am to explore every aspect of life with you, I know just what to do, I will be your Stress Reliever, just say

D. C.

it and I will deliver My Sweet Lady just say the words and I will pleasure your canvas, stroking your curves making sure no place on your body goes untouched, I don't miss, my love will have you sitting at work reminiscing, I am your King here on this earth, My Sweet Lady, I know your worth, no matter the cost, the purse, I will pay it just to have you next to me where you belong, forever together you and I, a perfect love song, this love will never die, no matter the storm this love will love on.

MII: The Return of the King

ROYAL THERAPY

Sitting in my office waiting for my three o'clock appointment, I hear a knock and my door swings open, my secretary is showing my client in, our session is about to take motion, let's begin, I say please come in and sit or lay whichever you prefer, take a load off, get comfortable, leave all your stress, doubts and fears at the door, you are here for me to explore your mind, body and soul, just sit back and let go, now tell me what's on your mind, let's start there, as I gaze at your beautiful face, your pain will be erased once you leave my side, an Unforgettable Night is about to occur, as we begin you start telling me how you want to unleash the love that lives within your soul, but yet have come across that one who deserves you and all that you're worth, as you continue to go on, I sit back taking it all in jotting everything down on my pad with my pen, you are a strong woman who doesn't need a man to win, you want to let a man in, but don't know how is the impression I'm taking as you profess all that you have to offer, with being well aware of the hurt and despair that can come along with being with a man, choose your man wisely I say, you deserve to be treated with royalty and nothing less, never Settle For Less, it won't be all good days, with hugs and kisses, so find that one you are willing to go through the bad days with knowing that the storm will pass over and he is your heaven sent, that shoulder you can lean on when life presents obstacles, that one you can never let go, if only it was me I would show you so that you understand what I mean, let's proceed with taking care of your needs, you start to talk about your body, how you feel so erotic at times, wanting someone to come along and explore your fantasies, someone who can come and make you weak in the knees when he licks in between, a real man is what you need I see, you start to undress me with your eyes, you stand up walking over to the door to make sure it's locked tight, I ask what are you doing Ms. Right, you say I have been coming here for quite some time now, and in you I have found what I want, what I have been looking for, I want you to explore my insides, you already know what I want, I let you run free all through my mind, I feel it's time you give me what I feel is mine, as you glide over to my desk with your hands rubbing across my chest, up to my face to remove my glasses as you gaze into my eyes, your passion rises, kissing me on the side of my cheek, asking me to give you a drink, I smile and say are you sure, do you really think that's a wise choice, once I start you will scream my name, my secretary may hear your voice while I'm deep inside, with your eyes clearly saying yes, with a charming smile that I will never be able to forget, while I pour I continue to explore your deep secrets, buzzing my secretary to let her know to clear my schedule for the rest of the day, this patient is in dying need and want to stay for another session, you're blessing your lips with a sip, you remove your skirt and slip, showing me you're ready for this royal trip, walking over to my radio to play something slow, you motion my way with a sway in your hips, grabbing my hand placing it on your ass while you ask how can a man not want all of this, keeping my cool with one hand on the radio and the other holding my face as my eyes stare at your waist you're putting me in this place where I want to be, since you've been coming here you say when you leave my office and close your eyes all you see is me and the things I want you to do, I want you to invoke my heart with your love, sending a rush through my body as you push me back into my chair to straddle me, looking deeply into my eyes, you loving my lashes, calling me Snuffaluffagus with a kiss to my lips, removing my tie from over my head, putting it on yourself, unbuttoning my shirt, touching on my chest, your feelings are going berserk, showing my strength I lift you up to lay you down on my desk, ready I am to give you the best you've ever had, you have met your match, Taking My Time, no need to rush through the drill, I'm going to make sure you feel me deep in your spine, with each and every stroke, you will know when I'm Down Low, the way I flow through your body, deep inside your special place, my love can't be erased, going at a steady pace, the look you give when I touch your warm embrace is priceless, I can't form the right words to say, see you take the cake, the way you shake and bake, it's getting late, but I'm not worried about the time as I enter your spine from behind to give you more of a good time, you will never come to find another of my kind here on this earth, heaven is where I was birthed, I flew down to give you your worth, to give you a piece of my crown, the way I'm putting it down you won't hurt anymore, your stress has left the building, as I explore your deep secrets, I am the one you will forever be needing, giving you what you have needed for some time, our session is ending as I kiss you from behind, completing my Royal Therapy by giving you all that you will ever desire, putting out your fire, you scream out sire, your body I have devoured until next time I can enter your spine, your homework for the night is to dream of different positions that you will want me to have you in the next time I can hit you with my Royal Therapy, I will be invading your mind, this session unlike any other kind.

D. C.

EXPLORING YOUR FANTASIES

Deep into your mind I go, deep inside exploring Your Worth, learning your ways and your mindset, seeing what keeps those feeling burning inside, deep inside of your heart and soul, taking your dreams and turning them into reality, sex on the beach is one of your fantasies, soft white sand, close to the waves we land, we stand in each other's hands, a kiss to your lips, a star shoots by, your heart skips as I gaze into your eyes, my hands slide to your hips, causing a dip, a sway by the way if I can say, I am craving you in a different type of way, you make me do things I normally wouldn't do, turning me into a slave as we lay, dark blue water crashing, our tongues lashing with the water splashing, we're having the time of your life, I'm always going to give it to you Just Right, loving you all through this lovely night, with the stars and moon as our light, you're shining so bright, I'm swimming through your mind showing you how a night can be, Exploring Your Fantasies, that right there was the romantic side, I see you have some freaky tendencies that sit right here at the forefront of your mind, blindfolded while I hit you from behind, oh my, my, my, your fantasies are one of a kind, look at this find, you want me to tie you up with chains, spank you a little because you misbehaved, I'm your Stress Reliever, today I'm going to give it to you the royal way, speechless you become with no words to say, a smile comes across your face, bring it my way, give it to me in the worst way type of fantasy, thrusting you hard making it so that you feel me for the next three days, this can be your reality, Exploring Your Fantasies, driving down the highway at a steady pace up the coast, next thing I know you're giving me that sexy look, with your hands hooked on my flesh, rubbing on my body, kissing on my chest, I speed up my coast, you start to pull off your clothes telling me you want me most, no time I say we have to go, no worries Papi just sit back and drive I go, you quote, you go, I float, your hands go down below, pulling out your Royal pole, with a kiss, a lick, a slow suck to the tip, my passion erupts, he's almost fully equipped, becoming real stiff, your tongue hits me with another lick, up and down, your right leg swings round, on top you are now, cruise

MII: The Return of the King

control button I push, spreading your cheeks, elevating your levels, turning the a/c on didn't help, I still have you hotter than the devil, with one eye on the road as you explode type of fantasies, here's another one I see, up in a room, the twenty-sixth floor, with you and me on this balcony, the stars you want to see as I love you from behind, pulling on your hair lifting your head to the skies, sexy you are under the starlight, turning you around to prop you up on the edge wrapping your legs around my waist as I push inside your warm embrace, deep breaths you take, as we love the night away type of fantasies, there's one more I see, oh you little freak, I'm with it my Queen to be, let's find a place so that we can creep, no sheets needed, free is what we will be, park we are underneath this tree, kissing with lip biting, these urges we can't fight them, it's one a.m., the street lights are dim, you open your door telling me to come and explore, walking towards the hood of the car, standing there with nothing but your shirt and heels on, your curves are right on point, you point with your finger, signaling me to come, in my mind I run, but I play it smooth and cruise, a real cool dude, we're in this kissing type of mood, you drop down to pleasure, waking him up so you can weather your storm, you won't be able to measure to none, I'm not your norm, standing you up so that I can perform, placing you on top of my hood, spreading your legs to look at all that good, with my wood rubbing on your pearl, I'm about to take your world for a spin, pushing deep within, your nails are deep in my back, I stay on the attack, showing you I know where all your spots are at, I have you breathing harder with the way I'm freaking you, legs and knees are shaking, your heart I will never bruise, pulling out, you grab to kiss and suck with your mouth before you turn around, I look around, checking to see if anyone heard these freaky sounds, from the back I'm putting it down, I howl at the moon while giving you that boom, boom, clap, invading your map, taking over, you're loving the way I grip your shoulders type of fantasy, I will provide and succeed, give you what you need, when it comes to Exploring Your Fantasies.

D. C.

SORRY, I LET YOU DOWN

Listening to you fuss, scream and shout as you storm around the house in a rush, with more and more shouts about how I took your heart and drove it into the ground, a great woman in you I have found, but I choose to run around town with this one and that one, looking for what I had at home, bags packed you're ready to get on, saying this is your last chance to keep me here, what do you have to say for yourself, King? Taking a deep breath, swallowing that big knot that's in my throat, wiping the sweat from my palms on my shirt, in my mind I say I can't lose her, here I go, my love I have done some hurtful things, I swear to God things I didn't mean, I can't believe how I have betrayed your trust as I lusted the night away, this dame and that dame, none equals your name, without you I will never be the same, I hate I did you this way, please stay, let me wipe your tears away that I have caused, a slight pause, then I say it takes a real man to admit when he's wrong, but a real man should never had any wrong to admit to because he should be only loving that one, all the blame belongs to me, fronting while I ran the streets like it wouldn't matter if you stayed or went, all along I knew with you is where I belong, I am nothing without you, I need you to stay home so I can make some right out of this wrong, I know this is my last chance to keep you, from here on out I will cherish the ground beneath you, from a boy to a man I have grown, I'm ready to be with only you, no more lies, no more late nights, I'm ready to fight for what's right, what's right is us, give me those bags, baby unpack, allow my love back in, together we can win, I will never let you down again.

MII: The Return of the King

I CAN'T TAKE THIS PAIN

I was your Stress Reliever, Lazy Love all wrapped up in one, your Hey Now, your Showdown, putting it down when entering your town, but now you're nowhere to be found, I came home and found drawers empty, closet ram shacked, no more clothes on the racks, someone tell me where Aston Cushier at, am I being punked, I didn't see this coming, I gave her everything she ever wanted, I don't understand this merry-go-round, pleasing her to the core, I was the man of her town, how could she go and hurt me the way she has, walking down my stairs to the kitchen grabbing a glass and a bottle, popping the top to pour, but I ignore the glass and walk right past the counter, turning the bottle upwards, mumbling words to myself, trying to ease my pain, I feel the rain starting to pour and hit my Window Pane, the woman whom I adore to the core is gone, was it ever true love like I thought it was, it wasn't supposed to go this way, every day I wake without you by my side, taking your rightful place here at night, takes my breath away, oh how I wish someone can come change this day, my world is crashing down around me, so difficult to love another, now hurt is all I see this can't be, I Can't Take This Pain, walking through my den, I see my key and a note side by side and it reads, King, I can't lie, for some time now I've been living a double life, sneaking out here and there, using your car to meet my other elsewhere, as I read I drink, feeling rage and pain, she goes on to say, it's not you it's me, I will always love you for the things you did for me, but I must move on to find myself, I know you have dealt with this before, but I must explore my options, I'm leaving like this because I know those eyes of yours would have stopped me from leaving, drinking more and more I am, here I was playing the rightful role, but I guess her love grew cold, I should have been smarter, I should have known, now that she is gone, someone come and save me, as I drink I still miss the way things used to be, with you smiling all the time, missing our late night creeps, the way you would blow my mind between the sheets, the way you would put that thang on me, nobody is touching your physique, mystic, mysterious, I'm growing delirious, this is serious, I'm in need of your

D. C.

love, I need a drug, a single dose of you will hold me a lifetime, still I can't believe you betrayed me and gave away what once was mine, pulling my mind back together before I'm all the way gone her letter goes on to say, at the end of the day, you will always have a place in my heart, sorry we had to part, goodbye and I will always love you, what am I to do, lost I am now like art, what am I to do, I need a real one to play the Queen's part, drinking this Grey Goose, guess I have to find someone new, she will regret she ever turned me loose, I Can't Take This Pain, but I won't allow it to break me down, I wear a King's crown for a reason, I am every season wrapped up in one, the damage is done, mad burning like the sun, I am the one she will come back running to when dude turns her loose, another sip of the goose and another sip of the goose, I'm going to shake this pain, a King I will always remain, your highness.

MII: The Return of the King

TO FEEL YOUR TOUCH AGAIN

All I want to do is see you, I just want to feel your body close to mine, baby I don't need no wine, heavenly intoxicated with just one touch from you, your hold turns my cold days around, in you I have found the one I will forever need, the more I get the more I want, baby feed your love into my soul, attach your heart to mine, I will never find one as fine as you who stands before me, my heart is yours, my body is here for you to explore, your passionate noise is the song, I want to hear that moan, I have no fear when you're near, baby let's be clear, no lust in my body, I want you for years upon years to come, I love to make you cum how your body goes numb and weak with me in control, reaching that peak your love I seek, forever in a day and night this I want for life, your hold is something I can't explain, I haven't been the same, it's simple and plain to see, you have removed these dark clouds, stopping all the rain from pouring on top of me, To Feel Your Touch Again, swimming across the seas, dropping to my knees to please, waiting patiently, just for you to ease my pain, I said before never will I be the same, I hold no complaints, closing my eyes, just to see you, my love signs are pointed your way, escaping, lost in your love, no I don't want to be found with the way you put it down, I love seeing you on the mound, waiting for your perfect pitch, my pusher girl, rocking my world, I get that fiend inch and twitch when I can't feel your touch, it's a must have, I see you and just grab, taking a hit to calm my nerves, my special love, I place no one above you, take me high and above, now that it's just me and you, be my super woman, save me here I am not giving a damn about what the press may say, from this day I will always scream your name, you take away my pain every time you come with that touch, oh how I love you so much, I could never stop this love, until the next time I Feel Your Touch that sends a shock through my soul, know that I will never let go of you, my love is here to stay until my last day.

D. C.

YOU'RE INCREDIBLE

Amazing you are, the brightest of all stars, shining your light in my life, giving me more than I could ever hope for my love is forever yours, my heart will forever pour love in your direction, the affection you give is the reason I live, you are My Rib, this will never end, my happily ever after, my life's book with you in every chapter, bless the day our pastor said you may kiss your bride, beginning a new life with you by my side with one look into your eyes I knew this was Just Right, giving you my eternal love, you don't know what you have done, awakening a love that's so strong, forever holding you in my arms, my miracle woman, when cold I will keep you warm, my love will perform in ways you've never seen before, I adore you always and forever I will be yours, my full-course meal, I couldn't deal without your love, my rose this is true, my heart only wants you, now and forever no matter the stormy weather, together we will stay I belong to you, my heart is in the right place, You're Incredible, I want to wake up to your face every day, fall asleep to your smile when we lay the night away, your rightful place is here beside me on my throne, my kingdom is your home, this is where you belong, You're so Incredible, I never will let go, it's the way your words flow, the way you glide and float, You're so damn Incredible the way you coast, the way you're lips stay moist, you leave me no choice, for life I want to enjoy you forever my Cherie Amor, I want you more and more, your mind, body and soul I will explore, You're Incredible, this I know, I love your freaky love show, you love My Magic Show, My Twelve Royals Ways, going Down Low, You're Incredible, this I know, my heart tells me so, your heart I will never let go.

MII: The Return of the King

LIFT OFF, TAKE OFF, BLAST OFF

Sitting in this room alone, just you and I, my eyes going up and down your thighs, hold up let me set the mood rewind, you're standing there in your long black dress with a slit up the side, playing peek-a-boo with your thighs, sipping on your wine, your body is fine, those curves are perfectly wined, Just Right, your face, oh what a beautiful sight, as I stand there fresh, nice and tight, black button down on, open with my chest showing, it's snowing rose petals everywhere, I go all out for you I swear, a candle there lighting up the room just enough so that I can see you when I touch you, it's a must, your body I crave, ready to Lift Off, baby what are you saying, making that move smooth, intoxicated I love it we're on this freaky warfare, today launch you will be flying high in the air, ready for Lift Off we're rising higher and higher in the air, seducing me with your lips, you got me on fire, my hands on your hips, your love I desire, dancing to each other's grooves, our tongues doing all kind of moves, our clothes slowly being removed, equipped with the right tools, tonight, you win, never will you lose when dealing with me boo, laying you gently onto the bed, love is about to be made, forever wanting me for the rest of your days, my tongue becomes a maze the way I move up, down, left, right, side to side, moans and cries, as I Take Off in between your thighs playing with your pearl, making your passion rise, the temperature rises, the looks in your eyes brings joy to my life, you feel so right, the way I'm licking your Georgia peach, flying high, reaching to the heavens in the skies, squeezing your thighs tight, your passion starts to cum down and we're not done, I've just begun to Blast Off through your body, welcome to my Royal Party, kissing your lips, as I get started with a slight thrust, making sure you're feeling me is a must, in King you can trust, amazing you are when your naked, loving every minute, every second, concentrating on you, turning on your juice box, making you warm and hot, deep into your spot, my spot, your Erotic Zone is where I belong, pressing our bodies close with your hands, gripping me tight, I will be flowing through your body all night, acting a fool, breaking my own rules, Falling In Love, could it be true, deep in the inside of

D. C.

you, position after position, switching and tongue licking, never am I finished until you're finished, your happiness is my mission, taking you to another level, as we Lift Off I'm keeping you as hot as the devil when I Take Off through your palace of love taking you to the heavens above making you Blast Off into the night, my strokes are outta sight, hitting you with my might, making you feel nice, just the two, just me and you sounds right, I need you in my life, through the night we continue to take flight, this love will never stop, these feelings are Just Right.

CRUSHING ON YOU

I don't know how this came about, friends at first, but now I'm starting to see you in a different way, feelings are beginning to take place, scared I am to say, to let you know how I'm feeling here on this day, I don't want to ruin what we have, our friendship, that would be selfish of me, but these feelings are ready to rip, bust through my chest, I just have to have you, at night I can't rest, I feel you will complete me, I think you hold the key to my treasure chest, I see you going through the mess, tired I am of hearing about you're dealing with these unworthy clowns, in my arms is where you belong, I will never bring any harm to this relationship, I don't want our friendship to sink, so I sit back and let my ship sail off into the moonlight, I dream of you each and every night, knowing I can do you Just Right, not knowing if you even see me in the same light, not wanting to take that chance, holding my feelings in check, I want this dance to live on forever, holding my stance, I am here to help you weather any storm that you may go through, watching you prance around town, another fool has come around only to hurt you once again, with me you will win, your King is right here in front of you, you don't have to look any farther is what I want to tell you, with me knowing every quality that you are looking for in a King, I have them all with much, much more to give, your heart I want to explore, forever cherish and adore, I will always be yours to hold to have by your side, that look from your eyes takes me on a ride, Crushing On You I am, I want to know you from the inside out, giving you that ultimate satisfaction is what I am about, never will I deceive you, I'm what you need, only if I could work up the courage to feed you my thoughts, I would show you love doesn't cost a thing, I will give you what you have been waiting for, that ring.

D. C.

A REALLY GOOD FEELING

Just say the words my love, just say the words and I will take you high and above, giving you that Really Good Feeling you always thought of, A Really Good Feeling that you have only imagined, just say the words and I will be gladly to oblige your every wish, allow me to take a dip through your body, going places no man has ever gone before, soaring through when I roar, are you ready for me to explore your precious treasure, my love can't be measured with a stick, I will be breaking down your walls of bricks with the tip of my tongue, I twist where the sun doesn't shine, close your blinds, the world's not ready for this One Of A Kind show, spreading you wide so my tongue can make you Lose Control, around and around playing with your pearl, your jewel, at the end of this escapade you will understand why I rule, for what I have in store I'm going to make you do things you not used to doing, your heart has been ruined, my screwdriver will tighten up all your bolts, putting it back together again when I flow through, climbing on top of you to serve you up with one stroke, you begin to shiver and bust, calling me King as you erupt with Sounds Of Love making, Virgo baby, I am a plus, a must have as you grab the sheets tight, squeezing your thighs around me with all your might, tonight's the night, the start of a new beginning of life, damn your palace is so tight, hitting you with A Really Good Feeling that you will grow into love, as I fill you up making you bust, enough is never enough, I won't stop until you finish putting it down, I am wearing my crown, wiping away all your frowns with your nails deep into my back as I attack with my grooves, hitting your palace with my large and thick tool, you're feeling my moves, I stop, pause to kiss you slow whispers of turn around so I can spread her out to put it down, facing the mirror so I can see all of your love faces, pulling on your wavy long hair as I take you there, I'm going deeper than what you can bare, you start to run from my smoking gun, with a smile of pleasure from ear to ear, you fear of falling in love, I know it's near as I shift gears under hooking your arms from the rear, reversing on that thang, making you sang with no complaints, massaging your spine as I slow wind, Taking

MII: The Return of the King

My Time, you feel so right, Body To Body, kissing your neck down your back, stopping to pause for a second, are you ready for this love lesson, you will walk out professing, I'm testing your limits, turning you around to get back in it, picking you up pressing you up against the wall, lovely it is when making your waterfall, I have you climbing the wall, deep into your curves, I'm going up and down with my feet planted firmly on the ground floor, you let out a scream as I roar, exploring your sexual fantasies, making you believe, becoming weak you are, wrapping your arms around my neck, I take you off the wall, no we're not done yet, you feel the strength in my arms as I perform, ringing all your alarms, I'm weathering your storm, putting out your fire, forever you will desire the touch of this King, making that ass bounce, shout and scream, you would think my love acts are from a movie scene, giving you all of me is what you need, you see what you get when you just say the words my love, laying your head down on my pillow, thoughts of me when you dream, I know it seems unreal what you feel, I have skills, your last was an appetizer, I'm your full course meal, A Really Good Feeling is what you feel, my love making is just that real.

TEAM US
(INTERLUDE)

A moment of honesty, my heart tells me this love is real, you know the way to my soul, my spirit filled when you're near sending chills through my body, real love I can't hide it, Team Us, I can't deny it, fighting for our future, never knowing any ending, since the beginning I saw us living hand and hand, no one can stop this, this is God's plan, at first I didn't understand the power you hold, my heart is in your control, tell me baby that you will never let go, your love is all I want to know, your love making show puts me on float, cloud thirty three, that's how many licks it took when I was down low making your passion flow, your palace deep in I go, Team Us baby, yeah I know, you scream never letting go, this is a lifetime show, connected at our hearts, becoming one, nothing can tear us apart, you are my poetry art in motion, my camera is rolling, focusing on you, my love, our love I know is true, my feelings pointed directly at you, time stops when I'm pushing inside, you have that One Of A Kind, Second To None, my mind is wrapped up around you, the things you do make me Lose Control, as we float on cloud eighty-five, that's how many strokes it took before your love came streaming down my vine, showering me with all your love, you're blowing my mind, as I fill you up, overflowing your cup with my love potion, you have me Wide Open, addicted I am, this is no movie, my actions are not scripted, never will we finish, we will be going forever and ever, get enough I will never, kissing you, touching you, my heart belongs to you, love drunk, you have me in this intoxicating groove, the way your hips sway back and forth, the way you move with all the right tools, how can I lose with you at my side, that look in your eyes always takes me high, lost in your trance when pushing in between those thighs, passions are on the rise, through your eyes you tell me you're all mine, as mine do the same, baby Team Us, I have no complaints, waving that white flag, never will I go astray, forever I will stay for the rest of my days I will only say Team Us, making your passion erupt when I hit you with my thrust, pleasing you is a must, feeding you these chocolate-covered strawberries as I whisper in your ear, baby I love to love you, no one can ever compare to the things you do, having you here with me puts me at ease, no one will ever come in between Team Us.

D. C.

CHOCOLATE STRAWBERRIES

Ringing your phone, you pick up I say hey my love, you say hi my King I was just thinking about what's in between your thighs, we laughed and I say oh my I was hitting you to see what you were doing tonight, I need you here so that I can express the reasons on why I love you the way I do, there's something special I want to try my love, so hop in your ride, you're getting that King's Love tonight, without hesitation you say alright, waiting for you to appear, I get everything in gear, my room is filled with roses for you to lay across nice and soft, candles so that I can see your body appear in this mirror, I set up in my chair thinking to myself I can't wait to fill you up, I put that Remy V and Stella Black on ice the doorbell rings, there goes my Mrs. Tight, my Mrs. Right, looking at all that splendid sexiness through my peep hole, ready to attack, opening my door, my eyes begin to explore your everglades, I'm about to misbehave, becoming your royal slave, but I Take My Time, kissing you while touching on your behind, giving off a little grind, to my room I lead you where you find your Queendom awaits, give me your jacket baby and sit down, take your right place as I pour you a drink to put your nerves at ease, teasing your lips with a kiss, a lick as the flames flick and flick while the music plays slow, oh how ready I am to rock your boat, but I Take My Time with your body, but I can't wait to get inside it, I'm about to get you excited with what's next to come, sit right there my love as I run to the kitchen to grab my Chocolate Strawberries and whipped cream, ready I am to seduce your core, leaving you wanting an encore when I'm done, the party's just begun, laying you down loving that smile, kissing gentle, massaging your mental, your tension I am about to release, you have unleashed this love beast, unveiling your clothes, your body is now exposed, I'm going to make you Lose Control, powering up your inner freak, here we go, Turning Up The Heat as I splash your body with this whipped cream, placing these Chocolate Strawberries down your stream, my tongue is about to mark you up, turning you into a firecracker, my tongue is about to spark you up, spraying you down from your breasts, some has landed on my chest, you licked up the mess as I continue to impress, spraying down the middle past those hips in between with this whipped cream, placing Chocolate Strawberries in a few more places I will dive, I won't be coming up for air baby no worries I will survive, as I prepare to Take Off, I start off at your neck placing a passion mark there, kissing and licking everywhere, massaging your breasts, removing all cream as I eat the Strawberry that's in between the two, you start to fiend, your body is being put in my groove, to my rhythm you move, winning you are baby, you will never lose when it comes to this dude named King, winding down your core, exploring with more Chocolate Strawberries, playing with your cherry pop, going nonstop, licking that spot, going in circles, making you rock, you're running, I'm gunning with my tongue, giving you that number one love of ecstasy, no one can do it like me, they can't even compete, as I eat the last of the Chocolate Strawberries your cherry explodes with a waterfall of passion, screams as my tongue keeps lashing, giving you all of my satisfaction with the skills that I possess, pushing your limits to the test with my Lazy Love, my tongue just dug and dug until the sun came up, putting you to sleep with a blush saying King you're too much, you gave me such a rush with your touch, my love is all yours to hold my King you say as you fall asleep Blue Dreaming of me, forever I will be at your side, through the day I will stay constantly on your mind, when night falls your body will become mine, I will continue to be your reality whenever your King crosses your mind, Oh what a Beautiful find.

D. C.

MAKING YOU MINE

Caught up in an intense situation, there's no escaping these boundaries, I'm all in, here to claim what's rightfully mine, I'm here not only to make love to your body but to make love to your mind so that you become all mine, my better whole, Soul Searching, I'm not letting go of this love, where is he? Let me just tell him how we both feel and keep it real my love, wait babe you say let's play it safe, tonight in your arms I will lay, I say, the strong type, I hope you like, tonight I will become lost inside of you, here just visiting for one night, he thinks we're family so it's cool, he comes out calling you boo, come to the room, unpleasantly replying with okay, I say damn fool, playing it cool knowing I'm going to lay the boom, quietly saying later you and I in the other room, my thoughts consume, it's a must we ride this voyage tonight, hearing us while he sleeps, he just might, as the night fades away, patiently I lay watching the time creep, waiting for you to sneak and lay next to me, Tic Toc, Tic Toc, the clock strikes three, here you are climbing into my sheets, whispering baby I need you to be lost inside of me, opening my eyes from dozing off, who said love doesn't cost, your actions is the money, the transaction is what you bought, our tongues twist and toss, gazing into your world, becoming lost inside of you my girl, with my tongue I start to lick and lick, your body I want to explore, I'm about to adore your canvas, no place will go untouched, I don't miss, well-endowed and fully equipped, you're going to feel all of this, spreading your thighs as I kiss in between your inner thighs, I become locked in a place when I get to touch your prize, when I'm freaking you, all I know is you, the world becomes you, lost inside, taking me to an unpresidential level, when I'm freaking you nothing else matters, our sound waves shatter the Window Pane, going crazy insane when I'm freaking you, turning you into my fiend, no worries I will supply this drug anytime of the day, this new flame can go on for nights, I'm your Just Right, my tongue starts to take flight, with your pearl tongue I fight, don't fight it baby, call my name girl, say it, as I lick faster in between your walls back to your pearl, but my name you held back, didn't call, trying to resist the

MII: The Return of the King

temp, knowing he may hear me giving you that new thang, this new flame, he's exempt, I come harder with my attack, giving you that up, down, round and round flip, my tongue doesn't miss, your heart skips, legs tighten, the pillow you're biting I say again, call my name so the neighbors can hear, I have no fear of what's to come, you and I will forever be one, going deep making you explode like a gun, grabbing me tightly, you still don't call out what I want, I stunt, flipping you to the side, it's about to get harder and harder for you to keep it inside, opening you wide so deep in I can go, pulling in slow so that you feel every inch, I feel you twitch when you feel my tip, this is only the beginning, there's no ending to this Royal Love, with each second that passes, grabbing on your thighs and ass while loving you from the side, I slide on top chest to chest we come together forever, your palace I weather the stormy waterfall, busting down your walls, I can see it in your eyes that I'm driving your body crazy, standing right in front filling your cup, as I go harder your palace is about to erupt, placing your legs above my shoulders, your beauty is in the eyes of this beholder, going deeper, yes I'm thicker and longer than what you had before, can't you feel me deep even when I extend out, there's no doubt, I know you're ready to scream and shout, yell as loud as you want, exploring a part of your cave that you didn't even know existed, I told you I don't miss, as I rip through your walls, I say let me flip you right side up, I want to hear that ass go boom, boom, clap, look what you've done to me, look at where I am at, in your house with your man in the other room as I sit here and give you what your body needs to consume, me, Remy V and you, pulling on your hair as you look back and stare, I guess chemistry is true, I don't know if it's the Remy V or you, but this groove is times two, I say to you as I long deep stroke from the back, say my name, let me hear that fall from your lips and say it like you mean it, I want to feel that shhh, in and out as I dip, your nails rip through the sheets as I attack with that Royal passion, giving you a pleasure beating, you conceding, screaming out OHHHH KING, BOY YOU GOT ME FEIGNING, YOUR LOVE IS ALL I'M NEEDING, as we both give that Ultimate Climax, you fix yourself trying to relax kissing me before you sneak off telling me I'm yours, you creep away and pray he heard none of the above, climbing back

D. C.

into bed quietly as you can smiling knowing where your heart lies, as we both close our eyes saying I love you.

MII: The Return of the King

ENOUGH IS ENOUGH

Pulling up to your house, opening my car door, rushing to your door, opening the front door to find your living room in shambles, as I walk towards the kitchen, dishes are smashed to pieces, glass is everywhere, pictures torn over there, racing up the stairs to find you slumped over in a corner, oh the horror, what has he done to you, putting the safety on my gun as I slide it back in my holster, I bend down to become eye level with you, so I can consume your pain, what did he do, your face is black and blue, here for you I will remain, I'm here to take care of you, snatching the blanket off the bed to hide your flesh, your clothes are torn, this scene is a mess, you deserve the best, your worth is so much more than you think, he is weak for putting his hands on a Queen, Enough Is Enough, no more of him hurting you, I won't let it happen to you again, picking you up, holding you tightly in my arms close to keep you warm, going down stairs, your heart and faith I will repair, you can count on me I swear, a real man, a real King is here in your atmosphere, I stand here giving you my word, no more of this pain my love, I will give you A Feeling you Never Felt Before, you will never be the same, it's a shame what you had to endure, I will cure your sickness, you will never have to go through this with me as your King kicking the front door open coming to a halt, the animal who touched your greatness in the way that he did, vile, must be taught a lesson in manners and standards, sitting you upright against the porch, my strength has been lit, ripping off my shirt, he's about to get this work as I charge in with a left jab to the body, with a right cross that he slips and dips me with a right chin checker, I smile and say that's it, come on, he charges, I slide to the right punching him directly in his jaw, he falls, I continue to put these paws on him giving him a lesson he deserves, women are the most precious thing God could have ever created here on this earth, cherish their worth, knocked him out cold, sleep in the dirt, running to you so I can get you out of here, this lifestyle is about to be left in your rear, you whisper in my ear thank you as I'm opening up my car door putting you in letting you know it's okay now, you can relax, turning my ignition, there's no

D. C.

more hoping and wishing, your knight in well dirty armor, (we laugh), is here to give you more of what you deserve here on this earth, love is what you're worth, put your past behind you, he will never be able to hurt you again, Enough Is Enough my friend, I will always protect you until the end of time.

MII: The Return of the King

EYE CANDY

I get that sweet tooth when I see you, that body of yours is so tight, your hair is always laid right, those eyes of yours blow me outta sight, those curves are fit winding Just Right, they stay pulling me in breaking down my strength and might, swimming in your love rubbing on your butt in my mind, baby damn you're so fine, making me spill my wine as I pour losing track of time, wishing I can see you more often, I don't blink when I'm bless with your presence, not wanting to miss a thing, you pretty young thing, making a King drop to his knees, and sing the way you sway those hips when you walk, dropping my jaws, I'm in Ah, oh my, my, my how did you fit those thighs in those jeans, making me feign for what's in between, come to King for just One Night my Eye Candy, sipping on this brandy making me speak the truth, you're the truth, my heart sky rockets through the roof when you're near, no need to fear, I'm strapped with the right gear, those lips I want you to bring here to me, I love it when I see you enter my stratosphere, you are Second To None, baby you are the one, do you feel me noticing you each and every time you come close my Eye Candy, I want to do the most, leaving me with nothing, but the memories and the smell of your perfume, I will never forget you my Eye Candy, I need a taste, I want to come and take my place, I want you to sit it on my face, I need to taste, come feed my desire, come put out my fire, I want to hear you call out sire, deep diving into your water, roaming around your cave, oh the things I will do will make you misbehave, come and let me turn you into My Love Slave, let me show you why the world would pay for my actions, satisfaction guaranteed my Eye Candy, I will make it so that you can't stand to be without me, I wish you would notice me, all I can think when I see my Eye Candy is how I need you next to me, I close my eyes and see you as my Queen, my secret Eye Candy to be.

D. C.

YOU ARE MY DESTINY

Timeless days, stuck I am in this cave, my love for you remains the same, your love stays on my mind, counting down the time, with each passing hour, minutes and seconds, waiting for that very second that you come back into my arms to be mine, while I wait my love I continue professing, thanking God for this blessing, my angel in disguise, no matter where you are in this world, you won't be able to hide, my feelings are too strong, I know we belong, this love can't be wrong, my feelings are right, forever we will live on as the day turns into night, your room is filled with candle lights surrounding your bed, I take you by the hand, leading you to Lovers' Land as we stand close, a kiss to your lips, my love you have evoked, Ready, Set, Go, grabbing you low at the hips, I hope you are ready for this trip, lifting your body high, gazing into each other's eyes, beginning to kiss slow, here we go, you're rubbing on my freshly shaved head, I lay you on the bed, on top is where you will find me, your legs I spread, you're already wet as a rainforest, my love I'm going to keep pouring into your soul, adoring your canvas, this love is all I want to know, my beautiful butterfly, can't you see what you are doing to me on the inside, I'm in too deep, swimming in your cage of ecstasy, lockdown by you is where I want to be, splashing in your sea of love, You Are My Destiny, look at what you have done, you have me calling out your name, since that very first time I've never been the same, each and every time we make love it's never the same, you have washed away my past pain, your heart I claim, the apple of my eye, spoiling you rotten, those lips of yours are soft as cotton, my arms are underneath your legs pressed over the top of your head, I have you tangled up in my web with nowhere to go, as I push down low in your slip and slide, from the look in your eyes I have your emotions floating high, wrapping your thighs around my body, welcome to my Royal Party, slow jamming as we cut the night away, A Really Good Feeling, Our Chemistry taking flight, I'm pushing with more might, picking up my strides, deep inside your palace, three times a day, I just have to have it, I couldn't manage not being able to feel your soul, Losing Control, you have a hold on me, promise to never let go, your world is all I want, just you and me, my love you have set free from that first day, you became My Destiny.

D. C.

WHEN MY LOVE CALLS II

Awakened by the ringing of your phone, you answer hello clearing your throat, oh I say did I wake you babe, I'm up you say what's wrong my King, my love I really I need you close to me, I need you to come and tame this inner freak that you have unleashed the last time When Your Love Called, a quick pause as you yawn, just say the words my King and I'll be on my way, I say my love I want you to come fulfill your position, I know it's a mission, but I'm hoping and wishing that you come through, I'm in the mood for some of you, prove that I can call on you when in need, indeed my King, I'm on my way, prepare the room for me, for tonight it's all about you, I'm going to show what I can do, hanging up with a be safe, I can't wait to see your face, split screen me in the mirror getting clean, you putting on your lace everything with a black trench coat, red pumps and purse to match, while I spray cologne, knowing it's about to be on, lighting my candles with a match, laying out the scene with a trail of rose petals leading from the door to the room, waiting patiently with a drink in hand, music is playing, lights are down low so that the candles will make our bodies glow, ready I am for your Queen show, hearing you pull up, listening to you getting out the car to close your door, I hear you walk getting closer I can't wait to adore, you open and come in closing the front door, I can hear your heels as you glide across the floor, closer and closer you are for me to adore, you walk in to see me sitting up with nothing, but my silk boxers on, puffing on my cigar as I sip my drink admiring how fine you are, you start peeling off your coat, my eyes are focused on watching you coast, moving slow, teasing me to the music, pleasing my eyes, making my royal rise to no surprise, my baby is banging, looking right, keeping you in my sights, moving closer and closer until our bodies touch, becoming one, no lust, this is love in the making, cherishing every second, you say I'm about to teach you a lesson, kissing me slow, going down, pulling my boxers completely off, stroking me slow and soft, with a smile, giving me X's and Oh's for a while, curling my toes with that tongue of yours, you have exposed my spots, baby don't stop, with your head in motion,

MII: The Return of the King

strong is my devotion, damn those circular motions got me going, I wasn't knowing, you never showed you had it like this, without missing a beat you climb on top of me, sliding me in deep into your wet and warm palace, from the look upon my face it says you can have it, baby have it all, It's Yours, do as you please, explore this love, fitting tight with no glove, taking me to a place I never heard of, is this love, grabbing you tight around your ass, you're moving those hips fast, splashing all over my stomach, I have you Cuming from the bottom to the top, rocking nonstop as you Tic Toc, Tic Toc, rotating those hips like a never-ending clock, I won't tap baby, I'm not going to quit, you just keep hitting and don't miss, telling me to raise up, we're not done, sit in this chair, strap up, I'm about to shift gears, the room is hot, sitting down, you turn around and slow wind down on my royal, I feel spoiled due to the show that you are giving me, pleasing my throne, I'm glad you answered your phone, feeling that ice cream coming on, the faster you start to perform, leaning back as I rub up and down your body, deep inside it, I deliver a heavy package, kissing your back thanking you for performing your love acts
When My Love Calls II.

D. C.

I CAN'T GET YOU OUT MY SYSTEM

It's the strides in your walk, that sexy tone in your voice when you talk, for your love I would pay the cost, it's the rhythm of your heartbeat, I get lost when we are in between the sheets, you complete me, I love to see that smile and those pretty white teeth, on down to those beautiful feet, you make me complete, your legs and thighs firm and thick, just my type, you have everything that I like, you're my Mrs. Right, running my hands through your long straight black hair, into your eyes I stare, I can't compare, you take me there, to a place where I never want to escape, allow me to take my rightful place beside you, every little thing you do brings me joy, from the way you laugh, I love seeing those dimples with your crazy ass, with your personality we will never clash, I know we will outlast time, forever mine, we will grow strong, I love the way you perform, with you I can weather any storm, you give me what I need, feeding my soul with your love, I love how you are a professional, never can I let go, but when you get home you leave it all at the door, my freak comes out behind closed curtains, I'm certain I will love you for life, making you my wife, without thinking twice, I will fight and fight for only you, oh how I love the things you do, there's nothing I wouldn't do just to show you it's you who I love, trust, giving you my heart until the end of time, we will never part, we will never become lost like precious art, you are my Sparta treasure, never can I measure the love I have inside, you are in for one hell of a ride, for all life time I won't be able to Get You Out My System, you are my Back Bone, my equilibrium, you keep me up right, standing tight, this love, your heart is my life, here to please you and your needs, to be your servant, I'm down on bended knee.

MII: The Return of the King

MY SPANISH ROSE II

I should have been more of a man about this situation I have us in, loving two, there's no way either can win, at the end we all lose, to gain back My Spanish Rose trust it took such a cost that I couldn't afford, but still I adore her love, she showed me the meaning of Honest Love, from the pain I caused everyone, hearts on pause, I've shattered walls, broken down mountains, conquered all, to lose it all again, having to make a decision, the choice needs to be in, what is it going to be, as we stand outside looking each other in the face with me saying baby just wait, I will go back in there and tell her I choose you, silence for a few tics, which felt like an eternity, baby tell me what you think, as my ship begins to sink, she says I'll call you with a date and time, I'll be fine, go to the family you chose, I'm no longer your Spanish Rose, exposing my feelings as she slams the car door, my heart is torn, walking back towards the house, into my room I go, without thinking twice I begin to punch the wall with force and might, this just isn't right, the other that's in my life comes in to console me saying it will be alright, it's okay, we can start anew from this very day moving forward, even though I know you're not looking forward to the choice she made, that's her bed babe let her lay, with no words to say, but can I be alone for some time, I got to get my mind right, roll me one so I can take flight, smoking now, high as a kite, thinking about all of our nights, My Spanish Rose was Just Right, how did I mess up what was mine, no matter what, all the time, you never know when, but what's done in the dark will eventually come to the light, knowing I wasn't living a straight arrow, I hated to see her go, knowing another is going to take her out from the cold, still she has a hold on me that I can't shake, never will I forget our days, months and years, I will always be here, if ever you are in need you can reach out for me, even though I may be the last you will ever want to see, my love will never cease for you My Spanish Rose II, love and peace be with you.

D. C.

TURN UP THE HEAT

The temperature will rise soon, as you step foot inside of my castle, my love will hit you, commit to flowing through your veins and body, going limp feeling numb, as you cum again, I'm not stopping with all my rocking, my boat crashing into your shore, your insides I explore, wanting more and more, as I adore you to the fullest, sending my rocket fast as a shooting bullet, your hair I'm going to pull it when pushing in deep from the back, fitting tightly we are a Perfect Match, the one for me, as I Turn Up The Heat, you grip the sheets, pulling on the pillow with your teeth, I pound deep, thrust hard and sweet, sweat rushing down our bodies, we're dripping wet, it's a Royal Party, your King is about to get naughty by nature, taking a break from the strokes, the temp is about to rise for where my tongue is about to go, wrapping your legs around my head, you're holding on tight, baby don't let go, my tongue possesses a different type of motion, watch me coast through your river, your palace will become wet as the ocean when I'm done flowing with these circular motions, in and out, going fast just to slow it down, playing with your pearl tongue, I found it makes you quiver, pushing with my fingers, as I make you deliver, that shiver, pouring down rain like it's December, turning your oven hot like it's the middle of July, this night you will remember as I raise your spirits high, I cannot lie you caught me by surprise, loving the way you taste inside, I can write in cursive all night if you're the pad and paper, my tongue is the pen, singing my name as you cum again, standing up so I can go in, feeding your soul, pleasuring your palace so smooth and nice, double tap twice, long stroke, the heat is hot tonight, showing you love in many different ways, my strokes are on another level, making you misbehave, pushing into your cave staring at your pretty face, that smile will never erase, your eyes roll off into space, taking you to another place, hitting all spots, old and new, doing things your last couldn't do, making you squirt as I flirt with your clit, with my tip, back in with my fully equipped, legs around my hips, hands joined together, fingers locked, lips and eyes engaged, in and out at a fast but yet steady pace off into the night we will be

Turning Up The Heat in this place, you will always hold a special place in my heart from this day forth, this feeling will never part.

BREAK YOU DOWN II

I have been racing through your mind since the last time, you're thinking about the next time you will find yourself in my arms, reminiscing on how I broke you down when you stepped foot into my kingdom, my town the last time, press play baby no need to rewind, this time I will Take My Time part two with no tongue action between the hips, for this time my fully equipped will hit all your spots, I won't miss, I don't miss, taking your feelings for a trip, as I grab you at the hips, kissing you slowly, putting you in that mood, excuse my hands for doing what they're about to do, see they have a mind of their own, seeking out their mark, inside your palace my fingers start their motion, in and out they're coasting, you're already soaked and wet, telling me your mind is already set on this mission we're about to embark on, tonight I will perform in ways that will make you say baby I'm Yours for the rest of my days, go ahead baby press play, I'm about to steal your body away, pulling off your clothes, I'm going to Break You Down so that I will put a forever hold, a forever smile on your face, taking your heart to another place, I lay you down so that we can escape together, ready I'm to weather your storm, pulling out, I'm not hung like the norm, hope you can handle the way I'm about to perform, I'm all yours, spreading your wings slow and easy, pulling into your palace with a meaning, see this is real love, sexual healing, from the top of the ceiling, to the bottom of the floor, deep into your cave I explore, with no flashlight I can see just fine when massaging your spine, at the end of this escapade you will be mine, calling me the truth as I flow through your warm embrace with care, into your eyes I stare, taking you there, baby I swear you say you're deep into my palace, keep your strokes on repeat, keep going deep inside of me, never will I escape your hold, never will I let go, baby just go, wrap your hands around my throat, Break me Down, a King in you I have found, when you slide through my town, pushing your legs past your shoulders, it's about to get wild, Pleasure all the while you're screaming loud, I'm about to cum without you using your tongue, where have you been the way you feel deep within, rubbing on your smooth skin, nails in my back, sliding you to the side with one leg up so I can show you where it's at, a different attack, cruising, going with a slow rock, allowing you to catch your breath here in my Royal Room, putting down the boom, boom, pow, you're loving my style, going for a while, hours, to be exact, sliding to the back, putting that arch down, head up, as I pound and pound, grabbing your shoulders so there's no running, yes baby I feel you Cuming once more, you call out I adore your stroke, baby It's Yours, just flow in and out, showing you what I'm about, leaving you with no doubt, as you shout and moan to the rhythm of this love, I'm Breaking You Down so that you can never place no one above, I am your King, here to give you all that you need, turning you into a lifetime feign When You Call On Me, I will be here to please, weak in the knees your ass I squeeze as I erupt filling your cup, round two baby, you just can't get enough.

D. C.

WONDERLAND II

Welcome back to my throne, I see I have your mind on nothing but thoughts of me, what must I do for you this time, I just want you to please me as I sleep Deep Dreaming of your Wonderland, you stand out without a doubt blow my back out when you're arching my spine from behind my King, give it all to me as I wander off, no worries baby, but this time it will cost, no not money, but your heart which I see has been lost for quite some time, I love it when you allow me to enter your mind to claim what's mine on this side of my Wonderland, I have the master key to make you weak in all the right places, love faces you will be making, taking you for an all-night voyage, sailing your sea, deep diving between your knees with my tongue, blazing you are hotter than the sun, taking you far the way my tongue is doing waves, through your everglades, soft and smooth as I persuade you to Lose Control, holding on tight to never let go, as I coast through your desire, igniting your fire with my tongue twists, not missing a beat, as I come up to give you more of me, as you sleep in my Wonderland, interlocking our hands, loving the plan that I map out, kissing you before I push in to make you scream and shout, sliding in with no extension, Body To Body, rubbing on your smooth soft skin, I want in to your heart, as I rip your palace apart with passion strokes Down Low, but taking you high, floating through the sky, through my eyes in my Wonderland there's no limit on how high we can go, giving you a Royal Show as I explode through your dark hole, deep in I go, can you handle my flow, trying to evoke all your passion with all my in and out action and tongue lashing, leaving you with an Everlasting memory, your alarm rings, waking you with a smile, looking around to see if I was really there, was it reality, you and me, or a dream, removing your covers to find your thong removed, soaked are the sheets, asking yourself could this be, how did I become nude, was King here, did he really put me in the groove, his Wonderland has me singing the blues, each night I will leave my window open, so that he can climb in and show me those moves, hoping he comes back I don't want to lose my

King and his Wonderland, seeing him each night is my plan, if you ever felt his touch, then you will understand my Wonderland.

D. C.

PALACE OF PLEASURE

Your Palace of Pleasure becomes a stormy weather when I start to move up your thighs, staring into your eyes moving closer so you can feel Mr. Right doing your body nice and slow, once I start to go performing my best show kissing you slow, putting your passion on cruise control, in control I am, ripping off your clothes so I can invoke your pleasure from the top of your head to the bottom of your feet, precious you are to me, as my tongue begins to dig deep inside your inner thighs, about to take you on a never-ending ride, for when I'm done and you're alone closing your eyes you will feel, see, smell me inside, leaving an impression on your life, with the way my love goes, my tongue just flows in and out, around and around, seducing your palace, licking and tongue kissing your lips that are between your hips, your wetness is dripping from my chin, I'm going deep within your pleasure, showing you I can weather your storm, pinning your legs back towards your head, in the middle of my bed, your hands rubbing on my head with moans and groans, legs begin to shake, that undying flow is about to come on, licking it all up, sucking on your lips while you erupt, I'm coming up to all smiles, it's about to get wild, you spread your legs with your finger you gesture to come closer, as I slide in all your moisture, Palace Of Pleasure, we French kiss, as I hit that spot, stopping I will not, pinning your arms to the bed, wrapping your legs, deeper I head in with short extended burst, my beautiful lady, I'm giving you all my worth, as we change positions, I place your legs on my shoulders, letting your arms go as I raise to extend in that pushup position, no more hoping and wishing, what you're about to feel is real, touching spots that you thought were lost, going soft until you can take it all, you will go through withdraws when I'm not in between your walls, lost in your sauce I become, harder I go breaking your bricks, no tapping baby, I won't quit, giving you that yellow light stick shift, going slow again, half in with just the tip, here comes that Greenlight Special again, as I rip through your Palace Of Pleasure, I can handle whatever you pitch, as we switch, flipping you over to hit you with my extended clip, with my hands gripping your ass firmly, spreading you widely, sliding right in again with that yellow light special, soon you will feel the might and power I hold, you grab a pillow to hold, as I go slow, a little deeper, but slow, it's almost that time for me to hit the gas and go, but for now I'm going to Take My Time and go slow so you feel how deep my strokes will go, coasting, flowing, I'm knowing you're loving these pleasure acts, the way I'm about to attack will put me where your heart is at, here we go, I know you didn't think I would come this hard, picking up my flow, petal to the floor, arch in your back so I can go deeper into your core, giving you more of what you deserve, some real back and forth action, splashing in your pool of love, pulling your head up by your hair so we can stare into the mirror, I want to see those love faces you make as I Break You Down, in me you have found a real King who wears the crown of real love making, back breaking, headboard shaking, my strokes are escalating, before I start to shaking I turn you around quickly wrapping your legs to my waist, taking my place in your palace, showing strength, picking you up, Lift Off into your Palace Of Pleasure, I can't measure, going where no one has ever taken you before, turning you out, as you scream and shout, as I bust into your Palace Of Pleasure house, giving you more than enough to talk about with your girls, you can't get enough of how I just rocked your world.

D. C.

ONE SPECIAL NIGHT II

Remembering that day we had, you phoned me late into the night, hoping I might answer, ring, ring and ringing my phone goes on, your face shows up on my screen, my eyes light up, hitting the answer button on the screen saying hello my Queen, my love is everything okay, it's real late, she replies with saying I need to escape, can I come over so you can fill my palace, I need you on this One Special Night, excited I become with hands in my pants saying yes baby come over we can dance, little did I know she was already at my door, you sneaky girl, welcome back to my world, we're about to lose the power for a few hours, your body I'm about to handle and devour, conquer your love and soul, I told you after that One Special Day I will forever have a hold on you with the things I do, making you come back to take your rightful place, you're standing in nothing but some leggings, heels and a trench coat, I know what you're here for, walking through my bedroom door, your coat hits the floor, stripping off your heels and leggings, ready you are to perform, telling me don't be alarmed, walking over to me slowly, swaying your hips that don't quit, making my fully equipped rise, dropping to your knees staring me in the eyes, telling me you have a surprise, rubbing up and down my thighs, pulling my boxer briefs down, the royal pole you have found, beginning to lick him up and down the shaft, your tongue plus me that's easy math, long like a giraffe neck you stroke with your mouth down south, showing me what you're about, with me saying baby it's your body, you can do whatever it is you like, loving the way you singing into my microphone, feeling at home, curling my toes, taking me to limits I thought I couldn't go, you're putting on a show, it's my turn to flow, you come up slowly, kissing my abs and chest, all the way up to my neck, our lips and tongue meet, walking you over to the bed where passion is made, turning into your Love Slave, laying you down kissing and licking down your neck and breasts, past your stomach to those thighs, opening you wide as my tongue goes inside, teasing you a little, tickling your fancy, it's not about me, it's about you, see cupid has nothing on me, digging into you with real love, my arrow is my tongue, making you hotter than one hundred suns, I am your only one, coming up with that sticky face, making you bust uncontrollably with me is where you will forever be, my royal shaft is about to creep deep, inside is where you will find me, in your world exploring every twist and turn, you yearn and moan for more, on this One Special Night, I'm giving it to you Just Right, pushing with a little might, Taking My Time, it's about to be a long night, a freaky night, anything goes, touching every hole, lighting up your soul like it's the fourth of July, in the sky we rise, flipping you over so that I can go deeper inside, what's that you say, you want me to try a different place, you say it will make you explode in a different way, I say okay, lubing up so I can make you erupt, sliding slow, tight as hell, here we go, her screams she can't hold, pushing slow, in and out, you shout I'm about to cum, playing with your pearl tongue, as I go wild pulling out to go back deep into your Palace Of Pleasure, I can feel that creamy weather streaming down, a freak in you is what I have found, on this One Special Night, feeding you my pipe, going all night until the morning sun, for life I will be that one.

D. C.

I DIDN'T MEAN IT

How could I allow you to split, I know I have done some foolish shit, baby I Didn't Mean It, saying that you can walk, names I called you, taking it too far, give me those keys to the car, baby I Didn't Mean It at all, wait a second, just pause, baby willing I am to drop my pride, allow my feelings and love to come back inside, pushing my ego to the side, I need you in my life, don't you say goodbye, I know I have taken you for granted with Lies and Deceit, I'm here begging on my knees, as I cry out change is overcoming inside of me, you open up my eyes and now I can see, love is a two way street, without you it will be the death of me, I couldn't breathe, I wouldn't eat, my mind wouldn't allow me to sleep, you see how you will be the death of me, I know I was supposed to be more understanding, caring and all, believe me baby I'm breaking down my walls, no more tears running down your jaws, I won't cause any more pain to your heart, I don't want to see us part, become a lost art, a better man I will be playing that part, your King I want to forever be, I'm supposed to be, no more late night creeps, I Didn't Mean It baby I was weak, will be even weaker if you leave, allow me to do what I need to prove you belong with me, give me one more chance, take my hand and I will see to it that you will never regret that you didn't leave, I Didn't Mean It baby please say you will forever stay with me, complete my home, don't leave me empty, stay beside my throne, together we are royalty, my Queen forever you will be, I will spend the rest of eternity loving you the way you need.

MII: The Return of the King

KRYPTONITE
(INTERLUDE)

You gave me a taste, now I know there's no resisting you, inside your palace I consume all of you, all the freaky things we're going to do tonight will excite your feelings, ignite your passion, light your soul on fire, can you imagine this sexual healing, tonight I will play the role of a villain, you're the hero, I am your Kryptonite, you're trying to fight it, but my Tongue Lashing has you Just Right, let your guard down baby, don't fight it, allow me to hit you with my power and might, I want to show you my strength and raise you higher when I go inside, deep inside, high with your hands to the ceiling, I'm feeding you what you've been missing and feigning with your legs wrapped around my waist, crowding your space, uplifting your soul, taking you to another realm, out of space, giving you that undying feeling, Pleasure, I can see it written all over your face as I blessed you through the night with my Royal pipe, this night will be an Unforgettable Night, this memory will last the rest of your life, busting all over my mic, twice, going on number three, can't no one do it better than me, a blessed King, well endowed with that boom, boom, pow, equipped with that know how in between my hips, I aim to please, call on me when you're in need, I have the recipe to feed your soul, coasting as you exhale and breathe, come Float with me and you will see why they call me King.

D. C.

FLOAT

Could it be your smooth Carmel tone that puts me on this level of undying want, I need more of you, with these distant nights and late night texts over the phone wanting you to come home and Float with me, coast through my world of love, down your passion river as I Fed Ex deliver this package you have been looking and waiting for, baby I'm yours, come Float with me, let's defy the laws of gravity, just you and me above the clouds going wild when we touch each other, baby I love you like no other, could it be true love that I have discovered or could it be that sweet, sweet moan, that heavenly tone you give off when I'm inside of your Erotic Zones that makes me Float, Float on high, opening up my favorite bottle so that I can make a toast to these feelings that feel oh so right, baby I feel your fire burning inside of me, all I want is you see, look through my eyes my love doesn't hold no lies, forever Floating we will be in the sky, this love is strong, I'm holding on with all my might, as we Float on through the night, we coast, wrestle and play fight, that rough stuff you like, here I am to give you what you need, when you sing into my mic, you take me to different heights, you Break Me Down, you take hold of my crown, your Showdown is no match, to your love I am attached, you make me bow down, that's no easy task, that's why you're no match, can't no one compare, you hit spots that I didn't even know that were there, when we Float you take me there, you take me to a place where I never want to come back from, you are my one, I need you like the world needs the sun, when we Float I become a new person, I become certain in my capabilities, you fulfill all my needs every time you come Float with me, I'll be waiting for you my Queen.

MII: The Return of the King

UNPREDICTABLE

Unpredictable is what you can call me, I never give my all to one see, I always leave them wanting more, with the way that I explore they can tell I have more in store in my bank, I come strong like a tank, you think I'm playing, this isn't fake, cutting with me you will faint, fall into a deep sleep, If I were to hit you with my Everlasting, If I to give you all of me, searching for that one who can handle my creep in between the sheets, your body will become weak once you are lying next to me, knowing you heard around town about me, my freaky reputation is true my pretty sexy thing, tonight you will find out what it means to be loved by a King, patiently waiting you were for this day, are you ready to give your love to King, sire is what you will call me once I enter in between giving you what you need, craving me you will after I release this royal passion, giving it to you from your favorite position, face down as I hit it from the back I pound, your screams become loud, through the pillow the neighbors down the street can hear your type of loud, your palace can't take all of me, this is going to take a while, in and out, in and out, slow with my rock, Tic Toc, Tic Toc, you're getting a taste of what I'm about, you let out a loud shout, high above my throne when I mount, a mountain you will have to climb, time after time losing count, can't keep track of your eruptions, your Palace Of Pleasure busting, I will be at the top of your discussion when you're lunching with your girls, deep into my Wonderland, forever my girl, you never know what's next with my twist and twirls, I hold the master plan, my Masterpiece, with my Unpredictable abilities I will make you release, taking away your stress when I dig deep, your moans sound so sexy to me, I can tell from your actions you have never had it this way, trust in me as we lay the night away, putting you to sleep with just a tease of my Unpredictable capabilities, your heart I freeze until the next time we meet, leaving you as you rest to sleep, dreaming of me, King is all you will see.

D. C.

SOUNDS OF LOVE MAKING

Your sounds put me at ease, soothes my soul when I'm deep in between, sing soft and sweet as a mockingbird, the greatest sound here on earth, when in your presence you take me to another level, can't no one do it better, the sounds that you give off when I'm deep inside your womb, playing inside your treasure, giving you that boom, boom, clap, with my tongue going everywhere on your map, hitting designated spots, making your palace pop, your Sounds Of Love making doesn't stop, from the bottom of your moans, to those screams at the top of your lungs puts me in a dream, synchronizing our vibe, playing my rhythm to the beat of your drum, making those trumpets sound, as I make love roll off your tongue, your legs become weak, I'm about to make you cum, you grab my pillow trying to fight and run, I show my strength in these arms as I held you down moving my tongue faster than a machine gun, you cry out King you're the royal one, sire this is your palace for the rest of your days to come, I'm making you cum again, you squirm as you squirt, I flip you over to give you that work, I wrap your legs around my head, I stand to be fed, you grab my shaft with your hand, you starting to follow my master plan, can you imagine the sounds that are being made simultaneously going ham, in my Royal Room it's going down, a Royal Lover you have finally found, I am that one smoking gun when the dust settles, my flow, my touch, my melody is soft as rose petals, I hear your echoes when deep in the middle, a lucky fellow I am to be blessedly serenaded by your cords, oh my Lord I look forward to your Pleasure, always wanting your Pleasure, even in stormy weather I can hear your moans and cries over the rain, pressing you up against my Window Pane, I love to hear you sing my name when I'm landing my plane into your Erotic Zones, your Sounds Of Love making plays over and over again in my mind, I can't get your tones out my head, it's on constant rewind, repeat, repeat, inside of your Pleasure is where I forever want to be, without your touch I will become weak, I need to feast off your Palace Of Pleasure, I am your vampire, drawn to your blood,
I can't measure how high you take me up,

MII: The Return of the King

I just can't get enough of your Sounds Of Love making.

D. C.

THE PURSUIT

I can chase you forever, I wouldn't mind The Pursuit, my eyes are stuck on you, my mind was once confused, my heart was torn and bruised, I know with you I can't lose, no need to wonder what will be my next move, ready set, I will be your iron knight, your heart I will protect, the best is yet to come, I am that one, locking you down and throwing away the key, all I see is you and me, pause, wait, slow it down, what I meant to say was all I see is you on top of me, with me Pushing Inside Of You from down under, Deep, Deep, into your palace, there's no cure, your love is what I have imagined since the First Time that I ever imagined a love, the chase is on, I can endure anything that is thrown my way, look into my eyes, they will tell you all that I have to say without speaking a word, your love, yes I defer, I bow to, my queen it's you I'm trying to get a hold, a grip on your heart as I rip and run through these streets looking for you, my main squeeze, I get a glimpse in traffic, my nerves I try to ease, I'm on The Pursuit, I can't lose you, baby please, moving fast, dipping while I dash trying to catch up to your beautiful ass, green, green, yellow lights flash, you're moving too fast, RED, once again I lose your sexy ass, stuck, dead at this light, time passes, I'm still thinking about the smile I caught last knowing my life belongs to you, you're my type, I can call your heart my home, I want nothing more than for you to ring my phone, to choose me to be your King as your lifelong partner, on the throne we will sit, in traffic again I sit as I reminisce, you pull up alongside of my ride, I don't want to blink my eyes, I have to take this chance, I can't lose you again my wife, you look and smile as the light turns green, here's the scene, moving fast my feelings for you will outlast your last, in hot Pursuit, this time I'm on you, this King you will choose, I can be your dreams and fulfill your fantasies, breaking down your walls showing you that last you had wasn't reality, they tried to be me, but couldn't measure up, I'm catching up, your cup of love is about to run over, yellow light, RED, we're stuck, your beauty is in the eyes of this beholder, windows roll down, Royalty is in your presence, no more colder days and lonely nights, you see that I'm no clown, for your love I will fight, showing in you many ways that I am your Mr. Right, this pursuit I can run for life, green light, you smile and go, on the chase again this will be a never-ending show, one day you will feel what flows through my veins, until then your smile will hold my heart while we are apart, the start of a never-ending Pursuit of happiness.

D. C.

FEEL ME

I'm going to make you Feel Me even when you are using your hands to do that erotic dance in between your thighs, this King holds all types of surprises, the heat will keep rising higher than you could have ever imagined, tell me do you want to be bad baby, I'm going to make you Feel Me enough to call me daddy, Papi, King, can't no other top me, those others are floppy, I have that hard disc copy, there's no stopping once I go there yes there, sweating while I'm down there, no need for air I can dive for days, this King will have you misbehaving, Deep, Deep into your cave with my tongue doing the wave, giving you the best you ever had, yes the royal way, the way your body is moving, I'm pursuing your feelings, feeling the tension, like you forgot to mention you never had it before, your body I continue to explore, I realize you never had this before, from jump I told you I'm nothing like you ever had before, you will Feel Me after four strokes, the lump in your throat is your heart telling you to let loose, let go, this King that's giving you this Royal Show is for sure the real deal, explode and let go, I'm a full-course meal, we coast, I flow through your palace, Body to Body, can you fathom the scene, close your eyes so that you can Feel Me as I stroke slow, rocking your body coast to coast, words really can't justify this Rollercoaster Ride, pushing inside taking my time with what will remain mine for all time, no one shall ever come in between this divine union, The Pursuit is done, you're about to bust again all over my loaded gun, this King has you calling out, "YOU'RE THE ONE," this Feel Me joint has just begun, I plant my feet firmly to stand, under hooking your legs with my arms pulling you close to the edge so that I can perform that Lazy Love, hit you with something that is sanctified from on high, pulling inside at that yellow light speed, red light as I say take a deep breath baby, breathe, here comes that Greenlight Special, spreading you wide as you open up your eyes to see me grooving inside, you love the way my body winds, up and down, side to side, I'm changing your life here tonight, you Feel Me my love, my thrust, my might, giving you a different taste of love, outta sight, opening your eyes to another side of love, they call me Mr.

MII: The Return of the King

Right, we're going to continue this love action until the candle lights burn all the way out, I grip you close to do the most, showing my strength, later to your girls you can brag and boast, I lift you up, in the air you float, strong I am, yes I know, your face shows a glow, yes I know, your thoughts are surrounding my ceiling, I see them, yes I know, you never heard it like this before, this is King's Love that you explore, I'm going to make you Feel Me to your core, you scream you want more, pushing your body up against the wall, kissing you soft and slow, your waterfalls, I withdraw all your hurt, heartache and pain, you will never be the same, there's nothing plain about this catch, throwing you over the bed so that I can stretch you over from that backside, I can feel your love streaming down, a real one is what you have found, in love thoughts around floating around your mental from the way I'm putting it down, in and out you moan loud into the pillow, deep and hard inside I go your arch is high, my arm is hooking your thighs, from the back and the side, giving you that Everlasting Night, relieving your stress, dropping your legs so that you can Feel Me, my pipe with long lasting strokes, yes baby I will go slow so that you feel every inch, pinch yourself love this is no dream, this is your reality, actually you will Feel Me when you dream, in your dreams it will seem as if I'm there inside, giving you that delight, that's Just Right, hitting you with that thunder at lightning speed, breaking you down to your knees, begging please, while I please you with Pleasure, for me to never leave, gripping your real hair, yes no weave, I lay you flat, chest to back, close with my stroke, the deeper I go with a small arch as we float, damn you say baby go, this is your palace just go, I flow, in and out without a doubt I gave her what the town is buzzing about, this is King's, the Royal Lover, house, from the west to the south, they can hear you shout I'm taking you there, to another place, to those others farewell, loving you with grace as this race is about to come to an end, even when I'm finished you will Feel Me in it, I'm the realist, letting go as you feel this, feel all of me inside, closing your eyes with a smile on your face this is just the beginning of this race, leaving you with Royal Memoirs until the next time I can take you far.

0-100
(REAL QUICK)

I want you to come to me, you know if we do this one more time that you will love me for all time, that first time I wined and dined, pleasured you with a fine time, Taking My Time with your canvas, making sure no spot on your body went untouched, I don't miss, each smiled that you let off when I went off down below to give you more than you ever hoped for, something very impossible to ignore, as I explored your everglades, putting on my shades before I entered your maze, wait, wait, damn I just went 0 to a 100 (Real Quick), let me slow it down so you can see how we came to me getting ready to enter you're maze, putting on shades, you will be amazed, my speed will have you in a daze, listen closely, I will not repeat these quotes, fast as lightning I go to pick you up, open your door, kissing and touching racing through traffic, to my home we go, I open my door, in we go, keys I throw, kicking off my shoes while spinning you around to kiss your lips slow, but fast this feeling will outlast three lifetimes, I snatch off your clothes, then mine, lay you down kissing around and around your canvas, I just can't stand it when you're not in my presence, you are my heaven sent, this is meant, closing your eyes in love, your feelings are spent, I'm cashing in, I grab my shades before I pull into your maze, to give you a taste of what you crave, the best in the west, the rest is no threat, I hold the crown putting it down, I pound 0 to a 100 (Real Quick), let me slow it down, I just loved you in a few different ways, did you catch that, yes you have met your match, the others couldn't light your match, I'm that fire you will always desire, deep in you, the west is where I'm at, my back you scratched, your walls I caved in, deep within, I stroked which felt slow to you, but fast as I float, you can't fight this flow, you felt me in your throat, deep in I go with every stroke your feelings I invoke, giving you what you have been craving for all your days, putting your legs over my shoulders so that I can put you farther into a daze, grabbing my crown by the way as I put it down, my hat is turned around, your arms and hands are around my waist as I give you a taste of my well-endowed, I can tell from that shock frown upon your face you never heard of King, the one who runs this town, forever you will feign for what's in between, you will want to become my Queen, I'm putting it down 0 to a 100 (Real Quick), slow it down, let me show you how I showed out in this scene, yes your screams give me what's in between, you are my drug and I am your feind, you are my King and I want to be your Queen, damn you're in me so deep, she recites, pushing in slow but fast with both of her legs on my shoulders, who me, my feet I stand on the floor, firmly holding those thighs tightly together so that she Feels Me, feel it, this wood, giving that good, good Pleasure, however that was not a frown but a look of satisfaction, saying It's Yours with no words, to you I defer, I bow at your feet, kissing your neck down your valley, rubbing and touching on your alley, you look with a glare telling me I am taking you there, yes there, I swear this went 0 to a 100 (Real Quick), watch closely, I was doing the most you see, going so hard, going so fast to where I dashed around the world and back again, watch as I sent her love to the south when I hit her in between with my New Orleans partying down her strip, ripping down her mardi gras, the love didn't stop y'all as she falls going to your Niagara falls, stopping in Australia as I kiss down your neck to the valley of the west, giving you that one Unforgettable show, the faster I go, explode up, down low, my love is sweet, your ass I will keep, your scent will sleep with me in between my sheets, thinking about you for weeks, damn I just went 0 to a 100 (Real Quick) with ease, check my memory please, back I go giving you that Unforgettable show, faster than slow, explode I did, this I know, clothes back on from the floor, in the car we go, kissing you so sweet your ass I grab saying your love I will keep back home at last in my bed I sleep with your scent overwhelming me, I just went 0 to a 100 (Real Quick), my love game is the Shhh.

D. C.

#923

Romance fills the air, pulling out all the stops, showing you that I care in more ways than one, this night has just begun, anxious with a hint of suspense, after tonight you will reminisce of the things to come once you enter my Royal Room, I put so much thought into pleasing you, I'm feeling everything about you, it's the things that you do, the talk in your speech, your smile which makes me weak, the strides in your walk, no other woman can compete, your love I seek, the time has come for you to be alone with me, without anyone to intrude or disturb, I know your worth here on God's green earth, your body is about to become my turf, my playing field even with my strength, will and might, I'm nervous about this night, this isn't me to be nervous, but you I hold high, flying above the sky, thoughts of being in between your thighs (mmmm), I cannot lie, I feel that you are Mrs. Just Right, that's why tonight has to be Just Right, every word that I speak, every move that I make, no mistakes, for today is the day that I crown my wife, doing the Unthinkable, my phone rings and it's you, My Love, My Beautiful Dove, hello as I answer, hey babe you say with a slight tremble in your voice of nervousness, a soft kiss and touch is what you have missed for quite some time now, I was put here for you to be found by me, I can't wait to give you what your heart has desired for so long, these were my thoughts, are you ready to explore my love and let go? As you say I'm here parking on level number three, can you meet me in the lobby, but stay on the phone, okay hold on as I slide my shoes on anticipating the night as I make a slight right to the elevator, it's seems later than time reads, trying to keep my feelings at ease, I've been waiting for this one for quite some time, a year to be exact, waiting patiently before I attack, as you speak saying sweetie where are you at, turn around I say, right here as your face lights up the night, looking amazing shall I add, your smile is so right and bright, blushing from ear to ear, Follow My Lead My Love, this way my dear, walking side by side with a little space in between, as we wait for the elevator to take us up, I can't get enough of that beautiful smile of yours, my thoughts are going wild as we stand silently apart, admiring

MII: The Return of the King

your body, a work of art, our hearts will be joined to never part, I can't wait to explore that other smile of yours, oh how I'm going to adore your palace, hold, I'm getting ahead of myself, ding is the sound as we exit and take a left, Slow is our pace as we walk and get closer to that desired place, our hearts are at a race, redness takes over your face, beautiful you are, can't any other take your place, ready I am to take this love affair far, approaching the door, #923, do you dare enter? Take my hand, close your eyes, and prepare yourself, I drop the key to let it scan, I am nothing like your last guy by far nothing like the normality your used to, more like your fantasy come true, you're with a real man, a King, who will romantically Pleasure your soul, not with just love making, but with an emotional and mental connection, entering #923 with me saying you're now in the land of sweet soft affection, after tonight you will be professing your love to me, your eyes open as you peak to see a trail of rose petals all over the bed and floor, leading out to the balcony, open up My Love this night is all yours, priceless is the look upon your face, your heart begins to race, I set the pace by pouring you a glass of Belvedere, to the balcony we go, talking about many things as the wind blows softly, you walk back in towards the bed kicking off your shoes, taking a sip of your drink, starting to get loose, giving me a look, that look, which has me shook, as I sit near, another glass My Love you say to erase your fear, you never had it like this and you never will, your King is here to stay, those bad memories I will take away, putting your glass down as I come closer to ignite your fire, I want to be all that you desire, kissing you slowly, rubbing on your body, here we go, I stand grabbing your hand, pulling you up so that you can watch me pull off my shirt to throw it to the floor, you take action by pulling off yours, your body I'm about to explore, Body To Body, Taking My Time, you have that look in your eyes, you are about to earn what's been yours for so long, what we're about to do is no surprise, I lay you back down across the rose petals unbuttoning your pants as I slide them off, my tongue is about to dance in between your thighs, starting from your lips to your neck, down to your perfectly shape breasts, no rest tonight, you're having King all night, that Just Right, out of sight, making my way down your valley, licking all over your canvas, spreading you wide so *that my fingers and tongue can go inside, damn baby you're so wet and tight, where have you been all my life, making Love Faces as I give you that delight, my tongue has your feelings moving in my direction, so much affection, I'm giving you a Lesson In Love, my precious dove, I come up after making your body quiver, tongue kissing you slowly before I deliver my gunslinger, into the middle of your darkness I go, slow, caressing your body as I stroke, your legs and thighs are around my waist tight, as I take my rightful place, your passion I have evoked to the Tenth Power, your walls I crush and devour, we have been going for about an hour, changing positions, we are on a mission, taking off like a rocket, I'm hitting your pocket, raising your legs above my head, in with my royal tip, kissing your lips, hitting you with my fully equipped, you flip the script giving me a taste of how it will be with you in control, you drop low teasing me with your tongue, curling my toes as you give me a show, up you come with your tongue to my chest, you're the f****** best, sitting high with that arch in your back, your body is amazing, your hands are in the air as you ride my waves, you are becoming My Love Slave, I rise with my hands on the small of your back, kissing you as you push back, you say baby I want you to attack from the back (pause), taking a shot I do before switching positions, go slow you imply as I spread your ass and thighs, deep inside is where I want to be, your juices are flowing all over me as I swim your sea like a shark hitting my mark, taking you there, to a place where you've never been before, I am all yours you say, flipping you back over so that I can see your face, with each hour that passes I erase your past, smacking your butt with a great feeling, giving you that sexually healing, that love you have been missing, dashing faster, almost there, this feeling I can't compare, you are my air that I breathe, exploding as we lay the night away, embrace in my arms as we to sleep, waking up the next morning with you next to me, looking deep into your eyes as you say can we press repeat, with no hesitation I give you all of me, #923, until the next time we meet I will be thinking of you my sweet Beautiful Find, it took a long time to make you mine, a greater love I will never find, I'm yours.*

HAPPINESS

When your name is spoken, something on the inside of my body calls out Happiness, ever since I found the key to your heart, your love, there is only one you, I can't compare, a sweet summer breeze when you come near, girl it's true, I'm ready for you, I place no one above, shining brighter than the sun when you smile, I love everything about your style, you put a smile on my heart each and every time we come together from being apart, beautiful you are, perfect in my eyes, the only star I see at night, it's no surprise that you're my Mrs. Right, you can take me seriously baby, this is serious, for in this lifetime I want you for the rest of my days, gazing deeply into your eyes as I drop to my right knee, I want to share vows with you my love, I want to be blessed by the heavens above, let's go before the hand of God my love, I want you for the rest of my days, your heart I will never replace, here I am to stay, this love that I feel burning inside for you is real, you can kill all doubts and fears, Happiness when I look at you, tears form on the inside, so much joy on the inside, you are the love of my life, I need you each day, every night, your King, your love, your friend, is here to cherish you for eternity, look deep into my eyes and you will see that we are Soul Mates, Happiness is written across your face, that smile always leaves me with a loving impression, I'm confessing my all, you fill me with bliss, my heaven has sent me what I waited for, my angel in disguise, I thank you for entering my life, never thought twice, since that day we exchanged numbers, so many thoughts and wonders without you even knowing I secretly fell in love, it all started on a hot summer day, you drove right by, but I caught your gorgeous face, that visual I couldn't escape, waiting to get a glimpse of you the unknown, just seeing you that feeling alone gave me life, that split two seconds made my mornings, wave and smile, driving me wild, only if you knew I would say, I couldn't shake my feelings and emotions, taking a chance at Happiness ever after, nothing, but good memories and laughter, take my hand, make me a better man, you are the center of my life, I will never fade from this choice I've made, you are my wife, you don't have to look any farther than me, I have all that you will ever need and want, your beauty is in the eyes of this beholder, I will be your shoulder that you can lean on in your time of need, taking away any pain that you my endure, with me you are secure, I am perfectly blind with only your guidance to lead me, visions of you and I walking through life hand and hand, together we will withstand any type of weather that may come our way, it can't get no better than you, my thoughts, my feelings, my heart is true, I want no one else for as long as I live, but you, so much compassion, so hard to hold all this inside, waiting for the perfect night to unveil all that I possess, heart pounding through my chest, the rest don't stand a chance, this will be a lifetime dance with no ending, we will just keep replaying the beginning, is that okay with you? Will you comply with all that I want you to do? I don't need to wait for time to tell, hell I know right now, I'm still on bended knee to the ground, my love just flows with your heart intact, at this very moment this is where my feelings are at, can you match that? She replies and says..............

To Be Continued...

MII: The Return of the King

A DESIRED FEELING

I have Desired this Feeling that's growing inside of me for so long, waiting for the right heart I can call my own, my home away from home, one who can sit aside me on my throne and rule on high, a woman by day, My Love Slave by night, your lips, hips and thighs have me on rise, shhh baby you're the shhh baby, I tell no lies, you have that spark, that fire in your eyes, your passion I desire, allow me to enter your love zone, where I belong, in your world, I'm far from what you're used to my girl, the way my tongue twirls when touching you there, yes there you will never be able to compare this King, the things I can do once I go in between will make you sing hit notes you never thought to imagine, can you imagine the ride I can take you on, close your eyes and listen to my voice so that you can visualize and watch me in your dreams as you sleep, this roller coaster you will want to repeat, wet you are, deep as the sea I am, diving with no scuba gear, pulling you near, playing with your pearl, tasting your flavor, one major night is in store, you're in store for that Desired Feeling you have been searching for, oh how I adore your precious jewel, I fuel your fire, I swear each and every time you are in need you will think of me, your desire, once I begin to stroke your buried treasure in search of your gold, your legs I fold, deeper into your stratosphere, whispers takes over my ears, putting my rocket in gear shifting with my motions, grooving to the rhythm of your heartbeat, Taking My Time, making your body, mind and soul all mine, you will never find another of my kind here on this earth, for what it is worth, I know your worth, your value, I have you tangled in my arms as I perform these Desired strokes, I want you to release and let go of what you have been holding onto for so long, I'm going deep, going long, can you handle this show I'm putting on, take what I pitch, this desire will make you tap, call it quits as I hit you with my royal passion, no wall will go untouched, I don't miss, I bare a Gift, that will have your mind all in a twist, we kiss, I'm the shhh when it comes to this loving tip, it's written all over your face, you're loving this desire that's in between my waist, the

D. C.

*sun's coming up, digging you until the next day, A Desired Feeling
you will never be able to release nor escape,
this King can't be replaced.*

SNEAKY & FREAKY

I want to love you and only you, but first I want to freak you like you've never been freaked before, your core I want to adore, tonight you will feel my might and hear me roar, Sneaky is what we will have to be, Down Low on the creep, with your man asleep in the next room, let me show you that I'm the strong type, I know you will like the way I lay down the boom, I will leave your mind and body Just Right, tonight I will become lost inside of you, here just visiting for one night, it's a must we get it in tonight, hearing us he just might, late night creep and sneak quietly so that you can lay next to me, patiently I watch the time Tic Toc, dozing off as the clock strikes three, feeling someone climbing into my sheets, is this a dream or my reality, I quickly peek my eyes to see, playing sleep so that she can wake up the beast, moving slowly, she's close, kissing me on my cheek as you whisper baby I need you to be lost inside of me, opening my eyes fully so that I can gaze into yours, kissing your lips, our tongues start to twist, I lick and lick your lips while sucking on your tongue, yea I am that one, your body I want to explore, from your head to your feet I will adore, your canvas will be painted with my love, no place will go untouched, feel free to lead me where ever you want me to go, I want to be lost in you, give me a lifetime show, low you go, your eyes to my eyes with your hands moving down my abs to my thighs real slow, pulling my pants to the floor, that kiss you just gave to my inner thigh makes me adore those lips of yours, explore my love, take me for a ride, a rush goes up my side, a lick from left to right, both hands grip my royal pipe, dreams of this you will have every night, your lips to my mic, singing Just Right, you have me like hands in the air on the highest rollercoaster do I dare, damn baby I swear, yes there, right there, grabbing your hair, moving it to the side, so I can see you slip and slide, deep throat as you take me inside slow as far as you can go, just flowing back and forth you go, that freak in you is about to show, telling me to stand without ever letting go with your jaws, you need a standing ovation with an applause, you have me in awe, seeing stars in all, pushing me back down to the bed as you crawl up my body to place me inside of

D. C.

your walls, so warm, so juicy and wet, the best I've ever felt, making me melt on contact, my legs shake, in my head I say, no King relax, not just yet, you're a vet, Ready, Set, Go, I don't miss, you're about to feel my extended clip as I hit you with my left then right stroke, deep diving when we coast, submerged inside of your world, twirling our tongues, you're about to become sprung, our bodies intertwined all over this bed, spreading your thighs as I kiss in between, you're about to get that supreme, that royalty type of treatment, no worries I'll be open for business whenever you need it, you will become my feign, I will supply exactly what you need, I'm your Just Right, my tongue starts to fight with your pearl, I want you to say my name my girl, don't fight it baby call my name, say it, you hold back as we continue this Sneaky & Freaky episode, flipping you to that backside, in this position you're about to be fed that long deep only hit you with the tip for a bit stroke, I'm loving this view while I smoke, passing it to you so you can take a toke, deep, deep is the flow, pushing in, here I go picking up my coast, speed boat, running this marathon through your valley, this love scene is right up my alley, so outta sight, I'm going to go all night/morning until you call my name, are you ready to say my name, do I need to dig a little deeper, I know my love is a keeper just say it my freak, as you grip the sheets pressing your face into the pillow to let go a Sneaky scream, you're making me earn it, but you deserve it, be free, be with me, as we both climax at the same damn time with you yelling out King you're all I need, it's yours forever in a day, I'm claiming it's mine, as you climb out the sheets just to Sneak back into your bed, dreamland is where I head, waking up with a smile on my face wondering if last night really happened, satisfaction as I smell you all over me, Sneaky & Freaky is what we will forever be.

POISONOUS LOVE

THERE'S SOMETHING IN THIS LIQUOR, WITH EVERY SIP THOSE THIGHS ARE LOOKING THICKER, MY FEELINGS ARE GROWING DEEPER, THERE'S SOMETHING IN THIS LIQUOR OHH YEA, I CANT HELP BUT STARE AT YOUR FIGURE, WHAT DID YOU SLIP UP IN MY CUP OF LOVE, I CAN NEVER HAVE TOO MUCH, BUT THERE'S SOMETHING IN THIS LIQUOR, MY FEELINGS ARE GROWING DEEPER, I KNOW YOU'RE NOT A TRICKSTER, ALL I WANT IS YOU, ALL I SEE IS YOU, ALL I NEED IS YOU, BABY WHAT DID YOU DO? MY LOVE FOR YOU IS GROWING THICKER AND THICKER, THERE'S SOMETHING IN THIS LIQUOR, I CANT HELP BUT STARE AT YOUR FIGURE, DAMN YOU LOOK SO GOOD, BRING THAT JUST RIGHT HERE, SO I CAN GIVE IT TO YOU LIKE A REAL KING SHOULD, I WISH I COULD SEE YOU STRIP RIGHT NOW, I CAN HELP YOU OUT AND RELIEVE THAT STRESS RIGHT NOW, PUT THIS KING TO THE TEST, SO I CAN WORK YOU OUT RIGHT NOW, I WILL SHOW YOU NOTHING BUT THE BEST, THE GREATEST SEX OFF THIS LIQUOR WHEN I LICK YOU THERE, YES THERE, THE AIR IS GETTING THICKER, SWEATING AS I LICK YOU THERE, I SWEAR ALL I WANT TO DO IS DRINK AND LOVE, DRINK, DRINK AND LOVE YOU, ALL I WANT IS YOU, WHAT HAVE YOU DONE TO ME, IN THIS VERY MOMENT I WANT YOU OFF THIS LIQUOR, MY LOVE IS GROWING DEEPER AS I FLOW DEEPER THROUGH YOUR PALACE, CLOSE YOUR EYES AND IMGAINE MY STROKE, YOUR LOVE I WILL PROVOKE, I CANT HELP BUT GO DEEP INSIDE OF YOU, IT'S BECAUSE OF YOU THAT I FEEL THIS WAY, ALL I CAN SAY IS YOU COMPLETE ME, NO IT ISN'T THE LIQUOR TALKING, MY BODY IS WALKING THROUGH YOUR VALLEY GIVING YOU A LESSON IN LOVE, SHOWING YOU THINGS YOU NEVER HAD BEFORE, KING WILL GIVE YOU WHAT YOU'VE BEEN MISSING IN LOVE, THIS TREASURE I HOLD TRUST IT'S ENOUGH, TAKING MY TIME, NO RUSH, THIS ISN'T A HIGH SCHOOL CRUSH, BUT LOVE FROM THE GATE NEVER LUST, IN MY LOVE YOU CAN TRUST, WITH ME IT'S A PLUS, 3, 2, 1, IT'S YOUR TIME TO ERUPT, AS I BUST THROUGH THE CEILING, I HAVE THAT

D. C.

SEXUAL HEALING STORED INSIDE OF ME, WHEN I TOUCH YOU WILL FINALLY BE FREE, I LOVE EVERYTHING ABOUT YOU FROM YOUR HEAD TO YOUR FEET, DAMN IT'S SOMETHING IN THIS LIQUOR, WHAT HAVE YOU DONE TO ME, MY LOVE IS GROWING DEEPER OHH YEA, ALL I WANT IS YOU, ALL I SEE IS YOU, ALL I NEED IS YOU.

MII: The Return of the King

LET ME LOVE YOU

My Love, my heart, my soul, yes it is you that holds my love, my thoughts are only of you, all I want to do is love you, Let Me Love You, show you a love that will take you on a journey, a voyage that you will never want to come back from, Let Me Love You and show you that you will never have to run again, I am him, the one they call King, your King I'm willing to be if you allow me to love you, oh Let Me Love you my Beautiful Find, say that forever your hand will be mine, let me protect your precious heart for all time, those others didn't do you right, I'm here to stay with you all through the nights and days to come, let me be that one, Let Me Love You, the sun shines upon you, your glow, your essence takes me to a place where I never want to leave, say that it is me you need, the only time you will feel weak is when I am in between your knees, legs and thighs giving you all that I have stored inside, shifting and stroking with all my might, can you picture that on many nights to come, even when the sun is up I will continue to make your body erupt, bust like an uncontrollable gun, yes I am that one who will love you like never before, Let Me Love You and adore the very ground you walk on, you have my feelings on fire, my life's desire is to make sure you go through this life the rest of your life with no more hurt, your past is six feet under the dirt, allow my hand to slip up under your shirt, now rubbing on your breasts as I caress your lips with my lips, this kiss is One Of A Kind, blowing each other's mind, never will I come to find another of your kind, my queen it seems you have finally come to me to give me what I need, and that is to show love for just one, that one is you, accept My Gift, you are my Rib, I'm going to give you the world, you are my world, my everything my girl, my Queen it seems that you have stolen my heart, never will we part, from this day forth I will prove my love in ways that you could imagine only or see in a movie, you're my groove theory, let's make some Unforgettable memories.

D. C.

FOR YOU I WILL

So Perfect In My Eyes, so worth going through any fight, no matter the storm, my love will prove its might, just to have you by my side, I see no one but you, confused I think not, this love will never cease, my feelings can't stop rising to the top, an angel from up above, you're the cream of the crop, in you I have found My One And Only, I had to go through a few phonies to prepare for you, it is so true, my love for you that is, you're my fix, the perfect fit, I can never get enough, sending a rush through my body to your body, those love chills, my potion, my tonic, you want it, I got, For You I Will show my skills, my abilities, and answer that question that's lingering in your head, why do they call him Royalty? For You I Will, close your eyes so that I can take you on a ride, no peeking, no you can't see, you got me feigning like Jodeci, in between your thighs is where I want to be, slow it down let me repeat, I got you feigning like Jodeci while in between the sheets with your thighs wrapped around me, deep in your pleasure is where you can find me, my love is the key to your heart, For You I Will unlock that buried treasure, my limits can't be measured, admiring everything about you as I stroke your core as if you're priceless art that can't be bought without love, Never Duplicated, I'm so faded off your kiss, those lips have my feelings in a twist, I Can't Resist, For You I Will make sure no spot goes untouched, I won't miss a spot when licking your canvas from your neck to your breasts, kissing, sucking, and rubbing as I give you my all, For You I Will deep dive until you erupt twice, all night long loving with my lavish tongue, you have earned this one, your temptation is so persuasive, taking me in new directions, you are the new essence of perfection, without question all that I will ever need, my heart is sincerely in its entirety yours for the long haul, For You I Will never fall, never fail your love, never turn your trust, my loving making you can trust is yours, no lust, no fight, no fuss, each and every day I will make your body erupt, my feelings are here to stay, my heart will never change, my mind will remain, body, soul and love you will always hold, I am yours, all of me, from the depths of my feet, I come up to give you more of me, my tongue I

MII: The Return of the King

release, in between my thighs I unleash the freak in me, kissing you slowly as I pull into your palace in slow motion, coasting with my stroking, arching with a long extension, For You I Will take your mind and body on a mission, hitting you with this royal healing, A Feeling You Never Felt Before, V shape at the corner of the bed is where I explore deep into your core, taking you to that other side of love, ready you are to erupt and bust, stretching you out to the limit, giving you a lesson in love, For You I Will be the log for your fire, turn over baby from the back is what I desire, showing you things you didn't know, hitting spots you never knew you had before, arching your back, making you throw it back, giving you the most amazing love, stretching you out to the limit, For You I Will show you why they call me Royalty, turn around open your eyes and see, spread your legs and wrap them around me, this is the grand finale, I hope you like the strong type, place your hands around my neck, I'm about to make you love me, look at what you are in for, standing firm as I raise you high towards the ceiling, stretching you out with this royal healing, giving you that falling in love feeling, pulling on your hair as I stroke you slow than fast, slow than fast, spreading your cheeks, smacking your ass, giving you that I never had love, throwing you to the bed so that I can spread and go deep, one, two, three, your staring into my eyes, deep, four, five, six, I'm shifting my hips as I kiss your lips, seven, eight, our hearts skip to each other's tune, nine and ten explode deep down inside your womb, consuming all of your love, showing you why my For You I Will always be above the rest, kissing the night away, as you lay on my chest, For You I Will give nothing, but the best.

D. C.

SINCE I MET YOU

There can only be one of you, oh my love listen to what I am saying to you, there can only be one of you because Since I Met You I haven't been the same, my life has changed for the greater good, my past couldn't make me feel like I feel now in this very moment while stroking these keys wishing I was stroking in between your knees and thighs, but back to my Since I Met You, my love for you will never be the same, baby listen to what I am saying, with each and every day I am granted to see your lovely face, I will love you in ways that will never leave you with any complaints, our love will grow and grow to never stay the same, but I will always remain yours, Since I Met You I was yours, I knew that your heart was scorned, I could feel it, you hid it well, but I could tell you needed me just as much as I needed you, coming together us two, not ready but willing, chemistry is so different not to mention all this sexual tension, I'm sensing you're feeling, needing that touch, that healing, how long has it been, a year, you're feigning, my dear, come here, Since I Met You I have no fear in love, to love, to fight for love, I will fight for you, Since I Met You I see no one but you, going through withdrawals when I can't have you, so much passion when I am around you, nothing even matters when we are together, no matter the weather, through rain and storm I will perform, my love is strong for you, these love acts are only for you, Since I Met You it's been all about you, my heart belongs to you, when we are Body To Body and I turn you into My Love Slave, the feeling you give me when you drop low after you misbehave, oh the things you do with your tongue have me in a daze, that stroke has me amazed, you tend to turn me into Your Love Slave from time to time, but Tic Toc Tic Toc that love is mine when I flip you around and arch your back just to hit you from behind, that wonderful spot, oh my lord, that Lazy Love, Since I Met You there are so many things I want to try, so much I want to do, only with you, I see you as my life's treasure, no one will ever be able to measure up to your stature, I just have to have it, I just have to have you, Since I Met You I am blind, these other chicks are not worth my time, I'm too busy trying to find new ways to

make you mine, hold up baby you're not listening to my rhyme, you're my One Of A Kind, that Beautiful Find, a goddess, My Queen, my everything and I never want this flame to burn out so I turn out, show out in ways that you've never seen before, just to win your love each and every day, like a fat kid eating chocolate cake, feed me more, baby I need more and more, Since I Met You I have no problem with letting the trumpets sound so that the crowd can hear me roar as I confess my one and only true love, the heavens above have ordained this love, Since I Met You you're all I can think of, your kiss takes me high floating above the clouds, your gentle touch sends that rush through my body deep down to my soul, you have a hold on My Gift, my heart, My Rib you are, we will never part, together forever, I will never steer you wrong, Since I Met You I knew where my love belongs, forever going strong, this loving will live on and on, and on and on, a soft kiss to your lips I kiss the sweetest thing I will ever know,
I Love You Baby, forever my Lady.

D. C.

INHALE ME

Tonight, the focus is all on you, Sh*t tonight I hope you notice it's all yours, you finally get to explore a different flavor, this flavor will make you go and tell your neighbor about the taste, Sh*t tonight we will be going for hours, no time on this clock will be wasted, your body I'm about to devour, there will be no separating us tonight, your love is mine for the taking, love is what we will be making, your walls I will be breaking down, a lesson in love is what you have found, with every touch a barrier I will break, how much can you take? We're going to war tonight, look at what you are in for, I'm going to stretch you to the limits, showing you things you didn't know, Giving You A Feeling You Never Felt Before, welcome to King's Royal Show, here I go kissing you from head to toe, finding your hidden treasures, giving you what you deserve, knowing your worth, to be treated like a Queen dropping down to my knees to pull you towards the edge of the bed as I say It's Yours, "Own It" as I kiss in between your thighs, licking on your Hot Zones, loving those moans and sounds you give off as I dive off into your palace of love, gripping at your thighs kissing them as I spread you wide, saying It's Yours, as I get ready to adorn your love, adore your core, this lick is sent from the heavens above, sending chills through and through your body as you grip the sheets I say guess whose it is, baby Own this as I try to find out how many licks it takes until you Tick Tick boom, stroking my finger deep inside as I play with your pearl, your eyes focus on me then roll back as I suck and kiss with a lick soft and gentle, baby just Inhale Me while I stroke your mental with no words, all physical using my tongue as a pen writing in cursive, doesn't it feel so good, you're taking me like I knew you would, showing you my skills making your wheels turn faster and faster, knowing this is your First Time of having a shade of my kind, you are in King's hands, I'm going to do your body fine, this palace is all mine, showing you nobody can love you like King, climbing upon your canvas to kiss your lips, Body to Body, I can feel your heart skip, beat to my beat, you belong to me as I to you, you're gazing up at me, loving what you see as you peek at my well-endowed fully equipped *with that extend clip between my hips, Royal Love, yes my love I am that one here to give you what you have never tasted before, saying baby I will give it to you slow, no rush, this is your First Time with my kind, never will you be able to find another, none left like this brother, baby let me fill you up, hold it in, now take it down, I'm trying to make that waterfall come down, damn doesn't it feel so good, taking it like I knew you would, baby Inhale Me as I dwell in your palace of love kissing as I stroke you from above, here to explore your core in ways that will turn you into My Love Slave, giving you this mountain of pleasure, changing your life forever, opening your eyes up to the other side of love, giving you more than you ever could imagine, so much passion flows through the air, as we stare into each other eyes with a kiss to a whisper of love, taking you high and above, showing you that love is all that I am made up of, taking you deeper, my love is a sleeper, as I spread you wide to fill you up inside, baby take it all in, Inhale Me, let me fill you up with every back and forth action, satisfaction is guaranteed, after this you will be sound asleep, changing position to the back I creep, showing my strength under locking your legs with my arms to slide in deep with this elevation your love will fall down with no hesitation, love faces is what we are making, pulling you in front of the mirror so that I can see those looks, your heart I stole like a crook, your mind is shook, your body is caving, this love we're making is amazing, I have your feelings blazing, your river at a flow, the deeper I go, giving you just a little more of my Royal Show, turning you around kissing you hard, past that gentle stage, your My Love Slave on this Unforgettable Night, giving you My Everlasting, picking you up off the floor wrapping your legs around my waist to give you more, bouncing you slowly, I told you that I would rock you slow and steady, I hope you're ready, showing you my strength, I told you that I am your Heaven Sent, now my love just take it all in, I won't rush, Inhale Me baby, let me in, now take me down, doesn't that feel good, you're taking me like I knew you would, no limit to where we can go, taking it deeper, here we go, baby you're loving this flow, picking up my coast, faster I go giving you that put you back to sleep show, as I explode into your core,*

D. C.

this is only the beginning, I have more in store, with me there's never no ending, I am Truly Yours ...RL

MII: The Return of the King

MY EGO
(INTERLUDE)

My Ego runs high, but for you I will set it aside along with my pride just to find out what you are really feeling on the inside, your eyes don't lie, catching me as I stare, that glare tells me all that I need to know, I feel that you are ready for an all-night Royal Show, My Ego will show every ounce of me once I begin to touch your canvas, I promise no place on your body will go untouched, I don't miss sealed with a kiss, well-endowed and fully equipped with the right tool in between my thighs to show and prove that this feeling I give to you, you will never lose, your love will never stop, nor quit, I am your heaven sent, sometimes it's good to have an Ego, especially when you're good at what you do, watch my love, just listen to the things I want to do with you, kissing your lips for one, soft with my touch, let me open up your eyes to that other side of love, I can make you erupt with just one touch, this love is a must have, I must know more about you, ever since I saw you I could do nothing but think about you, what a strong attraction, satisfaction is guaranteed when I drop to my knees to go in between your thighs with my tongue, hotter than the sun I will have you, gripping and pulling on the sheets with you busting all over me, I wrote the book on how to love you up, I am that number one lover, there's no other, I'm the Champion lover, I love to taste you when I go deep down under, coming up with that sticky face, on repeat you say, no pride here, don't mind if the world watches me while I play through your Wonderland, I am that man, your King, My Ego is making you weak, your heart I seek with each and every stroke, I will evoke that lost love, showing you a different type of love in many forms with different positions, I never finish until you're finished, I'm nothing like your past, those dudes were the norm, I will outlast what you used to have, My Ego you will hold and grab on to, your palace is something I want to get used to, you see how sometimes it's good to carry around that Ego, it's that pride that people hold inside which makes them Lose Control, with you I can let it go so you can see me for who I really am, damn you have my mind in a frenzy, ever so

D. C.

tempting, I want my lips to know every inch of your body, this feeling I can't fight it, My Ego says just let go don't hide, show her the side of the Royal guy, for tonight we will sleep Naked so that I can explore your world to the fullest, I am the realist,
tonight you will never forget it.

MII: The Return of the King

NAKED

A perfect night, you and I alone, I've never seen something so beautiful that I can call my own, like a drug I'm drawn to your nakedness, I Can't Resist your temptation, I love the way the candles are bringing out your skin tone, giving my feelings an overwhelming sensation, love is what we will be making, the neighbors will be hearing some wall banging tonight, your body is so desirable that we don't need no protection tonight, damn did I just say that, come here, I love the way you sound when you let me in, I will be doing some eating at your table tonight, I am able to handle everything you throw my way, don't ever put your clothes back on my lady I say, Forever Yours, I'm Ready to explore your core to the fullest, taking you to a limit that you thought I wouldn't exceed, there's no limit when I'm feasting on your body, Naked we are, Ready, Set, Go let's get this started, indeed I'm in too deep with my tongue, but I'm not coming up for air, loving that stare you give with your hands in the air bringing them down to grab me around my head, your legs begin to shake, your thighs becomes tighter, my tongue is the fighter, doing circles around your ring making you Cum for the first time, cultivating your mind, all I have is time, making love slowly, giving you a show you've never seen before, your nakedness has my body exploring A Feeling I've Never Felt Before, this right here is all yours, all nine and a half inches not to mention these strokes I send from up above, digging and digging deep I've dug going low in your stratosphere, picking your body up off the bed to place you on my soft rug, to the floor we go, getting it with every stroke, I evoke your passion, thrashing and smashing your palace, can you imagine what I'm going to do next as your legs grow tighter with a shake ready to release all over me once more, it's not over just yet, I'm nothing like the norm, putting your legs in that V shape, pulling out to lick my tongue all over your plate, a quarter past eight, tears rolling down your face of joy as I enjoy you being Naked, never will you question my love and what I can do, my dove I'm so into you, coming up kissing and licking on your breasts, neck and lips as I stand up to flip you to your back side, straight as an arrow as I

D. C.

spread your thighs to slide in with just my tip, no rush, I will rip through your hips, you about to feel me so deep that you may tap and quit, my love game is the Shhh, to where you won't want to go anywhere else, I wear the crown and hold the belt, with each stroke you felt my power as I devour your walls, breaking them down, grooving to your rhythm as I take you down, putting that arch in your back hitting you with that red, yellow, Greenlight Special, giving you that Everlasting treatment that you deserve here on this earth, showing you what you are worth, making you squirt, more and more, this passion is all yours as I explode off into your core, you being Naked makes me want you more and more, oh how I adore your body my love, just thinking about it takes me high and above.

SO IN LOVE

This is my story, non-fiction surely all facts, my life has changed since you have come and enter my life, you are My Backbone, your heart I call my home, you have made my life so complete, you are so sweet, no one can compete, your smile takes my breath away, you are that Special One, kissing you from your head to your feet, I knew when I first laid my eyes on you that you would be the one, a feeling came over me, (Love), I just had to have you next to me, by my side, you have opened me up to another side of love, I have to be honest, before you I never thought about settling down, but now I'm so ready, I put you first now, I owe so much to you, I want nothing but to prove I'm worthy enough to have you, God has blessed me, he was so good to me when he sent me his angel, you, your love, I'm So Addicted to your love, So In Love, so deep in love, you are my heaven from up above, my pretty dove, you made so many differences in my life, My Gift, is yours, all I want to do is please you, constantly on my mind, how such a Beautiful Find came to find my heart, my eyes are perfectly blind to the rest, your love is all the art I need, so cultivating, the more you give the more I want, baby I will hold your heart to never break it, kept safe with mine, together we will spend a lifetime of sharing, caring, honesty, trust, loyalty, affection, love making so breathtaking, you are it for me, the one I have been searching and seeking for since I knew what love really meant, you were put here just for me, my sweet Virgo Love, I place no else above, you have me flying high, past cloud nine, soaring on high, roaring to the world about this love your love our love, I want them all to know who it is that has me lost in her love, twisted up with love, I will pay the cost even though I know your love can't be bought with money, honey I'm paying with all that I have in store, all that I hold inside, my love, it is all yours, I can't say it enough, you give more than I ever had before, I Can't Resist your touch, you are a must have in my life, my Queen be my wife, I see you as my wife, walking down that aisle making me the happiest man here on this earth, I know you're worth so much and I'm here to give it, to show you a love that you will forever adore, baby I am yours for the

D. C.

taking, my heart was breaking before you showed up, right from the start is was love never lust, my sweet lady, say that you will be mine for the rest of my lifetime, So In Love with you, I will never find another of your kind, so hooked on you, playing this game for keeps, I never want to lose you, the greatest love I will ever come to know, Lessons In Love I will always show, you have brought out this other side, and I love the guy you have turned me into, forever baby me and you, you and I, My Queen, My Wife, I will love you for the rest of my life.

MII: The Return of the King

KING

Once you enter my world, my girl, my woman, my Queen you will want to become, I am KING, just ask around about me, and they will tell you that I am that one, that one who can send a single chill down your body with just the thought of how I've touched your body and soul, let's get this party started, are you Ready, Set, Go you walk through my door, instantly your clothes hit the floor, you're about to hear me roar as we soar through the clouds up to the heavens, we're on Level 7, soon we will be past 11, I will be your heaven here on this earth, showing you how love is supposed to be given, you're worth all this sexual healing, pulling you towards me as we stand close in each other's arms, a soft kiss to your lips as we perform these acts, what they say about me are facts, you're falling deep into my trance, light as a feather your body becomes, showing you my strength by picking you up to hold you high as we continue to kiss, laying you down ever so gently, looking deeply into your eyes, I can see your heart starting to intertwine with mine, I don't miss, your feelings I'm about to equip and hold, never to let go, your soul will rise high with every stroke I deliver, your body I will conquer as you quiver, shiver and shake, that body I'm treating like an oven on 350° we bake no timer while eating your cake, rolling my tongue down your neck to your breasts, your canvas is next, spreading you wide so I can go where the sun don't shine, your palace is all mine, my tongue is doing flips, your hidden passion I'm about to find, these aren't tricks, this isn't my Magic Show, down below as I coast through and through your love, you're clenching my sheets throwing my pillows to the floor, while your body is contracting I'm pulling, holding you firm so that you can't run, giving you more and more, you're screaming I am that one, Calling My Name, KING, you're everything that word describes, damn boy no lies you're putting it down, you wear the crown well she says as she yells as I bring that waterfall flow of yours down in streams down my chin dripping onto my chest, putting your doubts to rest, as you explode with passion, your looks and reactions says it all, but I ask can you handle more? My Royal pole is about to explore your deep

D. C.

dark seas, dropping my pants to the floor, your eyes say OMG, as words flow from your lips, is that all for me, yes my love are ready to feel what so many want to feel, I'm about to make you evolve, your puzzle I'm about to solve, the Royal Lover is about to give that service you so desperately need, open up my love so I can feed you all nine, that feeling you're feeling in your stomach is me discovering a whole new world inside your body, breaking down walls, again you're Calling My Name, KING, with these words rolling off your tongue, you're everything that word means, clenching my sheets with no pillows to throw you let out a loud moan before you scream as you explode all over Mr. Royal, holding me close your thigh, I'm so deep inside, looking deep into your eyes, our hearts are fully intertwined, all mine you cry, as I flip you to that back side, you hop up and say wait a minute, I want to see if I can take it all for a ride, pushing me to the bed as you crawl up my legs with your tongue, I say taste yourself, I'm still dripping with your passion, you grab Mr. Royal firmly and stare as if you're asking yourself do you dare, starting off with a kiss to the tip, my toes curl, my eyes flip to the back of my head, to the side you go with your tongue wrapping Mr. Royal up, damn I say as you stroke up and down with both hands, this dance you're doing with your mouth and tongue has me calling out number one under the sun, slow it down I'm not trying to bust my gun just yet, we have some more to do, I have something I want to show you, a few more strokes and deep throat licks before you hop on and start doing a few tricks, moving those hips in a circular motion, you're coasting, rocking your boat back and forth, north and south, showing me what you're about, you twist around without getting off moving into that reverse cowgirl position, I see you're on a mission to keep me, KING, with the things you're doing, popping that ass slow, booty so soft, I'm deep hitting that spot gently but hard, my feelings have been caught off guard, you're taking me far, but watch this as I show my strength and stand up with you in this position, your legs wrapped tightly around my waist, deep into your cave is the place I want to be, putting you on the bed so you can look back at me as I dig deeper and deeper, you're Calling My Name once more, KING, with these words falling from your heart, this palace, my palace is all yours to explore whenever you see fit, I will

MII: The Return of the King

never tap nor quit, you're making me forget as my legs get weak about my past, OMG I'm about to bust all over you, KING you scream out, this is more than just sex, you're the best, the greatest I ever felt, more is being dealt, as I grab your hair to pull it towards me placing your back into a deeper arch so I can attack with a deeper stroke, here I go baby I'm almost there, you yell I swear there is no one I can compare you to KING you're everything that word means as I let out a roar from my core pulling out to bust all over your back side as I kiss the side of your lips, what a ride, what a trip, your heart, your love will forever be equipped with mine, each and every time you close your eyes, you will remember why they call me KING.

D. C.

PRIVATE PARTY
(OUTRO)

My party is coming to an end, the DJ is about to spin the last song, I left my Queen that I have chosen by giving my rose, my heart, a show you will get to know, handling that problem my brother came rushing to my door with, escorting everyone out (0-100) real quick, the party isn't over with, the last guest is out, I start to walk quick, stopping real quick to pour me a sip, I hope you're ready to Omit, your walls I am about to sink like a ship, walking through my double doors, standing equipped with my drink in hand in front, entering so that I can explore your every desire, you call out sire what took so long, I've been waiting for you to climb into your throne, I had to send everyone home my love, rushing I was, trying to get back to you, I had to make sure everyone was removed, you know everyone wants to rule, my crown I will never lose, giving you a sense of how real love should feel, walking up behind you, embracing you with my arms wrapped around your body, holding you close, staring at us in the mirror, I couldn't see anything more clearer, my Queen you are supposed to be, will be here with me, my kingdom is yours, saying this while kissing from your neck to your shoulders, your body I adore, taking off my shirt, dropping it to the floor, grabbing you at your waist, twirling you around so that we are face to face, gazing into your eyes, smiling on the inside with my heart I am, damn baby what are you doing to King, I love our love making schemes, anywhere you can get it, the world is are scene, putting me in this love making groove, making me want to give you everything, watching the moves I put on you, forget about those other dudes you will, nothing or no one can exceed my skills, imagine a big wheel with all that you desire on the playing field, all that you spin and land on I will take care of, I will take you high and above, I hope you're really ready for this King's Love, note that I won't be finished until your finished, this is no game, this is no gimmick, after my body party in my Private Party you will never be the same, no I can't explain, but allow me to show you, moving closer, your eyes focus, from my lips to my chest, your hands caress, Stress Reliever, to the mountaintop I will go to make you a believer, you're going to call out you're the best, shouting without a doubt, your hair is about to become a mess, my silk sheets will be soaked with just a few strokes, provoking your inner love, raining down you will, your cloud above will sit still, with my steel I will Break You Down, your willpower will come falling to the ground, a new love you have found, kissing your lips, removing your shirt, slipping it right off, ready I am to give you this work, lights on, removing my shirt, you're about to get this work, kissing you soft, your ticket has been bought, you are worth the cost, I've been watching you from across the room all night, picking you up to lay you across the bed showing you my might, pulling those heels and leggings off, leaving your thong on, rubbing up and down your thighs, massaging you Just Right, the night has just begun, your feelings are telling you I'm the one, passion burning hot like the sun, never could you find another of my kind, I am that guy, that one of a kind creeping in between your thighs, I'll be your Dream Catcher each and every night, finally the time has arrived, your reality isn't a fantasy anymore, pulling your thong to the side so my tongue can play inside and out, around and around doing circles, passion screams you let out, I had no doubt that I will make your palace wall fall, coming up from being down and working your walls, I got that sticky face with your juices dripping, I'm on a mission to make you Fall In Love, to make your dreams come true, take you high and above, crawling between your legs, no baby I don't want your pleasure mouth, oh I love it when you're down south, but tonight It's All About You and the things I'm going to do, pulling in slow with a deep stroke, your hands on my hips, you can't handle my dip, well-endowed and full equipped with a real love tip, tap and quit is on your mind, I'm Blowing Your Mind, feeding you deep into your spine, now your hands are grabbing and clenching my behind, baby you're the epitome of fine, now you're all mine, turn over so I can hit you from behind, spread you wide, my head slides deep, deep inside, you let out a loud cry, pushing with all my might, I grab your hair tight, pulling your head back to gaze into your eyes, taking you for a Rollercoaster Ride of your life, running you are, but can't fight this feeling, I'm giving you sexual healing, love baby I know the meaning, feigning you will be, Jodeci, I'm all you will ever need, you're loving every bit of my Private Party, the way I serve you when I'm getting naughty, I love our Body To Body, as we creep through my sheets, holding you close until you fall asleep, thinking about the love we both just received, I have found my one true Queen, you give me what I need, Soul Searching for what it seems like for an eternity, with just one look my lady you took my heart, I realize I never want to be apart, you are the Queen, my Queen I need here for the rest of my life, I was talking about you throughout this whole book, your love is priceless, you have me shook, a hard fought battle it took, turning this one down and that one down, only to you I give and place my crown, opening my eyes you have, on this day of my return I have found my one true Queen, I thank you my lady, you are everything I will ever need, I will forever be your one true King.